SPORT IN GREECE AND ROME

H. A. Harris

72

T & H

THAMES AND HUDSON

© 1972 THAMES AND HUDSON

PRINTED IN GREAT BRITAIN BY
THE CAMELOT PRESS LTD, LONDON AND SOUTHAMPTON

ISBN 0500 40022 9

CONTENTS

LIST OF ILLUSTRATIONS

PLATES

FIGURES

THIS BOOK
IS DEDICATED
TO THE MEMORY
OF
DOUGLAS ROBERT JARDINE
CRICKETER
1900–1958

PREFACE

THIS BOOK IS A NATURAL SEQUEL to *Greek Athletes and Athletics*, extending the field of enquiry to cover all the important sports and games of the ancient world. In a work entitled *Sport in Greece and Rome* it would have been impossible to disregard Greek athletics, and inevitably the first chapter covers the same ground as the earlier book. But in the last ten years fresh material has come to my notice, and it is included in this new treatment.

None of this additional evidence has led me to make any significant change in the views which I put forward in *Greek Athletes*. I have slightly modified my interpretation of the method of deciding the winner of the pentathlon, and I welcome the opportunity to correct a serious mistake about technique in the earlier volume, when I wrote that the discus was spun with the little finger of the throwing hand. The origin of error is often interesting. In my young days, the only ball I was able to deliver in the nets at cricket was a leg break out of the back of the hand, spun with the little finger. When in my late fifties I first tossed a discus experimentally, it was natural for me to throw it with the same action. No doubt I ought to have reflected that the vast majority of cricketers bowl from the front of the hand and spin the ball with the first and second fingers, that a leg break out of the back of the hand is never a fast ball, and that speed is the essence of discus-throwing; no doubt also I ought to have watched more carefully the action of experts with the discus. But I did none of these things.

I am grateful to the discus-throwers who have pointed out this mistake to me, and to the many athletes who have discussed other practical details of technique. Nothing has given me greater pleasure than this interest of active sportsmen in the early history of their pursuits, and I hope that this book will have a similar appeal. Because the evidence for the games dealt with is so slight and its interpretation often depends on the detailed examination of single words and phrases, it has not been possible entirely to exclude Greek and Latin from the text, but I have tried to present the material in such a way that even readers innocent of those languages will be able to follow the arguments.

Space does not allow me to thank individually all those who have widened my understanding of the subject, but I must express my gratitude to Professors L. A. Moritz and A. D. Cameron for enlightenment on several points, and to Professor H. H. Scullard, the General Editor of the series, for invaluable help and advice. Once again I have to thank the Society for Hellenic Travel and its agents, Messrs Fairways and Swinford. The Society's cruises and tours have made possible the personal inspection of sites and museums for which there is no substitute.

I am grateful also to the Pantyfedwen Trust of St David's University College, Lampeter, for a grant towards the provision of illustrations for the book.

Oxford

H. A. Harris

ATHLETICS

CHAPTER I

GREEK ATHLETICS

BY DERIVATION THE WORD 'SPORT' covers every diversion by which a man disports or amuses himself in his leisure time; it is essentially the antithesis of work. In English, however, the word has tended to become specialized to denote such of these activities as involve physical strength and skill. In the remote past the survival of the individual man, of the community and of the species depended on these qualities, and even now occasions sometimes arise when the same is true. It is perhaps for this reason that sport appeals to something very deep in many of us.

There are three ends to which the development of muscular strength and skill can be directed. A man may pit himself against the inanimate forces of Nature in pursuits such as mountaineering and potholing. Alternatively he may match his powers against those of other living creatures in hunting, shooting or fishing. Originally these were utilitarian occupations undertaken in order to obtain food. When they are followed for enjoyment they are often called field sports, but the modern tendency is to separate them completely from the rest of the world of sport. The Greeks and Romans enjoyed hunting and fishing as sports apart from the food value of the animals they pursued; but ancient field sports constitute a very specialized department of study, and they will form no part of this book. However, Man's association with animals in sport has not been confined to attempts to catch them. An important human acquirement has been skill in the training and management of horses. When this is directed to competition, either in ancient chariot-racing or on the modern Turf, it may fairly claim the name of sport. Whether the same can be said when the horse is replaced by a mass of ironmongery in car racing is a matter of opinion which happily does not concern the historian of sport in antiquity. The third application of physical achievement to purposes of enjoyment is the most widespread, that in which man challenges man in contests of strength and skill. In all ages this has happened in the fundamental activities of running, jumping and throwing, and in such combat events as boxing, fencing and wrestling. Here too the connection with survival is obvious, since these activities are basic in primitive warfare. In modern times the chosen field is more often that of ball games, either between individuals or between teams of several players.

These three categories are by no means mutually exclusive. Swimming and diving, sailing and canoeing, for instance, are enjoyed by many thousands simply as a challenge to develop skills to meet the hazards of wind and water, but they are also media for racing and competition. The same is true of skiing and skating. There are many who hold that these sports are at their best when the competitive element is kept out, and most people would agree that the intrusion of international rivalry into mountaineering has had none but unhappy results. The case for the delight to be gained from the mere attainment of such skills has never been better expressed than by Water Rat in *The Wind in the Willows*:

> Believe me, my young friend, there is *nothing*—absolutely nothing—half so much worth doing as simply messing about in boats. Simply messing, messing—about—in—boats.

Yet however much we may admire those who are content with the exercise of skills for their own sake, anyone who has ever experienced the excitement of the man-to-man struggle of a race or a team game will feel that they are missing something. So it is right that these should be the activities to which the term sport is especially applied.

Play appears to be an instinctive function of the young of most of the higher animals; as an adult pursuit it is pre-eminently, though perhaps not exclusively, human. It is found even in primitive society as soon as existence escapes from the stage where all human energy has to be devoted to merely keeping alive. The games thus evolved have been moulded by generations of pragmatic experience; their rules are handed on by tradition and modified at the whim of players of forceful personality. The result is a proliferation of primitive games as multifarious as that of languages and dialects. The study of them is a matter for the anthropologist. The historian of sport can only begin his task at the point where society has been able to produce some degree of organization in a game, which ensures that a code of rules for it is widely accepted. In Western civilization this happened first among the Greeks. Accordingly it is with the Greeks that a history of sport proper must commence.

For several reasons it is convenient to take as a starting point the traditional date of the first Olympic Games, 776 B C. It is true that this was by no means the beginning of Greek athletics. We know from Homer and from legend that the events of the Games had been practised in the Greek world for many centuries before that. But now for the first time some measure of organization became essential. The first Olympiad came early in what it is fashionable today to call a population explosion in Greece, which compelled many Greeks to abandon their country and seek a home in some distant part of the Mediterranean world. The new cities which they founded were self-contained sovereign states, independent of their mother cities. Like all Greeks, the new colonists quarrelled constantly with their Greek neighbours and were sometimes at war with them, but in spite of this they always retained a consciousness of their 'Greekness' which distinguished them all from the rest of mankind, the non-Greeks whom they called barbarians. The most important element in this Greekness or Hellenism was the Greek language; their religion, in spite of its dozen or more gods and goddesses, was also a unifying influence. This no doubt is why the great religious festivals of the homeland, at Olympia, Delphi, Delos, Epidaurus, Nemea and the Isthmus of Corinth, become prominent during or soon after the age of colonization. They attracted visitors from all over the Greek world, even from its furthest-flung cities in the south of France or round the Black Sea. Some of these visitors may have come with the same motives as genuine medieval pilgrims, some as an unconscious assertion of their Hellenism. Before many centuries had passed, the majority came simply for the enjoyment of a great experience.

There were two reasons for the connection of athletics with these religious festivals. The Greeks were strongly anthropomorphic in their conception of their deities, and assumed that what gave pleasure to themselves—music, drama or sport—would equally be gratifying to the gods. Even stronger was the consideration that the large crowds which assembled for the festivals provided spectators for the Games and audiences for the music and plays. Emphasis at the different festivals varied according to the deity worshipped at the place. Apollo's shrines at Delphi and Delos gave great prominence to music. Athletic sports and chariot-racing were important at all these centres, but at Olympia they were supreme. The assembling of athletes from so many widely separated cities clearly imposed the necessity of some standardization in the rules of the events of the Games.

The link between athletics and these festivals has often caused the connection of sport and religion to be exaggerated. The descriptions of athletics in Homer show that no such link existed in the age he was depicting. His Games in the *Iliad* are part of a funeral ceremony, with the purpose of distributing the belongings of the dead Patroclus to the heroes most worthy of them. In the *Odyssey* athletics are an after-dinner entertainment. The connection of sport with religious festivals in later times is probably as accidental as with us. The congestion of football fixtures at Christmas and Easter is due simply to the fact that spectators have time to spare at those festival seasons. It does not betoken any link whatever between soccer and the Christian faith. We must remember too that many Greek athletic meetings had no connection with religious festivals. During his campaigns Alexander the Great is recorded to have promoted such sports for the entertainment of his troops on nineteen occasions; one of these meetings was part of a funeral ceremony.[1]

The supremacy of Olympia had one important result. Its athletic programme and its rules for the various events were accepted without question all over the Greek world, as the authority of the Marylebone Cricket Club was long acknowledged in the modern world of cricket, or that of the Royal and Ancient Club of St Andrew's in golf. But there is one notable difference. In the modern examples, authority has passed within a century to other bodies; the programme and rules of Olympia, however, survived unchanged, so far as our evidence goes, for over a thousand years. Here the inclusion of sport among religious observances possibly had some influence. Divine ceremonial is extremely conservative; there is great reluctance to change it—the word 'solemn' fundamentally means 'customary'—and this same reluctance was very marked in Greek athletics compared with our own. In most athletic events the rules can be simple; in running, there must be a prohibition of interference with another competitor, in throwing and jumping a rule against overstepping the line. But in the combat events such as boxing and wrestling, rules must necessarily have been more elaborate, and it was here that the prestige of Olympia was most important.

We have little enough evidence about athletics at the great festivals before the fourth century B C, and practically none for the rest of the Greek world at that time. The stadia of the chief religious centres survive, and a few others. But we know the name and home city of at least one winner at every Olympiad from 776 BC to AD 249, and it is reasonable to suppose that any city which produced an Olympic victor must have had its own sports ground and athletics meetings; as some of these cities were small and unimportant, it would seem that a stadium of some kind was as inevitable a feature of every Greek city as a football ground is of every town and village in England today. Certainly when Alexander spread Greek civilization all over the Eastern Mediterranean at the end of the fourth century BC, every city in the newly Hellenized world took steps to provide itself with a stadium and to inaugurate athletics meetings.

These stadia differ considerably in shape from our modern running grounds. We are accustomed to a track consisting of two straights joined at the ends by semi-circular curves, with a large area of dead ground in the middle. The Greek stadium was in essence a rectangle about 200 yards long and 25–40 wide, with a starting line at each end and a turning post in the middle of each line. In races longer than a single length of the track, the runners had to make an abrupt turn round the post, a feat which would dismay any modern athlete. In the mountainous terrain of Greece a flat stretch of the required size was not easily found, and most stadia had to be artificially constructed. One way of doing this was to level the floor of a short valley, the sides of which then afforded excellent accommodation for spectators. When this is done with the minimum of soil-shifting, the upper end of the stadium is left as a curve set into the hillside, and this gives the U-shape which we regard as being characteristic of the Greek stadium. But by no means all stadia were of this design. It was sometimes more convenient to site the track along a terrace on a hillside. The hill slope provided spectators' banking on one side of it, and the only construction needed was the raising of an artificial bank along the other side and at one or both ends for further spectators. With a terrace stadium it did not matter whether the ends were rounded or square. Olympia is of this pattern, with both ends square (*Pl.* 2); so too is Delos. At Epidaurus the stadium was set into a short valley, but the upper end was squared, the lower being left open. The builders of some terrace stadia unnecessarily adopted the U pattern, with one rounded and one open end; Aspendos affords an example of this. Two stadia in Hellenistic cities of Asia Minor, Aphrodisias and Laodicea, follow a more logical plan and have rounded embankments at both ends, giving the greatest possible number of spectators' seats (*Pl.* 3). The city of Laodicea is known to everyone because of the words of the Spirit in the Apocalypse:

> So then because thou art lukewarm, and neither cold nor hot, I will spue thee out of my mouth.
>
> (*Revelation* III, 16)

The Spirit certainly spued out Laodicea to some effect, for the site is now utterly desolate. Yet the stadium remains strangely impressive; it is the largest known, with a floor well over 300 yards long. We can still see a number of the spectators' seats, which, as a surviving inscription informs us, were installed in the first century A D by a generous citizen, Nicostratus. The authorities at Didyma, an ancient religious centre on the coast of Asia Minor, chose an unusual but ingenious site for their stadium. They placed it alongside the enormous temple of Apollo, so that the steps of the temple podium provided admirable accommodation for spectators, some of whom scratched their names in the stone to lay claim to their seats. Many of these names, and some of the blocks of the runners' starting line, still survive (*Pl.* 4).

A second great difference between Greek athletics and our own is that Greek competitors were completely naked. This was not true of the earliest sports meetings. Contestants in Homer's Games wore shorts, which are depicted in some later vase-paintings (*Pl.* 5). The practice was still followed when the Olympic Games were instituted. Two stories were told to account for the change, which appears to have taken place before 700 B C. One was that in the first race in the

Olympiad of 720 BC a competitor's shorts fell off and he went on to win the race; the runners in the next race, thinking that this was the secret of his success, discarded theirs. The other story was that the same accident happened to a runner in the Panathenaic Games at Athens; he tripped over his dropping shorts, fell and was killed, and the magistrate gave orders that shorts should never again be worn. Whatever the reason, Greeks always looked on their readiness to strip in public as one of the traits which marked them off from barbarians.[2]

The third feature of a Greek meeting which would seem odd to a modern visitor is the very restricted programme of events. At almost every festival in the Greek world the Olympic programme was followed. In addition to the races for horses and chariots, it comprised three combat events— boxing, wrestling and the pankration—four foot-races— 200 yards, 400 yards, a long-distance race and a race in armour —and a pentathlon consisting of javelin, discus, long jump, a 200 yards race and wrestling. At a few meetings at some periods there was a further race of 800 yards. This programme was usually repeated for different age-groups; at Olympia it was doubled for men and boys, at most festivals it was triplicated for boys, youths and men. In the Christian era, either the boys' or the youths' class was often further subdivided, but Olympia seems never to have gone beyond its two groups. Even stranger than the narrowness of this programme is the fact that it was never improved. It was established by 600 BC, and, as far as we know, it was unchanged when the Olympic Games came to an end a thousand years later. Yet in the equestrian events the Stewards at Olympia were willing to innovate, dropping some events and adding others as late as 264 BC. In athletics the only late addition was the race in armour in 520 BC. For some centuries the pankration at Olympia was confined to men, presumably being thought too dangerous for boys, but it was common as a boys' event elsewhere, and in 200 BC Olympia at last included it. On the other hand a boys' pentathlon, to which there appears to be no possible objection, was held in 628 BC but immediately abandoned. It never returned to the Olympic programme, though it remained a popular event for boys and youths all over the Greek world for many centuries.[3]

WRESTLING

Classification by age was the only one known in Greek athletics. In the combat events there was no division into classes by weight, as is normal in the modern world. The result was that success at the highest level in these events was possible only for big men. The Greeks themselves called them the 'heavy' events. This became even more marked as athletics fell more and more into the hands of professionals, and standards of skill rose. But wrestling remained a widespread activity of ordinary young men who had no pretensions to competing in the top circles, and no doubt at this level these amateurs normally took on opponents of their own size. In many respects it was the most characteristic Greek sport. The 'palaestra' or wrestling-school was for many centuries a feature of every Greek city, and later the Romans adopted the institution. There young men met their comrades and enjoyed a friendly bout of wrestling with them, just as today they would play a set of tennis or a game of squash. The palaestra was in many respects the club-house of the young.

All Greek athletes oiled themselves before exercise as a hygienic measure to keep dirt out of their pores, and at the end of their exertions took a bath and scraped off the dust, sweat and oil with a bronze strigil (*Pls.* 8–10). After the oiling, wrestlers dusted one another with powder before a contest in order to ensure a good grip. The wrestling schools of the Greek world consumed large amounts of oil and of this special dust.

A wrestling match was for the best of three falls; the evidence appears to indicate that a fall was constituted by the shoulders of one of the combatants touching the ground. Holds, trips and throws were as varied as in modern wrestling.

The Greeks themselves recognized two main techniques, one in which a wrestler held off and tried to seize his opponent's wrists or arms (*Pls.* 6, 11), the other in which the contestants grappled at close quarters (*Pl.* 12). We can learn something of these techniques from painting and sculpture, but here, as in the rest of the field of ancient sport, we must beware of taking vases and statues too literally; they are works of art, not high-speed photographs or illustrations in a training manual.

BOXING

Greek boxing resembled our own in most respects. The chief difference, apart from the lack of classification by weight, was that a bout was not divided into rounds but went on uninterrupted until one of the competitors held up a hand in acknowledgment of defeat. Then as now gloves were worn to protect the hands. The evidence of paintings suggests that the gloves worn in competition in early days were long thongs of soft leather wound round the hands (*Pl.* 17). For the gloves of a later period, the third or second century B C, we have the evidence of a superb statue in the Terme museum at Rome, (*Pl.* 18), one of the finest examples of Hellenistic realism in art. When we first see the statue, our attention is naturally caught by the magnificent characterization, to which both the face and the whole pose contribute. For the student of the technicalities of Greek athletics, the hands and forearms deserve no less consideration. Here we have exact evidence for the boxing gloves of the period. The athlete wears close-fitting inner gloves of some thin material, extending from the wrist to the top of the fingers and thumbs; there are separate compartments for each finger, and only the top joint protrudes. To this inner glove is fixed the boxing glove proper, a pad of leather—which even in the bronze looks soft—about an inch thick and three inches wide, curiously narrow to our eyes. It is held in position by elaborate thonging, meticulously represented by the sculptor. An interesting feature of this thonging is the care taken to prevent any of the thongs from riding up on to the striking surface of the pad, where it might lacerate the opponent. Clearly the aim was to take every precaution against cutting the skin when a blow was struck, though the boxer's face shows that even the most careful precautions did not always succeed. The thonging is carried up past the wrist, and ends in a band of sheepskin round the forearm. The purpose of this was to allow the boxer to wipe his forehead to prevent sweat from trickling into his eyes; a similar device is used by tennis players today. The sculptor obviously worked on these gloves with loving care. Even the stitching round the inside edges of the fingers of the thin inner gloves is scrupulously depicted. It can now only be seen after considerable bodily contortions on the part of the viewer; clearly the arms were cast and worked separately and brazed on later.

It is strange that with their mathematical genius the Greeks never realized the importance in a knock-out competition of confining byes to the first round whenever there was an irregular number of entries. As a result it was possible for a competitor to draw a bye in any round, even at the semi-final stage, and to draw a bye more than once in the same contest. A man who drew a bye was called *ephedros*, 'sitting by'. An athlete who won an event without drawing a bye in any round claimed extra credit for being a victor *anephedros*, 'without sitting by'. The museum label of the Terme statue describes it as 'Defeated Boxer'. This is surely a mistake. As the eyes are lost, it is impossible to be completely certain about what the sculptor intended the facial expression to be. But the whole pose suggests an *ephedros* rather than a beaten man. The boxer is obviously a veteran of many fights. He sits without any of the excited tension which a younger man would show, awaiting the outcome of a contest which is taking place and chatting with someone standing beside him, possibly his trainer. No other work of art from antiquity takes us into the stadium with such intimacy as this statue.

Even today writers on Greek athletics continue to state that Greek boxing allowed only blows to the head. This

completely mistaken belief is based on a debatable interpretation of a silly aetiological myth related by Philostratus
in the second century A D. No doubt blows to the head are
more spectacular, but the Greeks were well aware of the exhausting effects of a sustained attack on the body. Several
vase-paintings depict these body blows, and there are a few
unmistakable references to them in literature. We do not
know certainly what was permitted and what forbidden in
Greek boxing. Vase-paintings show hitting with the open
hand (*Pl.* 17), and fights described in epics often end with a
downward blow, which suggests that the use of the side of
the hand in a hammer stroke was legitimate. It is even possible
that kicking was allowed. The medical writer Antyllus gives
this advice about shadow-boxing (σκιαμαχία), a favourite
method of training in antiquity:

> The shadow-boxer must use not only his hands but also
> his legs, sometimes as if he were jumping, at other times
> as if he were kicking.
>
> (Quoted by Oribasius, VI, 29.3)

A characteristic passage in the *Meditations* of the Emperor
Marcus Aurelius reveals two things which were forbidden:

> In sporting contests an opponent may have scarred us with
> his nails or butted us violently with his head. We do not
> appeal for a foul or retaliate or look on him thereafter as
> a man guilty of intentional unfair play; but even so we are
> on our guard against him, not regarding him as an enemy
> or suspecting him, but good-humouredly keeping out of
> his way. That is how we should act in other spheres of
> life.[4]
>
> (VI, 20)

We know something of the training methods of Greek
boxers. Like their modern counterparts they wore ear-
guards (ἀμφωτίδες) and softly padded gloves (σφαῖραι) for
sparring practice (*Pls.* 15, 16). Ear-guards were certainly not
worn in competition. The boxer of Plate 18 has the cauli-

flower ears which have always been the mark of his profession, and there are several references in Greek literature to the disfigurement. Boxers also used the punch-ball (κώρυκος) in training. Antyllus has left full instructions for its use:

For weaker men the punch-ball should be filled with millet or flour, for stronger men with sand. It should be hung from the roof of the gymnasium so that its bulk is opposite the eyes of the user. Those undergoing training use both hands, at first gently, then more vigorously, so that they attack it as it swings away, and when it swings back at them they give ground as they are thrust out of the way by its force. Lastly they punch it away beyond arm's reach, so that as it returns it falls with greater violence on the body as a result of its impetus. With a final effort after doing it all the violence they can, they hit it away so hard that if they were not very careful they would be thrown off their feet by the rebound. Sometimes they meet its onset with their hands, sometimes they draw back their heads and take it on the chest, sometimes they turn round and receive it on the broad of the back. So it can make the body muscular and give it tone, and it is a powerful exercise for the shoulders and the whole frame.[5]

(Quoted by Oribasius, VI, 33)

The combat events were controlled by referees who enforced the rules by flogging offenders. The forked sticks with which they applied this discipline are depicted in many vase-paintings (Pl. 32). A simile in Philo Judaeus reveals that, at any rate in Alexandria at the beginning of the Christian era, referees also used methods much more like those with which we are familiar in the modern ring. He is denouncing drunkards and their quarrelsome tempers, and says that they will go on fighting 'unless someone steps between them like a referee and separates them'.[6]

THE PANKRATION

This was a specialized form of struggle which, as its name

implies, included many combat devices, but it is clear that these were controlled by strict rules and conventions. The aim of the pankratiast was to put his opponent in such a position that he was compelled to admit defeat or else suffer strangulation or a broken limb. The event resembled wrestling in that the contestants grappled with one another and tried to secure decisive holds, but there was no attempt to impose a fall. Indeed, pankratiasts often rolled in close grapple on the ground (*Pl.* 20), and it is recorded of one of them that he gained many victories by intentionally lying on his back. Hitting with the fist was permitted; it seems to have been used mainly to compel an opponent to release a hold. Gloves, which would have interfered with grips, were not worn. An epigram in the *Anthology* celebrates the feat of Cleitomachus of Thebes, an Olympic victor in 216 BC, who won the wrestling, boxing and pankration on the same day in the Isthmian Games. Of this triple victory, the poet says:

> Immediately after taking off his blood-stained boxing gloves, he fought in the fierce pankration.
>
> (*Anthologia Palatina* IX, 588)

The only tactics which we know to have been banned were gouging—poking a thumb or finger into an opponent's eye —and biting; there may well have been other prohibitions. Little is known with certainty about the details of the event; it obviously had many affinities with judo, in that situations constantly arose involving the possibility of serious injury or even death, but the danger was averted by the imposition of a strict convention. Until the fourth century BC the pankration attracted many young men who would be called 'amateur' on any count, among them the aristocratic patrons of Pindar. But as the sport of the stadium increasingly became spectator entertainment provided by professionals, the event seems to have changed in spirit if not in letter. The crowds clamoured more and more loudly for violence, and the pankratiasts obliged them. Lists of prize money show that it became the most popular event in the programme.[7]

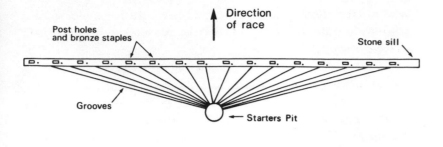

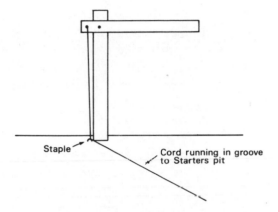

Figs. 1 and 2 *Above,
sketch-plan of the
starting line at the
Isthmian Sanctuary (not
to scale) and left, a
hypothetical
reconstruction of the
starting-gate.*

RUNNING

The two main points in which Greek races differed from our
own were the abrupt turn round a post instead of a gradual
bend, and the use by the Greeks of a starting-gate to prevent
'jumping the gun'. We can date the introduction of this
device to the middle of the fifth century BC. We know that
it was not in use in 480, because an anecdote about the events
of that year shows that at that time runners who started
before the signal were flogged. It appears that a mechanical
starting-gate for chariots was introduced at Olympia at about
the same time; it is impossible to say which sport may have
borrowed the idea from the other. Evidence of the existence
of this starting-gate for athletes, which the Greeks called a
husplex, have long been recognized in the post-sockets found

at regular intervals along the starting line in many stadia, sometimes but not always with grooves for the runners' toes between them. Excavations by Oscar Broneer at Isthmia in[1] 1956 made the interpretation of this evidence certain. In an early stadium there, Broneer found the ground-level apparatus of the *husplex*, sockets with grooves running from them to a central starter's pit behind the runners, all in excellent condition. The grooves had clearly accommodated cords, held in place by bronze staples which are still in their original position across the grooves. By far the most rational interpretation of this is that the cords controlled a pivoted bar in front of each runner, working like the arm of a railway signal, and that the simultaneous release of all the cords allowed all the bars to drop together and sent the runners off to a fair start (Figs. 1, 2).

This was the most usual pattern of *husplex*. Evidence for it is still to be seen at Olympia, Delphi, Epidaurus, Delos and Didyma. But there is also evidence of a later and different model. One of the most charming of ancient sites is Priene, a Greek city in Asia Minor which was once a port, but where the sea has now receded out of sight. The ruins lie on a hillside, exceptionally steep even for a Greek city, and its inhabitants must have been hard put to it to find a place for their stadium. The only possible position for it was a ledge at the foot of the slope, just inside the sea wall. Inevitably it was narrow; it could provide for only 8 runners, whereas most stadia accommodated from 12 to 20. In this stadium there was at first a *husplex* of the earlier type, and the eight stone blocks of the sill with their post-sockets for this still remain. This was replaced by a much more complicated structure, apparently working on a different principle. The excavators found the base of this intact (*Pl.* 21), and some of the upper elements lying about, including parts of an elaborate architrave. There are ten bases fitted on to a well-built sill. The central opening was clearly not intended for a runner. It was probably the entrance for the formal procession of athletes and officials at the beginning of a festival, and it may well have been suggested by the lay-out of the Roman Circus with its ceremonial archway in the middle of the row of chariot traps. The bases at Priene carried pilasters with square grooves running vertically down the inside faces of each runner's stall, linking with the grooves still to be seen in the bases and with a channel which runs along the sill and is carried without interruption under the bases. From this channel there are two outlets in the middle of the central opening, giving on to the stadium itself (Fig. 3).

Professor G. E. Bean in his *Aegean Turkey* has an interesting discussion of this starting-gate. He suggests that the purpose of the grooves in the pilasters was to support a wooden framework for a *husplex* very much like the older pattern, but worked by cords passing along the architrave and not along the ground. This is reasonable and may well be true, but it does not account for the channel in the sill. Bean interprets this as a drainage device to dispose of rain-water falling on the entablature; yet had this been its purpose, it would surely have discharged the water back off the stadium and not forwards on to it, where it would soak the stretch of ground on which the runners took their first steps. It seems more probable that the channel held the cords which worked the gate. We are accustomed to the starter standing behind the line of runners; here he can exert more control over them, and they

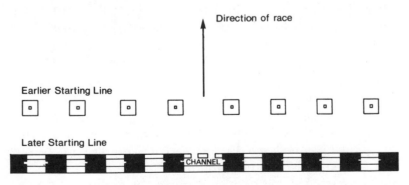

Fig. 3 *Foundations of the starting-gates in the stadium of Priene*

cannot secure an undetected 'flyer' by watching for his involuntary muscular movements just before pulling the trigger. But with a gate to prevent unfair starts there is no reason why the starter should not have been in front of the line, and with the layout at Priene there would have been no danger of his blocking the course of any runner. Another possibility is that the channel was designed to receive the bar of the *husplex* when it dropped. If this is so, the bar was not pivoted but moved with a guillotine action in grooves at each end and remained horizontal throughout. Some confirmation for this view is afforded by Statius' description of the start of a foot race:

> *Ut ruit atque aequum submisit regula limen,*
> *Corripuere leves spatium.*

When the bar fell and left the threshold level, the speedy runners leaped onto the track.

(*Thebaid* VI, 593)

'Left the threshold level' seems to imply that the bar dropped into a recess in the sill of the starting-gate.[8]

It should be added that at Epidaurus, where there is a fine starting-sill of the old pattern with grooves for the runners' toes and post-holes, the excavators found near this line a single block with a squared groove like those at Priene. It suggests that the authorities at Epidaurus may have experimented with a gate of the later pattern. At Athens too we know from an inscription that the *husplex* of the Panathenaic stadium was reconstructed about 100 BC. And Josephus may have been thinking of a starting-gate with an architrave when he compared Roman soldiers eagerly awaiting orders to march to 'runners *under* the *husplex* ready to start'.[9]

There is one minor problem of the Priene stadium. On most tracks, all races ended at the same place, so that, while the 400 yards, the long-distance race and the race in armour started and ended at the same line, the stade race—the 200 yards—started at the opposite end of the stadium. This explains why at Olympia and Delphi, for instance, there is a starting line with provision for a *husplex* at each end. At Priene and some other stadia there is no evidence of more than one. Obviously it was for the 200-yard sprint that the gate was most needed. Accordingly we must conclude that at Priene either this race finished at the opposite end to the others, or that the longer races started and ended at the finishing line of the 200 and did not use a gate.

A modern athlete might well wonder why a starting-gate is not used on our own tracks. A similar device has long been employed with success for greyhounds and is rapidly becoming universal for flat races on the Turf. An electrically operated gate should be well within the competence of our engineers. Its use would eliminate those unsatisfactory races in which a runner beats the gun without being detected by the starter, and those even more unsatisfactory occasions when a runner is disqualified for premature starts.[10]

Perhaps the most puzzling feature of the running in the stadium is that the Greeks appear to have been little concerned about the problem of the turn round the post. This may not have been very important in the *dolichos*, the long-distance race of some two or three miles, but in the *diaulos* of 400 yards, a race run at practically full speed throughout, to be first round the post must often have been decisive, especially at the great festivals where all the runners were of the top class and roughly equal in ability. Under these circumstances there must have been a great deal of bunching as the field approached the post, with inevitable bumping and colliding and many falls; there must also have been strong temptation to foul play. Yet Greek literature makes no reference to the problem. This led some writers in the past to suggest that each runner had a separate post to turn round, but this idea is untenable. Vase-painters too missed the opportunity which this point offered them. They sometimes depict a single runner at the post. A vase in Würzburg shows the post with an umpire carefully watching for fouls, but the runners are portrayed strung out in a line in the conventional frieze pattern.[11]

The two unmistakable references to the problem in literature written in Greek both come from the same unexpected source. At the turn of the Christian era, a learned Jewish theologian of Alexandria, Philo, wrote in Greek a voluminous commentary on the early books of the Old Testament for the benefit of Jews of the Dispersion who were more familiar with that language than with Hebrew. This hardly suggests a sporting figure, yet Philo uses athletics to illustrate his argument more often than any Greek writer whose works have survived. He must have been a devotee of the stadium and hippodrome at Alexandria, and he clearly expected that his fellow Jews would be equally well acquainted with the technicalities of athletics. We have already seen him illustrating a point by referring to an action of a boxing referee which is perfectly familiar to us and must have occurred constantly in the Greek ring, but which no other writer mentions. Twice in his works he drives home a point with an image drawn from the spills in the races in the stadium. Insisting that without God's mercy we all stand condemned, he writes:

> For no man unaided can run the race of life from birth to death without stumbling; we all have to endure being tripped, sometimes intentionally, sometimes accidentally.
>
> (*Quod Deus sit immutabilis*, 75)

Elsewhere he gives a splendid picture of a first-class runner who is able to keep out of that kind of trouble by accelerating quickly when it threatens:

> Rarely does God allow a man to run the race of life to the end without stumbling or tripping, and permit him to avoid both kinds of foul, intentional and accidental, by sweeping past the other runners with a sudden surge of speed which they cannot match.
>
> (*De Agricultura*, 180)

No man who had not often seen that happen on the track could possibly have written those lines.

The hoplite race or race in armour over 400 yards was a reminder that all athletics was in origin preparation for war; by historic times the full panoply had been reduced in the stadium to a symbolic helmet and shield (*Pl.*). The race was probably retained chiefly as a spectacle; as an athletic event it was clearly less esteemed as time went on. Another running event of the Greeks, and one which has had more influence on modern athletics, was the relay race. This formed no part of the regular athletic programme at Olympia and other meetings, but was held at separate festivals. Sometimes the course lay through the streets of the city; there is no evidence that such races ever took place in a stadium. Instead of our baton, the runners handed on a lighted torch, and in order to win, a team had to keep its torch alight to the end of the race (*Pls.* 24–28).[12]

THE PENTATHLON

The origin of the pentathlon is lost. Homer knows nothing of it; in the funeral games of the *Iliad*, the discus and javelin are separate events in their own right, and jumping is not mentioned. A feeble aetiological story related by Philostratus can be disregarded. It does not explain what it purports to explain, and it attributes the institution of the pentathlon to the Argonauts, who were earlier than Homer's world. The Greeks themselves sometimes represented the event as the supreme test of the all-rounder, sometimes as a consolation for the man who could not triumph in running or the combat events. Suidas records that a third-century mathematician, Eratosthenes, who almost achieved the highest grade in several disciplines, was sometimes called a Second Plato, sometimes Beta, and sometimes The Pentathlete. The source of the event is probably that the authorities at Olympia in its early days did not regard throwing and jumping as sufficiently important in themselves to justify separate prizes, and so grouped them together in this way and added a race and wrestling. In spite of every attempt to popularize them, field events have always been the Cinderella of athletics.

The Stewards at Olympia seem to have retained their prejudice against them even after they had invented the pentathlon. As we have seen, after taking the logical step of including
it in the programme for boys they immediately discontinued
it. This cannot have been on the ground that its component
parts were unsuitable for youngsters; the pentathlon for
boys and youths flourished all over the Greek world for
centuries. But in the long run, field events commanded no
more popular support from Greek crowds than with us. By
the beginning of the Christian era, when money prizes were
given at most meetings, the prize for the pentathlon was only
a quarter of that given for the combat events.[13]

There has been endless discussion about the method of
deciding the winner of the event. Two points seem reasonably certain. First places alone counted; the Greeks set great
store by victory and generally were little concerned even with
second or third places. Any system of reckoning points for
places is unthinkable. Also it is highly unlikely that they would
have assigned victory to any competitor who had failed to
win at least one of the three field events which were the
essence of the pentathlon; any system which would have
allowed victory to be achieved by skill only in running and
wrestling, which were events in their own right in another
part of the programme, must be ruled out.

The most likely interpretation of the evidence is this. The
pentathlon was conducted like a five-set tennis match; as
soon as one competitor had won three events, the contest
ended. The three events peculiar to the pentathlon—the
jump and the two throws—were held first. If a competitor
won all three, he was 'victor in the first triad', as the Greeks
put it. Otherwise, when this stage was completed, there were
either three competitors, A, B and C, with one win each, or
one, A, with two wins and another, B, with one. In the latter
case, these two ran a 200-yard race. If A won, he now had
three wins and was the victor. If B won the race, A and B
now had two each and they wrestled to decide the champion.
If after the triad there were three athletes with one win each,

these three ran the race. One of them, A, now had two wins, while B and C still had one each. B and C now wrestled in a semi-final; in virture of his two wins, A was given a bye and sat by as *ephedros*. He then wrestled with the winner of the semi-final, who now also had two wins, and the winner of this bout was the victor in the whole event.[14]

THE JUMP

In competition the Greeks practised only the long jump. Facility in this art was useful for travelling quickly across the Greek countryside, cut as it often is by small ravines and watercourses. As there were few walls and no hedges, high jumping was a less valuable activity; it seems to have been practised by both Greeks and Romans as a training exercise, but never to have become part of the programme of competitions. Pole-vaulting was also practised outside the athletic curriculum. Xenophon mentions it as a method by which a cavalryman could mount his horse by using his lance as a pole; this feat is depicted in vase-paintings (*Pl.* 29). Ovid describes how Nestor in his youth, while helping Meleager in the hunt for the Calydonian boar, escaped a charge of the infuriated quarry by pole-jumping into a tree with the aid of his hunting spear. Many centuries later, a man condemned to face a fierce animal in the arena won the sympathy of the crowd and escaped his fate by pole-jumping over the back of the beast as it rushed at him.[15]

The details of the Greek long jump are still a matter of much controversy. Modern experience does not greatly help to elucidate the evidence, because the Greeks always used jumping weights (*Pl.* 30). These can add considerably to an athlete's performance in a simple jump if they are thrown backwards in mid-air, but such evidence as we have suggests that the Greek jumper retained them until he had landed. Moreover, the only two jumps recorded from antiquity, of 52 feet and 55 feet, together with some other evidence, indicate that the Greek jump was a multiple one, double, triple or even quintuple, and no modern technique is known for the use of weights in such a complex activity. That the ancient technique was highly elaborate is suggested by the number of vase-paintings which depict athletes practising with them (*Pl.* 31).[16]

JAVELIN-THROWING

Of all the events of the programme, the javelin retained the closest link with training for war. From Homeric times until late in the Roman Imperial period, the thrown javelin remained an important secondary armament of the infantryman. He usually carried two, to be discharged before coming to close quarters with the enemy for sword and shield work. Accuracy was clearly of great importance, and in military training both Greeks and Romans practised throwing at a mark. But length of throw also mattered; to be able to throw further than the enemy was to be able to hit him before he could hit back. Accordingly the Greeks, like ourselves, made distance the aim in athletic javelin-throwing. Rather strangely, the javelin was not included in the programme of the first modern Olympic Games at Athens in 1896. When it was introduced at the London Olympiad of 1908, the Scandinavians had been practising it for some decades, using a technique different from the ancient one. The Greeks, whether in war or in the stadium, always threw the javelin with the help of a thong looped over the fingers of the throwing hand (*Pls.* 34, 36); but modern athletes have never adopted this method. The thong served two purposes. It increased the radius of the throwing arm and so added to the speed of projection. More important, because it was twisted round the shaft and unwound on the throw, it imparted spin to the javelin, like that given to a bullet or shell by the rifling of the gun barrel. This spin kept the javelin steady in flight and increased the probability of its landing on the point, which then as now must have been necessary to allow the throw to be measured. When using the thong, the thrower often has to push the javelin back with the free hand to keep the thong taut; this is shown in many vase-paintings (*Pl.* 33).

When the javelin was used in war or hunting, a fairly heavy shaft was needed to secure penetration. For war javelins, cornel wood is most often mentioned. For hunting spears, Grattius recommends cornel, myrtle, yew, pine, broom, wild olive or frankincense. Bacchylides reveals that elder wood was used for athletic javelins, and Theophrastus says that bamboo was employed for spear shafts; he does not specifically mention athletics, but bamboo would obviously be suitable for this purpose. It is true that while vase-painters often depict walking sticks made of jointed wood, the paintings never show joints in the shaft of any javelin, athletic or otherwise. But then, for athletic purposes the projections at the joints would naturally have been rasped down to diminish wind resistance. The paintings sometimes show an athlete throwing a pointed javelin, sometimes a blunt one (*Pl.* 33). Probably the point was demanded in competition, while the blunt end was a safety measure in practice.[17]

There is no record of the distance of any throw in antiquity, so we have no means of knowing what the Greeks achieved in this event. One of the most remarkable differences between ancient and modern athletics is the careless-ness of the Greeks about the measurement of throws and jumps compared with our feverish concern with records and record-breaking. In running the absence of standards was inevitable; fortunately for themselves, the Greeks had no stop-watches or electrical timing devices. But even where measurement would have been easy for them—they had widely accepted standard weights and measures—they seem to have been little concerned to apply them to athletic per-formances. The best Greek athletes were content to defeat those who were in immediate competition with them, and did not care what others had done at other times and places. Apart from the two recorded jumps, Philo Judaeus appears to be the only author who specifically mentions such measur-ing, also of jumps.[18]

THE DISCUS

Throwing the discus is a curious and illogical activity. It was natural for the Greeks to compete in javelin-throwing, because it was useful in war. It would have been equally natural to compete in throwing a stone of a size and shape to make a serviceable weapon, or in throwing a hand-ball such as is used in many games. A discus comes into neither category. The origin of the event is made clear by Homer. The weight thrown in the contest in his Funeral Games is an ingot of copper, which is also the prize for the winner. In ancient smelting, the molten ore was poured into a mould, usually circular, hollowed out in sand. The ingot thus formed had a curved lower surface corresponding to the bottom of the mould, and a flat top. Many such ingots have survived. Most of them are large, but several in the museum at Cagliari are of roughly the same size as the modern athletic discus.[19]

For the Greek method of throwing we have to rely almost entirely on works of art. The only clue afforded by literature is that discus throwers are described as 'whirling round', which suggests a way of delivery similar to our own. Painting and sculpture do not help us as much as we could have wished. Before throwing, an athlete always does a few preliminary swings with the discus to warm up and to loosen his throwing arm. This involves two moments of rest, one at each end of the swing. Painters and sculptors naturally preferred to depict these moments rather than attempt the much more difficult task of portraying the vigorous action of the throw itself (*Pls.* 37, 40). The few works of art which do show the throw suggest a rotary movement of the legs not unlike that of a modern thrower turning in the circle. To obtain maximum distance, the discus must remain steady in flight, without wobble. This is secured by the thrower imparting spin with his forefinger to the discus as it leaves his hand, similar to that given to the javelin by the thong.[20]

A possible difference between ancient and modern throwing is suggested by some of these pictures. Fundamentally

distance is secured by a combination of speed of ejection and
the optimum elevation of the throw from the horizontal.
Today, speed of ejection is obtained entirely by centrifugal
force, the arm being kept straight throughout the action,
while the thrower aims at the greatest possible speed of
revolution, with legs, body, shoulders and arms all contribut-
ing to this end. In the language of cricket, the discus is not
thrown but bowled. From time to time in the history of
cricket, fast bowlers have achieved additional speed by
straightening a bent elbow at the moment of delivery—by
throwing, in fact, instead of bowling. A number of paintings
of ancient discus throwers show the elbow of the throwing
arm bent just before delivery (*Pls.* 35, 36, 38). If cricketers can
achieve additional speed by the use of the bent elbow there
seems to be no reason why a discus thrower should not do
the same, and it is possible that the Greeks had discovered
this. In cricket the action is illegal, but there is nothing in the
modern rules of discus-throwing to prohibit it. Our athletes
might care to experiment.

Such was the programme of athletics meetings all over the
Greek world for a thousand years. The story of the place of
the sport in the social life of that world follows the same lines
as the history of organized games in the last two centuries.
Athletics was at first the leisure occupation of the classes
wealthy enough to afford the time for such activities and the
expense of travelling to the different festivals. But these
meetings were also the greatest spectator attractions in the
Greek world, commanding the same enthusiastic following
as chariot-racing among the Romans or football in our own
day, and, as with us, this caused the emergence of a class of
highly paid professional performers, whose standards of skill
drove the true amateurs out of competition at the top level.
It is not possible to give any accurate dating for this change,
which appears to have taken place rather more slowly than
with us; it probably happened between the fourth and second

centuries B C. When money comes in at the door, sport flies
out of the window, and the Greek athletic scene thereafter
exhibits the same abuses that are becoming only too familiar
to us in our big business world of so-called 'sport'. The
highly paid performers, the darlings of the crowds, were
ruined by success and by quickly acquired wealth, and
became insufferably arrogant. Plutarch records that in his
day the Spartans were the only athletes who did not hurl
abuse at umpires; when he wrote, Sparta had been part of
the Roman empire for some centuries, but the old discipline
still counted for something. Corruption permeated the whole
scene. Officials and rivals were bribed to 'fix' matches; col-
lusive agreements between boxers and wrestlers produced
tame draws, with the competitors dividing the prize money.
Yet the knowledge that conduct of this kind was common
did nothing to lessen the passion of spectators for athletics.
We have less evidence for this frenzy among the Greeks than
for the fanatical enthusiasm of Roman crowds for chariot-
racing, but indications are not wholly lacking. At the end of
the first century of the Christian era, Dio Chrysostom bears
witness to the behaviour of the crowds in the stadium, to
their yelling and frenzied blasphemies, the fanatical applause
for local athletes and malevolent abuse of their rivals. From
an earlier time comes a significant pointer to the place
of sport in the life of the community. In 224 B C, the island
and city of Rhodes experienced a severe earthquake which,
among other things, brought down the famous bronze
Colossus. Then as now, the rest of the civilized world rallied
round with funds to alleviate the results of the disaster.
Ptolemy III of Egypt contributed generously, mostly in kind,
but he earmarked part of his gift of corn 'for the Games'.
Hiero and Gelo, wealthy rulers in Sicily, sent 100 talents of
silver, 75 of which were to be spent on oil for the gymnasia.[21]
   It was perhaps the development of sport as an entertainment
for spectators and the desire to produce something to titillate
the fancy of the crowds that caused a growth in women's
athletics which appears to have taken place at about the

beginning of the Christian era. Before that time there had
been athletics meetings at Olympia for women, separate
from those for men; the competitors had worn a costume
described by Pausanias and faithfully portrayed in a famous
statue now in the Vatican Museum (*Pl.* 45). There may have
been similar festivals elsewhere, of which we know nothing.
A vase of the late sixth century B C, also in the Vatican, almost
certainly depicts a women's race (*Pl.* 46). It is just possible
that the women may be executing a vigorous dance, but
their arm action is exactly the same as that of men runners
on vases of the same period (*Pl.* 5). After that, except for
Plato's advocacy in the *Laws* of athletics for women, and a
few references to women's athletics at Sparta, there is silence
on the subject for some centuries. Our most comprehensive
piece of evidence, an inscription revealing the existence of
meetings for women at Delphi, Isthmia, Nemea, Epidaurus
and Athens, is dated to the first century A D. To the same
century belong other inscriptions attesting women's events
at Corinth and Naples, and in the same period the Emperor
Domitian included races for girls in his Capitoline Games at
Rome. A century later, in the Olympic Games at Antioch in
Syria, girls competed in wrestling and running, dressed in
shorts (μετὰ βομβωναρίων). When Malalas, our authority
for this, says that the winners of both sexes at these Games
were taken into the priesthood and observed lifelong chastity
he strains our credulity, even though he adds that their land
was tax-free during their lifetime. But there is no reason to
doubt that there were women athletes at Antioch at this
time. The well-known fourth-century mosaics of Piazza
Armerina in Sicily support the belief that women's athletics
in the Roman period had more to do with public entertainment than with sport proper (*Pl.* 44).[22]

The increasing commercialization of Greek athletics, and the
large money prizes offered at the meetings in the wealthy
cities of Asia Minor, caused the old 'sacred' Games of Greece

to decline in importance. For some centuries they continued to have a certain prestige value, and athletes in recording their achievements long adhered to the convention of putting Olympic, Pythian, Isthmian and Nemean victories at the head of the list. But as early as the first century BC even Olympia was in financial straits, and Herod the Great came to the rescue with a benefaction. During the long years of peace at the beginning of the Roman Imperial period, Greece and especially Olympia became a great tourist attraction for the Roman world—this is clear from the pages of Pausanias and Lucian—and the decline was arrested. But by the third century we hear little of these festivals, and there seem to have been no protests when the Olympic Games were brought to an end in 396. Elsewhere some meetings lingered on in the Byzantine empire. The Games at Antioch, for instance, were not suppressed until 520.[23]

Ten years after that we have a final glimpse of a Greek athlete. In 530 a Byzantine army under Belisarius was defending the city of Daras against a Persian force. The Byzantines were strongly entrenched, and after a preliminary skirmish the Persians did not dare to press on with their attack. Instead, a Persian horseman rode out from their ranks and issued a challenge to single combat. The only man among the Byzantines willing to accept was Andreas, the personal attendant of Bouzes, who was one of Belisarius' corps commanders. Andreas was not even a soldier; he was an instructor in physical training and the proprietor of a wrestling school in Byzantium. He was with the Byzantine army to help Bouzes to keep fit and to act as his masseur. The duel was fought on horseback with spears, like a medieval jousting match. At the first encounter, Andreas unhorsed and killed his opponent. The Persians then sent out a much bigger and more powerful champion. Against orders, Andreas went out again to meet this new enemy. In the charge both men were thrown from their horses, but Andreas, thanks to his experience in the wrestling ring, was well accustomed to being thrown; accordingly he was more quickly on his feet again and succeeded in killing this second challenger. So Greek athletics, which had had its origin in preparation for war, makes a final appearance on the battlefield. The wheel had come full circle.[24]

CHAPTER II

GREEK ATHLETICS IN THE ROMAN WORLD

IN 500 BC THERE WERE IN ITALY two thriving civilizations, the Etruscan and the Greek. The Etruscans occupied the northern part of the peninsula. The Greeks in their colonizing movement, which started in the eighth century, had seized all the most promising sites on the south coast, as they also did in Sicily. Some of these colonies had grown into cities of great wealth and influence, rivalling the mightiest on the Greek mainland, and this western extension of the Greek world into Italy was sometimes called Magna Graecia.

The origin of the Etruscan civilization is still a matter of dispute. One school follows the Greek tradition that it lay in Asia Minor; others—especially Italian Etruscologists—believe that it was completely indigenous to Italy. Our knowledge of it is necessarily limited; no Etruscan literature has survived, and the language of the inscriptions has not been finally deciphered. We have to rely on the statements of Greek and Roman writers and on what archaeological discoveries can tell us. Fortunately, these last are particularly rich. The Etruscans buried their dead in elaborate rock-cut or stone-built tombs, decorated with wall-paintings and sculptured reliefs, and equipped with lavish funeral furnishings. Many hundreds of these tombs have been explored; even more await investigation, and our knowledge may be expected to extend rapidly, if modern tomb-robbers allow.

This evidence enables us to form a picture of an Etruscan culture emerging in the ninth century BC and reaching its peak in the seventh and sixth centuries. Its heartland lay west of the Apennines and north of the Tiber, but in the sixth century a movement of expansion took Etruscan power as far as Capua, 100 miles south of Rome, and for a time Rome herself was under Etruscan rule. According to tradition, two of her kings were Etruscans, and the last of them was expelled in 510 BC. At sea the Etruscans were strong enough to deny their own coasts to Greek colonization. This clash of interests led them to ally themselves with the Carthaginians, the great rivals of the Greeks at sea, but Etruscan naval pretensions received a final blow in their defeat at the hands of Hiero of Syracuse in a battle off Cumae in 474. Rivalry at sea, however, did not prevent the Etruscans from conceiving a strong admiration for some aspects of Greek life, notably Greek art. Although Etruscan art is powerfully stamped with the characteristics of the people, the influence of Greece is equally unmistakable. Many Greek works of art were imported, especially vases and small bronzes; a considerable proportion of the finest Greek vases in our museums come from Etruscan tombs.

The wall-paintings in the tombs show that the Etruscans were especially attracted by the Greek love of sport and that they practised most of the events of the Greek athletic programme, running, wrestling, boxing with gloves of the Greek pattern, jumping with weights, javelin-throwing with the thong, and throwing the discus (*Pls.* 14, 35). The paintings in one tomb at Tarquinia are so exclusively dedicated to these subjects that it is generally called the 'Tomb of the Olympiads'; this evidence is supported by the large numbers of Greek vases with athletic subjects which have been found in other tombs. The Etruscans did not necessarily imitate the Greeks slavishly in their athletics. Certainly they did not follow them in insisting on their athletes being naked; many of the figures depicted, like the discus thrower in Plate 35, wear shorts. In the tomb of the Olympiads there is a scene showing chariot-racing. We must not take it for granted from this that here too the Etruscans were copying Greeks; they may well have developed the event independently. Nor is it known whether they followed the Greeks in holding meetings for athletics alone with the narrow Olympic programme. There was in the Etruscan temperament a streak of cruelty, shared or inherited by the Romans, which led them to delight in bloodshed in public entertainment. To satisfy this they promoted gladiatorial combats and wild beast shows; it is possible that they included some athletic events in such shows, as the Romans certainly did later.

Assuredly, in 500 BC no Greek or Etruscan can have envisaged the future that awaited Rome, an inconsiderable hill town which had recently secured its independence from the Etruscans. For the next two centuries, Rome was to be engaged in almost ceaseless warfare against her neighbours, including the Etruscans, to secure her future by making herself mistress of the centre of Italy. Then came her struggle with Carthage, long the enemy of the Greeks of Sicily and South Italy. For this reason, Rome was regarded as an ally by these during the wars, but when the wars ended with the complete defeat of Carthage in 200 BC these Greeks had been almost painlessly absorbed into the Roman domains. Macedon had given some assistance to the Carthaginians in the war, and the Romans determined that she must be taught not to interfere, though at this time it would seem that they had no intention of annexation. The Greeks of the homeland still regarded the Macedonians as intruders, enabled by their military might to exercise an undue influence on Greek affairs. For a time the Romans adopted this view and posed as champions of the independence of southern Greece. In an emotional scene at the Isthmian Games of 196 BC, the Roman commander Flamininus declared that the Greeks were once again free and independent. But independence was a gift of which the Greeks were now completely unable to take advantage. After half a century of increasing exasperation, Rome was compelled to convert Greece into a Roman province, and in order to make clear who was now master they destroyed one of the oldest of Greek cities, Corinth. Roman policy now changed. Annexation became the order of the day, and a century later still, when the Republic was being converted into the Empire, Rome had become the mistress of the whole of the Mediterranean world.

Much attention has been devoted to the problem of why the Roman Empire fell; less to the far more difficult problem of why it arose. Among the thousands of small towns in the Mediterranean countries at the beginning of the first millenium BC, why did this particular one come to dominate the civilized world? Certainly the reason did not lie in her possession of any perfect political system. Throughout her history Rome laboured under a constitution which by all canons of political science was fantastically absurd. It might be argued that the Roman genius for finding pragmatic solutions to political problems owed something to her long experience in making her own constitution work. Yet this is not an answer. Many other cities and nations had imperfect constitutions but did not rise to rule the world. Inescapably we are driven to the conclusion that the secret lay in the character of the Roman people. 'I do not know', said Burke, 'the method of drawing up an indictment against a whole people'; it might seem to follow that a general encomium of a nation must be equally faulty. Yet we cannot fall back on the only other solution, that Rome's greatness was due to the outstanding qualities of a few men. That judgment might with greater justification be made about the Greeks. The Greek world produced a remarkable succession of geniuses in many fields, to whom Rome can show no parallel; the Roman achievement is a high plateau with few outstanding peaks. But compared with the ordinary Roman, the ordinary Greek appears lacking in 'bottom' and staying power. It has often been remarked that in the military sphere, while the limelight rests on commanders of genius, the quality of a fighting force in the last resort depends on its non-commissioned officers. To the student of the ancient world it sometimes appears that almost any Roman was a born sergeant-major or chief petty officer.

At some time early in the first millenium BC there must

have been a chance combination of genes in this part of Italy which in the course of generations produced the Roman character. The qualities of that character have often been enumerated. There was a superb self-confidence and courage, without which none of the other virtues could have made their impression; a deep reverence for tradition and ancestral wisdom, which ensured the continuity of the virtues in the community; a moral earnestness and sense of duty which would have satisfied Thomas Arnold; a respect for property, combined with a passion for law and order; a desire for justice, allied to a conviction that, if law and order failed, justice was the first victim; a distrust of imagination and theoretical speculation, and a supreme ability to find a practical solution to any problem; a straightforward belief in religion as a sanction for morality, and, in particular, a respect for the sanctity of oaths; a conviction that older men had acquired knowledge and experience which made them far better qualified than the young to run the world, and a belief that the men most likely to serve the community well were those whose ancestors had proved themselves able to do the same. Today these virtues are highly unfashionable, and it is not surprising that the present generation, desperate to exonerate itself in its own eyes for its own deficiencies, seizes on and exaggerates the weak points in the Roman character, with the result that the enormous Roman contribution to civilization is now often vastly underrated.

However regrettable it may be on ideological grounds, it is a matter of empirical observation that those peoples which have given most to the world have generally, at the period of their greatest flowering, entertained a sturdy contempt for foreigners. A flabby internationalism is an infallible early symptom of the moral collapse of individual or nation. The feeling of contempt is based on an awareness of superiority inevitable at such a time. It is exacerbated if the superiority is not complete and there is some area where the ascendant nation feels inferior; then, in the popular jargon, it becomes a defence mechanism. The Roman attitude towards the

Etruscans was straightforward enough. They had once been ruled by Etruscan kings, and were well aware that there was Etruscan blood in many Roman veins, but they had comprehensively disposed of the Etruscan threat in a series of wars and absorbed them into their domain. Anything the Etruscans could do, the Roman felt he could do better. By the first century BC, Etruria was part of Rome's romantic past. Etruscan ancestry was even a matter of pride for some Roman families. The wealthy Maecenas, Augustus' unofficial Secretary for Culture and the Arts, was obviously delighted to have Horace call attention to his descent from Etruscan kings.[25]

The Roman attitude to the Greeks was very different. It was impossible to pretend that anything a Greek could do, a Roman could do better. Long before Rome had any military or political contact with the Greek world, intelligent Romans had realized the extent of the Greek achievement in literature and the arts, in mathematics, in philosophy and in speculative science, and had conceived a profound admiration for it. This attitude irritated the great mass of Romans, who were by no means intellectual in their interests, and by way of compensation they did exactly what we in our generation are doing to the Romans—they seized on Greek weaknesses, of which there were plenty, exaggerated them and so justified to themselves a contempt which emerges time and again in Latin literature. Perhaps the most extraordinary example of this is the passage in which Manilius uses the sun-tan acquired by naked athletes in stadium and palaestra as a reason for including the Greeks among the coloured peoples, Syrians, Ethiopians, Indians and Egyptians, who were not highly rated by the Romans:

> *Perque coloratas subtilis Graecia gentis*
> *gymnasium praefert vultu fortisque palaestras.*
> *(Astronomica* IV, 720)

The Roman conviction of their own general superiority over other peoples did not prevent them from experimenting with ideas borrowed from them, and if they served a useful purpose, adopting them. Both the Etruscans and the Greeks had gained experience in using sport as public entertainment, and the Romans benefitted from this. From the Etruscans they took gladiatorial and wild beast shows—if these can be called sport—which were to become one of the two great entertainments of the Roman world; the other, chariot-racing, may have been suggested to them by either the Greeks or the Etruscans. From time to time over a period of many centuries they experimented with Greek athletics, but these never became part of the social scene in the western Roman world as did the other two.

According to Roman tradition, the earliest public Games in the city were given by the Etruscan kings of Rome, the Tarquins, who laid out the Circus Maximus for chariot-racing. Livy tells us that the elder Tarquin extended the programme by introducing boxers from Etruria. From the Etruscans too came the custom of Games at funerals, and it was in this way that gladiatorial contests came to Rome. Moreover, if Livy is to be believed, the first stage performances in Rome were given in 364 BC by players from Etruria, dancing to the music of flutes. The Romans may have learnt something of Greek athletics from the Etruscans, but they also had plenty of opportunity to acquire the knowledge from the Greeks who lived in the numerous colonies in the south of Italy and Sicily. One of these colonies, Croton, produced more Olympic victors in the 'Golden Age' of Greek athletics, 600–300 BC, than any other city in the whole of the Greek world. The earliest recorded Greek Games at Rome were promoted by M. Fulvius Nobilior in 186 BC. The date is significant. Ten years before, Flamininus had proclaimed Greek independence, and the Romans were still flushed with enthusiasm for patronizing Greece. We hear of other Greek Games offered by Sulla in 81 BC, by M. Aemilius Scaurus in 58, by Pompey in 55, by C. Curio in 53 and in 46 by Julius Caesar. There is no reason to believe that these were the only occasions. No details of these festivals are known, but it is reasonable to suppose that the competitors in them were professional Greek athletes, brought over by the wealthy politicians who gave the Games, just as today British professional football teams are sometimes taken over to the USA to play exhibition matches there. The promoters may have used the same device to attract leading athletes as Herod the Great employed when he inaugurated festivals at Caesarea and Jerusalem—offering good second and third prizes, a feature not common in Greek athletic meetings—or they may have subsidized all competitors. The events at these festivals must have been those of the restricted Olympic Games programme used at all Greek meetings. But Dionysius of Halicarnassus tells us that shorts were worn by competitors at Rome until his own day— late in the first century B C.[26]

All these festivals were promoted and paid for by ambitious politicians in order to attract votes, and presumably they would not have included Greek athletics if the people had not understood and enjoyed them. Of the extent of their knowledge there is little evidence in Latin literature before the first century B C. Terence, it is true, attributes the failure of one of his plays on its first appearance to the rival attractions of a boxing display. A character in his *Eunuch* complains about the fashionable pencil silhouette of the girls of his day:

> Their mothers try to make them bottle-necked and flat-chested so that they shall look slender; if one of them happens to be a bit more curvaceous, they call her a boxer and put her on a slimming diet.
>
> (*Eunuch*, 315)

Plautus in his plays mentions boxers and pankratiasts, wrestling, javelin-throwing, discus-throwing and jumping. Both Terence and Plautus were translating Greek plays, but they would hardly have retained these technical terms if they had not been intelligible to their Roman audiences. Most conclusive of all is a threat in Plautus' *Rudens*:

I'll make a punch-ball of you and hang you up and go for
you with my fists.

(Rudens, 721)

At the beginning of the second century BC, the Roman
audience obviously knew something of a boxer's training
methods.[27]

For the social scene at Rome in the first century BC in the
last days of the Republic, we naturally turn to Cicero. He
has been called the most civilized man who ever lived. He
had every Roman virtue but one; from time to time he lost
confidence in himself. His one unpleasant characteristic, his
incredible vanity, may have been his defence against this
weakness in himself. Like all intelligent Romans, he had a
profound admiration for Greece and her past. Most of the
leisure he could find from political activity and the law-
courts he devoted to interpreting Greek philosophy to his
contemporaries in a series of works which present an invaluable synthesis of what was best in the Greek and Roman
attitudes to life. Unhappily his admiration for the Greeks
did not extend to their sports; this was scarcely surprising,
since by this time Greek athletes had become mere professional public entertainers. In July of 44 BC, less than four
months after the murder of Julius Caesar, Brutus promoted
Games in Rome. Cicero wrote to Atticus:

It is rumoured that there were not many spectators at the
opening of the Greek Games. That did not disappoint me
in the least, for you know what I think of Greek Games.

(Ad Atticum XVI, 5)

Earlier he had written to M. Marius about the Games given
in 55 BC by Pompey:

Seeing that you despise even gladiators, why should I
suppose that you minded missing the athletes? Pompey
himself admits that the effort and oil he expended on them
were wasted.

(Ad Familiares VII, 1)

(Evidently a Roman who promoted Games imitated a Greek agonothete in supplying oil for the competitors.)

Cicero's failure to appreciate these festivals may have arisen from his dislike of the nakedness involved. In one of his philosophical works he quotes with approval a line of Ennius:

> To strip in public is the beginning of evil-doing.
> (*Tusculanae Disputationes* IV, xxxiii. 70)

It is not to be wondered at, then, that we do not learn much from Cicero about Greek athletics in the Roman scene of his day. Yet when he finds an apt illustration from sport in his Greek authorities, he translates it, obviously sure that his readers will take the point. Thus he retains a simile in Chrysippus:

> If a man is running a race in the stadium, he ought to use every effort to win, but on no account must he cut in on a rival or push him with his hand. So too in life it is not wrong for a man to try to satisfy his needs, but it is not right for him to take anything from another.
> (*De Officiis* III, x. 42)

Moreover there is one passage in Cicero's letters which reveals the attitude of his contemporaries to the Olympic Games. In the August of 44 BC, undecided about what he ought to do in the confused situation in Rome after Caesar's assassination, he set out for Greece but turned back before he arrived there. He tells Atticus:

> Brutus and his friends were particularly glad at this, because by returning I escaped the imputation of being thought to have gone off to the Olympic Games. No conduct could have been more disgraceful at any crisis of the state; in this one it would have been indefensible.
> (*Ad Atticum* XVI, 7)

The implication of this is surely that many Romans did in fact go off to Olympia that August. And if this happened in that summer, far more Roman tourists must have visited the Games in Olympic years of less political tension. The colloquial phrase used by Cicero (*me existimari ad Olympia*) in itself suggests that the practice was well established— 'He's off to Olympia'.

A few years after Cicero's death the battle of Actium at last brought peace to the Roman world after a century of civil war, and left Augustus with the task of putting the empire in order. Much of this empire had been acquired during the wars, and machinery of government had been provided by rule of thumb for each province as it was gained. With great political tact Augustus, in putting order into the confusion, made as few changes as possible in outward constitutional forms. Broadly the situation which confronted him was an empire of two distinct halves. In the east Mediterranean, a number of provinces of very different origins had for a couple of centuries enjoyed the unifying influence of Greek culture and, most important, of the Greek language. In the west, Rome was still imposing the Latin culture and language as a unifying principle on a number of provinces of no less diverse origin. Among the minor differences between the two cultures was the disparity in popular entertainment. Festivals of Greek Games in the Roman Republican era had done little to invalidate the general principle that the West preferred gladiators, while the East was still loyal to its athletics.

For a century before the battle of Actium, Rome had been sending governors and their staffs into the Greek world, and they had of necessity to know Greek. But they had not always shown themselves sensitive to popular sentiment within their commands. Cicero's brother Quintus, for instance, took steps to discourage athletic festivals in his province of Asia, and Cicero congratulated him on doing so. Augustus took a very different line. When he founded the city of Nicopolis at Actium to celebrate his victory there, he re-inaugurated an existing athletic festival and reconstituted it as the Actia; like the Olympic and Pythian Games, it was held at four-yearly intervals, and at once it assumed an importance in the Greek athletic world equal to that of these and the other 'crown' festivals, the Isthmian and Nemean. At the same time he instituted a festival under the same name at Rome; for this and other athletic meetings which he promoted in Rome, he constructed a temporary stadium with wooden seats in the Campus Martius. Suetonius also records that whenever Augustus was present at Greek Games, he gave gifts to all the contestants; this must have assured a satisfactory number of competitors. Yet it is not easy to deduce from Suetonius whether the emperor had any personal enthusiasm for athletics. We are told that when he was a spectator at the Games he was always attentive to the proceedings, unlike Julius, who used to reveal his lack of interest by dealing with state documents in the Circus. Suetonius adds the curious information that Augustus used sometimes to watch from the top-storey windows of friends' houses which overlooked the Games. Dio makes the same statement about Tiberius, with whom it is much more in character; and it is probable that Suetonius, not the most accurate of historians, has slipped in transferring it to Augustus.[28]

Whether Augustus had a conception of sport as a unifying element between the two halves of his empire or was merely concerned that Roman officials should understand the pursuits of the peoples they would be called on to govern, it is impossible to say. He certainly encouraged active participation by Romans in Greek sports. According to Suetonius, he was particularly keen on watching Roman boxers, not only regular professionals, whom he used to match even with Greeks—the implied admission of Greek superiority in this event is noteworthy—but also impromptu bouts of ordinary unskilled townsmen in the slums.[29]

The new interest in Greek athletics is mirrored in the literature of the time. Apart from Terence and Plautus, the poets of the Republic throw little light on the subject: Lucretius, Catullus and Propertius hardly mention it. But with the foundation of the Empire there comes a change. Horace gives us vivid glimpses of young Sybaris, once renowned for hurling the discus or javelin out of the ground (*trans finem*), now reduced to effeminacy by his passion for Lydia, and of Hebrus,

> A better horseman than Bellerophon himself, unbeaten at boxing and running.
>
> (*Odes* III, 12)

He could rely on his readers' understanding an allusion to the pankratiast Glycon of Pergamum, a recent Olympic victor and also, as an inscription informs us, a winner at the Actia at Nicopolis. Similarly, two metaphors in his *Epistles* indicate that he could assume a knowledge of athletic techniques in his readers. Summing up his gospel of the Golden Mean, he writes:

> If you set a slow pace in the race, I shall not lag behind with you, and if you exert every effort to take the lead, I shall not run at your shoulder.
>
> (*Epistles* I, ii. 70)

Elsewhere he declares his refusal to argue with his critics in these words:

> For fear of being scratched by the sharp nail of my opponent [*luctantis*], I cry 'I protest against that pitch' [*displicet iste locus*] and demand '*Diludia*'.
>
> (*Epistles* I, xix. 46)

This passage contains one of the few references in ancient literature to what must always have been a risk to wrestlers —the sharp nails of their opponents, a danger which must surely have been guarded against in the rules. The phrase 'I protest against that pitch' is our only evidence that a wrestler who did not approve of the piece of ground chosen for the ring could refuse to fight on it. *Diludia* is found nowhere else. An ancient commentator says that gladiators used it for the postponement of a fight. Here it obviously means 'change

5 Detail from
left and runn
office.

1,2 Olympia. *Above*, view from above the old museum. The stadium, *below*,
is concealed by the trees in the centre of the picture. It is square at both ends
and completely surrounded by banking. Except for a small stand for officials,
there was never any stone seating provided here.

8 An athlete's toilet set, comprising two strigils and an oil-flask.

3 A[...]
from[...]
roun[...]

9 The gravestone of a young athlete. His left hand calls attention to his victor's wreath, while with his right he is scraping himself with a strigil after his bath. A small slave holds his oil-flask. Attic, fourth century BC.

4 Di[...]
podi[...]
be s[...]

10 Priene. Washbasins in the gymnasium with lion-head spouts still *in situ*.

11 A statue base from the wall of Themistocles in Athens (for an account of these bases see p. 101). *Left*, a runner on the starting line; his left foot is in front of his right by the few inches which separated the grooves in the sill of the *husplex*. *Centre*, wrestlers. *Right*, a javelin-thrower presses back the shaft of his weapon in order to tighten the thong.

12,13 A waist-lock and lift is demonstrated by the small bronze, *left*. On the impression of a gemstone, *right*, two boys practise a neck-lock and counter-move under the eye of their trainer.

14 A wall-painting in the Etruscan 'Tomb of the Monkey' at Chiusi shows jockeys and a wrestler throwing his opponent under the umpire's supervision.

15,16 Boxers with ear-guards. On the fourth-century BC gravestone relief, *left*, the boxer is depicted with ear-guards, but the sculptor has not been able to deny himself the pleasure of showing the ears. *Below*, this marble head may be a copy of an original by Myron. Here, too, the ear is seen as well as the straps of the ear-guard.

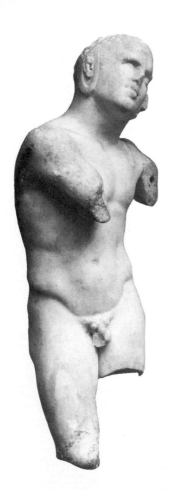

17 The outer rim of this red-figure kylix shows boxers striking with the open hand, whilst another winds on his protective thong.

18 This magnificent Hellenistic bronze shows an experienced boxer resting between bouts. He is wearing the elaborate boxing gloves of the period (pp. 22-3).

19 No satisfactory explanation has ever been given of why Greek boxing was sometimes accompanied by music. The disparity in size between the boxers on this vase is probably not significant, but simply due to the painter's need to place his central figure under the musician's pipes. Vases rarely depict boxers in such lively action as this; much more usual is the conventional attitude of Plate 6.

20 The scene on this skyphos represents the end of a pankration bout, with one contestant acknowledging defeat. Here the athletes wear no gloves; on the other side of this same skyphos, however, they do (*GAA*, Plate 21). The only safe conclusion is that we must observe great caution in using vase-paintings as evidence for any detail of Greek athletic technique.

of place'. A simile in Polybius reveals that the umpire could order the choice of a new site for the ring. Describing a situation of stalemate between the Roman and Carthaginian armies at Panormus in 247 BC, he says:

> At last Chance, *like a good umpire*, moved them from the position they had occupied to one where a decisive action was possible.[30]
>
> (I, 58)

While an unmistakable picture of the enthusiasm of wealthy young Romans for Greek athletics emerges from the pages of Horace, a great admirer of the Augustan regime and possibly an officially encouraged propagandist for it, he makes it clear that they did not confine themselves to the events of the narrow Olympic programme, but combined them with other sports and with traditional Roman pursuits mainly drawn from training for war. Horace's Sybaris has given up fencing as well as discus-throwing; Hebrus swims in the Tiber and is an expert hunter. To drive home the point that skill and training are needed in everything, Horace writes:

> The man who knows nothing of games keeps away from the weapons of the Campus, and being ignorant of ball-play, the discus or the hoop, he remains quiet, for fear that spectators may justifiably roar with laughter at his efforts.
>
> (*Ars Poetica*, 371)

He admits Greek superiority at their own sports, insisting that it would be absurd for a Roman to say, 'We are better at wrestling than the Greeks'. He is willing to grant that these Greek sports demand arduous preparation:

> The man who wishes to achieve the longed-for victory in a race must as a boy have trained long and hard, have sweated and groaned, and abstained from wine and women.
>
> (*Ars Poetica*, 412)

But he cannot prevent the Roman contempt for the Greek

from colouring his thought even on sport. When dealing with the Greek love of novelty he writes:

> It was when Greece laid aside her wars and began to devote herself to trifles [*nugari*], and prosperity caused her to drift into vice, that enthusiasm for athletics and horses flared up.
>
> (Epistles II, i.93)

Historically this is nonsense, but the Roman attitude is unmistakable. Again, praising the simple life, he advises hare-hunting or horse-breeding as pastimes, and then goes on:

> Or, if Roman pursuits wear you out because you are used to playing the Greek [*Graecari*], try the quick ball-play, which by its excitement makes you forget your exhaustion, or if you prefer discus-throwing, then aim high in the yielding air with your discus.
>
> (Satires II, ii.10)

But in spite of the occasional intrusion of this traditional Roman feeling about Greeks, there is no doubting Horace's genuine love of Greek sport. In this he was surprisingly followed later in Augustus' reign by Ovid, not generally regarded as the most athletic of poets. In the *Metamorphoses* he has a splendid description of Atalanta's race, and a spirited account of a wrestling match between Heracles and a river god, Achelous. Unhappily the end of the latter story is spoilt because the exigencies of the plot demand that the god, in order to avoid defeat, should metamorphose himself into a snake and then a bull. But one couplet shows that Ovid was acquainted with a detail of Greek wrestling procedure of which there is no equally explicit description in Greek literature. Achelous is relating the preparations for the fight:

> *Ille cavis hausto spargit me pulvere palmis,*
> *inque vicem fulvae tactu flavescit harenae.*

He picked up dust in his cupped hands and sprinkled it over me,

and in turn became golden as I threw the tawny dust over
him.

(Metamorphoses IX, 35)

Wrestlers, as we have seen, were allowed to dust their opponents to ensure that the oil with which they were smeared
should not prevent a firm grip.[31]

In exile on the shores of the Black Sea, Ovid remembered
sadly in springtime how the young men in Rome would be
enjoying themselves in the grassy Campus Martius:

> Now they are riding their horses, now they are fencing or
> playing with ball or hoop. Now, streaming with slippery
> oil, they bathe their weary limbs in the waters of the Virgo
> aqueduct.

(Tristia III, xii.19)

He pictures himself, compelled thus to watch busy life from
a distance, as an ephedros, a man who has drawn a bye in a
wrestling competition and finds it more exhausting to sit
idly watching a bout of his fellow competitors than to
engage in combat:

> The fresh wrestler on the yellow sand is stronger than the
> one whose arms are worn out by a long wait.

(Tristia IV, vi.31)

In another poem, cursing the unknown enemy who was
responsible for his banishment, he exclaims:

> If ever you hurl a discus into the empty air, may it hit you
> and fell you to the ground like Hyacinthus.

(Ibis, 589)

Several of Augustus' successors in the first century AD
followed his example in patronizing Greek sports. Tiberius,
it is true, gave no public Games of any kind and rarely
attended those given by others, even though in his youth
he had won the chief equestrian event in the Olympic Games,

the race for four-horse chariots, and his nephew Germanicus had achieved the same success. But Suetonius records of Caligula that he included matches between African and Campanian boxers in gladiatorial Games at Rome, and that he gave Greek Games at Syracuse and Games with a mixed programme (*miscellos*) at Lyons in Gaul, which included a contest in Latin and Greek oratory.[32]

If the programme of this festival at Lyons included athletics, it is one of the rare examples of athletics in the Latin cities of the Western empire outside Rome, though in the Greek cities of Sicily and south Italy athletics meetings continued at least into the second century AD. The younger Pliny tells us of such a meeting, also in Gaul, in the reign of Trajan, and his account reveals the characteristic Roman attitude to Greek institutions. A citizen of Vienne in the Rhône valley had left a sum of money to endow an athletics festival in the town, but a magistrate, Trebonius Rufus, a friend of Pliny, had decreed that the Games should be discontinued. There was an appeal to the emperor against the decree as being *ultra vires*. Trajan sat with a committee of judicial advisers to decide the appeal. One of these advisers, Junius Mauricus, when asked for his opinion, supported the ban and added, 'I wish they could be abolished at Rome too'. Pliny goes on:

> The decision was that the Games should be abolished; they had corrupted the morals of Vienne, as they corrupt everyone in Rome. But the vices of Vienne remain within their own walls; ours spread abroad. In the empire as in the human body, the worst disease is that which starts from the head.

> (*Epistulae* IV, xxii)

In strange contrast, Pliny elsewhere congratulates another friend on giving a gladiatorial show in Verona in honour of his dead wife, and sympathizes with him because the panthers which he had ordered for it from Africa were delayed by bad weather and did not arrive in time.[33]

Of all Roman emperors the keenest patron of Greek athletics was Nero, as might be expected in view of his enthusiasm for all things Greek and especially for the Olympic Games. In A D 60 he instituted the Neronia at Rome, a Greek festival which included athletic and equestrian events and also the arts—music, rhetoric and drama. He competed himself in the musical section and brought pressure to bear on Roman citizens to take part in the same events. Tacitus tells us that this innovation was widely frowned upon as likely to produce a degenerate younger generation:

> 'Our traditional morals, long crumbling, were completely overthrown by this foreign licentiousness, whose aim was . . . that our young men should be corrupted by these outlandish importations into becoming devotees of the gymnasium, of luxury and of unnatural vice . . . . The next stage would be that they would be compelled to strip naked, put on boxing gloves and practise that form of exercise instead of war and arms.
>
> *(Annals* XIV, xx)

In this passage we see old-fashioned Romans still nursing the belief, which had appeared from time to time for some centuries in Greek literature, that gymnasia were hotbeds of vice; we see too the fear that the traditional physical education of the Romans—training for war—was threatened by the introduction of Greek methods.

Nero made further efforts to promote interest in athletics by annexing a gymnasium to the great baths which he built in the Campus Martius. Tacitus adds the information that at this gymnasium he supplied oil for Senators and Knights 'with Greek liberality'. Here too stood a statue of the emperor until it was struck by lightning and reduced to a shapeless lump of bronze. Apparently he maintained a troop of athletes at his own expense. On one occasion he incurred unpopularity because at a time of food shortage a ship arrived from Alexandria carrying not corn but powder for the 'court wrestlers' (*luctatoribus aulicis*). One of this troop is known to us by name, Patrobius, an Olympic victor of slave origin; it is possible that the imperial patronage resulted in the relaxation of the rules governing qualifications for competitors at the great Greek festivals. The elder Pliny records that Patrobius was particularly addicted to the use of Egyptian powder. A similar association between an athlete and an emperor a few years later had a sad result. Plutarch tells us that a pankratiast named Regulus—the Latin name is noteworthy—died of apoplexy after being entertained by the Emperor Titus. In the next century the Emperor Commodus kept as his personal trainer an athlete named Narcissus. When one of the emperor's mistresses plotted to get rid of her lord, she bribed Narcissus to assassinate him.[34]

The festival of the Neronia at Rome seems not to have survived its founder. In AD 86 the Emperor Domitian inaugurated the Capitolia in honour of Rome's chief deity, Jupiter Capitolinus, with crowns of Jove's own oak as prizes. For a time at least these Games attracted the finest Greek athletes and were regarded as equal in prestige to the four great 'crown' festivals of Greece, in this respect usurping the place formerly occupied by Augustus' Actia. For the festival Domitian provided the first permanent stadium in Rome. Its familiar U-shape can still be seen in the Piazza Navona, which now occupies the site.[35]

The emperor for whose opinion of Greek athletics we have the firmest evidence is Trajan. When the younger Pliny was governor of Bithynia, he consulted the emperor about Nicaea, whose inhabitants were anxious to reconstruct their gymnasium on a scale far beyond their resources. Trajan's reply has survived along with Pliny's letter. He says that he can well understand the situation, for 'These wretched Greeklings are mad about their gymnasia' (*gymnasiis indulgent Graeculi*). The whole Roman attitude comes out in the contemptuous diminutive *Graeculi*.[36]

A generation later, the Emperor Marcus Aurelius was a lover of sport as well as a philosopher. We are told of him, 'He liked boxing, wrestling and running; he was a first-class player of ball-games [*pila lusit adprime*] and he hunted.' A tantalizing fragment which survives from a letter which he wrote to his tutor hints at a scene of which we should dearly like to have more details: 'My trainer was gripping me by the jaws' (*meus me alipta faucibus urgebat*).[37]

The Latin literature of the first century AD reveals a growing acquaintance with the technical details of athletics among Roman readers. In the spirited Funeral Games in his *Thebaid*, Statius shows a deeper knowledge of such details than any other epic poet, Greek or Roman. The subject of Lucan's epic—the civil war between Caesar and Pompey—gave little opportunity for the introduction of sport, but the poet contrived to satisfy contemporary taste by including a vivid description of the legendary wrestling match between Heracles and the giant Antaeus. The incident is somewhat inartistically dragged in by the heels, solely on the ground that one of the campaigns of the war was fought in a region traditionally associated with Antaeus. The other side of the Roman attitude to Greek athletics—their contempt for it as inferior to Roman weapon-training and potentially vicious—is well brought out in a speech to his troops which Lucan puts into Caesar's mouth before the battle of Pharsalus. Pompey's heterogeneous army included some Greek elements, and Caesar makes the most of this:

> You hope to conquer the world in this coming fight; you will not lose much blood in doing so. The young men of the army which is advancing to meet you are taken from the gymnasia of Greece and have been rendered effeminate by the exercises of the wrestling-school, and hardly able to carry their weapons.[38]
>
> (*Bellum Civile* VII, 269)

Even less promising as a source for evidence on athletics was the subject matter of another poet, Manilius, who wrote on astronomy and astrology, but he has one passage which reveals a more than conventional knowledge of sport. He is describing the influence of the constellation Lepus, the Hare, on those born under it:

> It almost bestows wings on them. Such will be the speed disposed throughout their bodies, speed like the wind's, that one will win a race in the stadium almost before he has started, while another will elude the harsh boxing-gloves of his opponent by the swiftness of his footwork, equally agile at evading blows and delivering them.
>
> (*Astronomica* V, 159)

Martial and Juvenal, after due allowance has been made for the distortion due to their satiric purpose, throw a great deal of light on the social scene in the first century. The former wrote several short poems to accompany gifts of articles connected with sport, various kinds of balls, a discus, a strigil, a wrestling cap and a warm cloak for putting on after exercise. In one poem he congratulates Atticus, a descendant of Cicero's friend, on confining his exercise to running, and not wasting his money on hiring coaches to train him in wrestling and ball-play. Juvenal, though his *mens sana in corpore sano* has so often been quoted to justify physical training and games as part of education, has nothing good to say of Greek athletics or indeed of anything else Greek. When he is expressing his dislike of the intrusion of Greek words into the Latin language, he takes his example from athletic terminology:

> *Et ceromatico fert niceteria collo.*
> [He wears his athletic trophies on his oil-smeared neck.]
>
> (III, 68)

He cynically suggests that the great runner Ladas, one of the heroes of the Golden Age of Greek athletics, would much have preferred hard cash to his Olympic crowns. His greatest contempt is for Roman women who conceived a passion for gladiators or professional athletes, or who themselves practised with gladiators' weapons or athletes' weights. For the rest, he throws in the public Games with chariot-racing and gladiatorial combats, which he deprecates.[39]

It is noticeable, however, that the prose writers of the period generally choose athletics rather than the other public entertainments to illustrate a point. Tacitus in his work on Oratory, suggesting that different speakers have different natural endowments, makes one of his characters say playfully to another:

> If you had been born in Greece, where athletics is an honourable profession, and heaven had granted you the thews and sinews of Nicostratus, I should not allow those mighty muscles, simply made for boxing, to be wasted on mere javelin- or discus-throwing.
>
> (*Dialogus de Oratoribus*, x, 5)

Quintilian uses a similar illustration to make the same point:

> The teacher of rhetoric will make the same distinction between his pupils as an athletics coach, who will make a runner of one pupil, a boxer or wrestler of another, or an expert at one of the other events of the 'sacred' Games of a third.

He elaborates the argument. The orator must not concentrate solely on those departments of his art for which he has a natural bent, but must develop his other abilities:

> To use the same example again, if the athletics coach has undertaken to train a pankratiast, he will not teach him only to strike with fist or foot, or merely instruct him in a few wrestling holds, but he will coach him in every department of that event. Some of these will be beyond the powers of some pupils; these must concentrate on what they can do. For there are two things which the trainer must particularly avoid. He must not attempt the impossible, and he must not cause a pupil to change from the event he can do best to another for which he is less suitable. But if a pupil turns up for coaching who is like the famous Nicostratus, whose veteran days we saw in

our boyhood, he will train him equally in all departments, and turn him out an undefeated champion in wrestling and the pankration, both of which Nicostratus won at the same meeting.

(Institutio Oratoria II, viii)

This Nicostratus won his double victory at the Olympic Games of AD 37. Julius Africanus tells us that he was the last man ever to do so, for the authorities thereafter banned double entries in these two events. Pausanias relates a romantic story about him. He came of a good family in Prymnessus in Phrygia, but while still a baby he was carried off by pirates and sold as a slave at Aegeae in Cilicia. Some time later his owner dreamed that he saw a lion's cub lying under Nicostratus' bed, a vision which foretold his athletic triumphs. Lucian adds the information that he was very ugly. The mention of him by Tacitus and Quintilian is interesting; it shows that Roman boys of the time had their sporting heroes among Greek athletes.[40]

It is natural that the battles of orators should be illustrated by imagery drawn from the fighting events of athletics. In a long letter to Tacitus about rhetorical techniques, the younger Pliny quotes a criticism of his own style made by a colleague, Regulus:

> He said to me, 'You think you must meet every argument of your opponent in a case; I see at once where his throat is, and put pressure on that'. He certainly does exert pressure at the point he has chosen, but he frequently chooses the wrong place. I replied that possibly what he thought was the throat might turn out to be knee, shin or ankle.

(Epistulae I, xx)

Here the metaphor is clearly from the pankration, in which victory was attained by compelling the opponent to admit defeat; threat of strangulation was obviously a very effective means of securing this. Elsewhere Pliny evokes a parallel from the ephedros, the man who draws a bye in one round of these combat events:

In some public Games, the draw separates one competitor
and keeps him apart to fight with the victor.

(Epistulae VIII, xiv)

He uses it to illustrate a situation in which a motion in a trial
before the Senate 'stands by' while an amendment to it is
voted upon.

The general attitude towards athletics among cultured
Romans of the first century comes out well in Seneca, a
moralist whose preaching was considerably better than his
practice. He denounces the popular passion for Games (*Ludi*),
but clearly it is gladiatorial contests which arouse his greatest
dislike. Once or twice he uses the fighting events of athletics
to illustrate the moral struggle in a way which suggests that
he had often watched them with interest. Thus he insists that
a man's courage must constantly be tested by confronting
the difficulties of real life:

> An athlete cannot bring true courage to his fights unless
> he has sometimes been beaten black and blue. The fighter
> who has seen his own blood, whose teeth have been rattled
> by a blow from his opponent, who has been thrown to
> the ground and felt the whole weight of his rival's body
> on him, who has not lost his spirit even when hurled about
> the ring, who, every time he has been knocked down, has
> got to his feet again more pugnacious than ever, this is the
> man who faces his next fight with confidence.

(Epistulae Morales XIII, 2)

In similar terms he reminds us that we must be prepared to
suffer in defence of our moral principles:

> Think of all the blows which athletes receive on their faces
> and indeed all over their bodies. Yet they put up with all
> this pain because they long for fame. And they do not face
> it merely because they are fighting, but so that they may
> be able to fight; for their very training involves pain. So
> we too must rise above all pains of the moral life, for the
> reward of them is not simply a crown or palm or the trum-
> pet of the herald calling for silence so that our name can

be proclaimed, but virtue, a steadfast soul, and peace of mind for all time, once we have overcome the buffets of fate in any single contest.

(Epistulae Morales LXXVIII, 16)

In another letter Seneca gives us a picture of himself sitting quietly in his study but able to hear the cheering and applause coming from the stadium. This makes him reflect on the contrast between the dedication of the athlete and the laxity of ordinary men about toughening their minds to face the moral struggle:

> I think to myself, 'How many men train their bodies, how few their minds! What enormous crowds flock to a corrupt [*non fidele*] spectacle provided only for entertainment, and what a solitude there is at any cultural project! What nitwits those athletes are whose muscles and broad shoulders we admire!' What puzzles me most is this; if the body can be brought by training to endure the blows and kicks of opponent after opponent [*non unius hominis*], to face the sun blazing down on the burning sand of the ring, and to last out all day, dripping with its own blood, how much more easily could the soul be strengthened to endure the blows of fate without flinching, and rise again after being thrown and trampled on!

(Epistulae Morales LXXX, 2)

(The Loeb edition of Seneca has a quaint mistranslation of the phrase *non unius hominis*—'of several opponents *at once*'. There is no evidence for any such combat against odds in ancient athletics. Seneca is obviously thinking of the opponents whom a victor has to defeat in the early rounds on his way to the final.) One of the most interesting points in this vivid passage is the phrase *non fidele*, 'untrustworthy', applied to these events. Seneca obviously believes that the results of these bouts were often 'fixed' beforehand by the professionals taking part. There is plenty of evidence for the practice at this period.

As a good Stoic, Seneca thought that the body should be kept fit by regular exercise. He gives us a delightful account of how he did this even in old age. He had a very young boy slave, Pharius,—'He says that we must be the same age, for we are both losing our teeth'—with whom he used to run races. But he laments that he will soon have to find another rival, because Pharius is treading too closely on his heels: 'Today we achieved that rare result for runners, a dead heat.' After the race he took a cold bath—'But nowadays a "cold bath" means "almost hot"'. In another letter he enumerates the exercises suitable for a man like himself, running, exercises with dumb-bells, high jumping, long jumping and 'marking time at the double'. Here we have one of the very rare mentions of high jumping in antiquity. The only other one known to me occurs in the *Thanksgiving to Gratian* of the fourth-century writer Ausonius. Praising the emperor for his excellence in physical pursuits, he asks, 'Who ever jumped so high?' (*Quis saltum in tam sublime collegit?* XX, xiv). It is clear that there was no neat Latin word for the high jump. Seneca uses a very clumsy circumlocution: *saltus, vel ille, qui corpus in altum levat, vel ille, qui in longum mittit* (jumping, either the kind which raises the body high, or the kind which sends it a long distance). This in itself suggests that it was not a common event.[41]

Sometimes a Latin author illuminates a detail of athletic technique for which we have no Greek evidence. When Seneca visualizes himself encouraging a man engaged in a moral struggle, he puts his advice in an athletic metaphor: 'Stand up, fill your lungs with air, and if you can, get to the top of that slope without drawing breath.' This appears to embody a method of 'endurance training'.[42]

Another interesting detail emerges in a passage of Quintilian, in which he is making the point that an orator need not use every device he knows in every speech. He draws a parallel from sport:

Trainers of wrestlers do not teach their pupils those moves

which they call 'numbers' [*numeros*] with a view to their
using every one of them in every contest—for success here
depends much more on weight, strength and staying
power—but so that they may have an equipment from
which they can use one trick or another as opportunity
offers.

(Institutio Oratoria XII, ii.12)

It is not clear whether these 'numbers', heard of only here,
were used of the same moves throughout the Greek athletic
world, as in modern fencing, or whether they constituted a
code known only to a wrestler and his coach, so that in a
contest a coach could indicate to his man the opportunity of
applying a particular trick by calling out its number, without
warning his opponent of what was coming.

Evidence of well-informed Roman interest in the Olympic
Games comes in the *Rhetorica ad Herennium*, a work which
used to be attributed to Cicero. The unknown author is
deprecating those who criticize others but never write
themselves:

It is as though a man were to go to the Olympic Games to
run and were to take up his position for the start, and then
denounce as impudent those who did start, while he
remained himself behind the starting-gate [*intra carceres*]
and told the others how Ladas or Boeotus ran at Sicyon.

(iv. 3)

This is unmistakably the work of someone who has watched
races. It shows that the starting-gate, the *husplex*, was still in
use at Olympia in the first century B C, and probably in Rome
as well. The Latin word used for it, *carceres*, 'prisons', is the
technical term for the starting stalls for chariots in the Roman
Circus. Boeotus of Sicyon won the stade race at the Olympic
Games of 124 B C. Two Greek runners bore the name Ladas,
a sprinter who won the stade at Olympia in 280 B C and a
much more famous long-distance runner of the fifth century
B C; it was no doubt the latter whom Juvenal had in mind.

The fifth-century sculptor Myron, celebrated for his discus-thrower, made a statue of the earlier Ladas which was equally famous in antiquity but has not survived even in copies. Moretti makes the interesting suggestion that this statue may have been carried off to Rome in the first century BC, along with many others of the same kind, and that this explains why references to Ladas are much more frequent in Latin literature from Catullus onwards than in Greek. Ladas came to be the typical great runner of the Golden Age, as Milo had long been the typical great wrestler.[43]

The most surprising of all Roman statements about Greek athletics occurs in Cicero. He is deprecating noisy weeping and all cries of pain:

> A brave and intelligent man does not even grunt, except perhaps when he is calling on all his resources for an effort, as when runners in the stadium shout at the top of their voices. Athletes do the same in training; boxers when striking an opponent grunt as they deliver the blow, not because they are in pain or their courage is failing, but because making the noise concentrates all their powers and the blow lands with greater violence.
>
> (*Tusculanae Disputationes* II, xxiii.56)

Here is a direct statement that runners in a race shouted with all the power of their lungs. When we remember that the shortest race in ancient athletics was over 200 yards, a distance which leaves little breath to spare, the allegation is hardly credible. Cicero, as we have seen, had no high opinion of Greek athletic meetings, but nowhere else does he betray ignorance of what went on at them, and in this passage his description of boxers grunting has a vivacity which surely comes from experience, at least as a spectator. There are two possible explanations. Shouting while running may have been a device of endurance training, as Cicero says, and he may have heard runners in a race utter a despairing shout as they dived for the line in a tight finish (the ancients did not use a tape). Or it may be that Greek athletes regarded these

meetings in the western Roman world rather lightheartedly
as holidays with all expenses paid, an attitude not unknown
among touring teams today. Cicero may have been present at
a meeting at which the runners did not treat the proceedings
with grim dedication but gaily shouted abuse at one another
as they ran, and may have supposed that this was the normal
practice.

It is now possible to appreciate the difference between the
place of athletics in the Greek world and its position in the
Roman. In Greece, athletics was the traditional sport,
hallowed by centuries of experience. It had links with
religious observance; it had enjoyed a Golden Age when it
had been the leisure occupation of the wealthy. Even before
the first impact of the Romans on the Greek world it had
become public entertainment provided by well-paid professional performers, but the change took place so gradually
that much of the earlier attitude to athletics persisted in a
situation in which the outlook had become completely
obsolete. The events of the athletic programme, derived
from the Olympic Games, continued to form the basis of
physical training in schools, where it played a much more
important part in education than with us. We have a close
parallel in the development of football. The modern game
came into existence a century ago, when men from the
British public schools and universities produced agreed codes
of rules which made uniformity possible over the whole
country and then over the whole world. Like Greek athletics,
modern football was for a time the leisure occupation of a
privileged class. Much more rapidly than its ancient counterpart, it became what it primarily is today, a spectacle for
mass entertainment provided by highly paid performers in a
scene where money is the sole consideration. Yet football
too retains something of earlier attitudes. It is still called
'sport', and most schools assume that it is natural for them
to provide football for their boy pupils.

In the Roman world, Greek athletics had no tradition of centuries and no belief in a Golden Age to lend a romantic glow. Athletics meetings were introduced by ambitious politicians as an amusement to gratify the people, in rivalry with gladiatorial shows and chariot-racing; a number of professionals were brought over to Italy to provide the spectacle, just as a company of actors might have been. Athletics meetings may have provided a change from other attractions, but there is no evidence that they ever seriously competed with them in popular esteem. Such appeal as they had was chiefly to the leisured and literate classes; this explains the number of allusions to athletics in Latin literature.

While the young men of these classes were quite willing to engage in some of the Greek events for amusement, they had a poor opinion of the professionals who practised them for a living. Seneca makes this clear in the letter in which we saw him advocating regular exercise as part of the good life:

> It is foolish and quite unfitting for an educated man to spend all his time on acquiring bulging muscles, a thick neck and mighty lungs. . . . Those who dedicate themselves to this way of life have many drawbacks to suffer. There are the hours of training which exhaust them and render them unable to concentrate on any worthwhile studies. The large amounts they are compelled to eat make them dull-witted. They have to submit to trainers of the lowest class, men whose minds cannot rise above the boxing ring and the bar, whose highest ambition is to get up a good sweat and then starve to make room for enough drink to put the moisture back. Drink and sweating—one might as well have malaria.
>
> (*Epistulae Morales* XV, 2)

It is the outlook of an old-fashioned don who thinks that the life of a professional footballer, however lucrative, is no career for a university graduate.

The Romans were selective in their choice of Greek events. No doubt at the formal Games the Olympic programme was followed; the imported Greek professionals would have demanded it. But long before the first Greek Games in Rome, boxing had been introduced from Etruscan sources into gladiatorial shows. This probably accounts for the vicious boxing gloves, loaded with lead and even with projecting spikes, which appear in Roman art; the spectators at these shows wanted blood. In Imperial times, the other Greek combat events, wrestling and the pankration, were included in mixed programmes. The Romans were equally selective in the forms of exercise which they borrowed from the Greeks to add to the physical training in their education and to the games they played in their spare time. Thus there is abundant evidence that they enjoyed running, jumping and throwing the discus, but little that they ever regarded javelin-throwing as an athletic event; Horace furnishes a solitary mention. For the Romans it was a military exercise; they threw at a target, and not, as in Greek and modern athletics, for distance. Moreover, the young Roman aristocrats do not appear to have made any clear distinction, as the Greeks tended to do, between the events of the athletic programme and other sports. Latin writers mingle these events freely with other games and pursuits, some of them also borrowed from the Greeks, such as ball games, swimming and the bowling of hoops. But these will demand separate treatment.[44]

BALL GAMES AND FRINGE ACTIVITIES

CHAPTER III

BALL GAMES

ALL BALL GAMES, from the simplest to the most complicated, arise from the uses to which a ball can be put. It can be thrown to be caught; it can be bounced on the ground or against a wall and be kept bouncing; it can be thrown, rolled along the ground, hit with a club or driven by some part of the body at a goal or target; it can be thrown or hit to a distance in order to gain time for some manoeuvre such as scoring runs. All these activities can be made more difficult by interposing some obstacle, a net, a bunker, a line on a wall or other players trying to intercept.

In the modern world, ball games are played at three levels. There are the sports organized by national or international associations, with codes of rules universally accepted. Matches are taken very seriously, and the result matters, for it produces league points, or progress to a further round of a competition, with the eventual hope of a championship, a trophy, medals or simply a reward in hard cash. When skill is at its highest, such games become spectator entertainment, and this is the sport which occupies so much space in our newspapers and time on our television screens. It is an important element in the life of society, and governments have to take account of it. Yet it is a fairly recent phenomenon. Games have been played from time immemorial, but always, with the exception of Greek athletics, on a local basis. Modern sport may be said to have begun in the middle of the eighteenth century, when a set of rules for cricket was published which gained general acceptance. Football had to wait another hundred years, until a century ago the laws of the two codes, Association and Rugby, were produced. During the next thirty years, many other games were similarly regularized, and by the opening of the present century the machinery of organized sport was in full operation. (The laws of Real Tennis go back to the Middle Ages, but in this game the construction of every new court with its very complex pattern necessarily brought the equally complicated rules with it.)

At the opposite end of the scale we have only to think of a large family party at the seaside with a ball. They will form a circle and start to throw catches to one another, and instinctively they will adapt them to the ability of the catcher; there will be easy lobs for the children and middle-aged mothers, but catches for the athletic youngsters to test their agility to the utmost. There is no wish to defeat anyone— nothing is easier than to throw a ball towards someone in such a way that he cannot possibly catch it; but a very pretty physical skill is involved in producing a throw of just the right standard of difficulty. If the party have a bat or some kind of club, they may improvise a game based vaguely on cricket or baseball, but adapted to take into account a groyne, an upturned boat or rocks sticking out of the sand. There may be some attempt to keep a score, but it will be forgotten as soon as the game is abandoned for refreshment. Much simple enjoyment is derived from the sunshine, the open air, and the fundamental skills of throwing, catching and hitting a ball.

There is another level of games important for our purpose, those played by children too young to be absorbed into the formal pursuits of organized sport. These groups of children differ from the family on the seashore, because in their games the rules are constant and are rigidly governed by tradition. The newcomer to the group learns the rules the hard way, and is soon in his turn imposing them on a fresh generation of entrants. We now know a great deal about these games from that charming book *Children's Games in Street and Play-*

ground, by Iona and Peter Opie. One ball game they describe under the name Kingy, adding that in different parts of the country it is called Hot Rice, King Ball, Dustbins, Buzz, Fudge, Cheesy, Peasy, Punch, Fisty, and—when played by girls—Queenie. The fundamental aim of the game is to throw the ball at another player and hit him; he is allowed to hit the ball away with his fist or in some districts with the palm of his hand or a bat or a dust-bin lid. Sometimes the game starts with one boy as 'he', who throws the ball at any of the other players, and anyone who is hit joins 'he' in the attack on the rest until only one is left. When a bat is used, only one boy is the target, and all the other boys join in aiming at him; the one who hits him takes over the bat and becomes the target. The Opies comment, 'This fast-moving game has all the qualifications for being considered the national game of British schoolboys; it is indigenous, it is sporting, it has fully evolved rules, it is immensely popular (almost every boy in England, Scotland and Wales plays it) and no native of Britain appears to have troubled to record it.' They add in a footnote, 'Children and teachers alike often regard the game as being special to their school, as well they might from the absence of literature on the subject.'

It is to the second and third of these modern levels that we must look for parallels to the ball games of the Greeks and Romans. Athletics and chariot-racing were as fully organized in antiquity as modern football, and records were as carefully kept, but nothing of the kind appears to have happened with ball games. Because of this, there is far less evidence for ball play than for athletics—even less for the Greeks than for the Romans; the few scattered references suggest almost without exception an easy informality. We are, for instance, instantly reminded of the family on the seashore when we meet in Seneca this passage, in which he is considering the difficulties of requesting and conferring favours:

I will use the comparison which our Stoic master Chrysippus makes between this and ball-play. There is no doubt that if the ball is dropped it is the fault either of the thrower or of the catcher; the ball keeps going only if it is thrown and caught by both with equal skill. But a good player will throw a long pass to a man at a distance quite differently from his short pass to a man standing near. The same applies to conferring favours. Unless the method is suited to the characters of both giver and recipient, the favour will not leave the one or reach the other as it should. If we are playing with a skilled and well-trained performer, we shall throw the ball with greater abandon [*audacius*]; for no matter how it reaches him, he will return it [*repercutiet*] with swift and agile hands. But if we are playing with an unskilled beginner, we shall not throw so hard or so wildly but more gently, lobbing the ball lazily right into his hands. We must do the same with our acts of kindness'.

(*De Beneficiis* II, 17.2)

A rather less pleasant picture of the same simple catching game is quoted by an ancient commentator on Hesiod's line, 'We give to someone who is himself a giver, but no one gives to a man who never gives':

Plutarch compares such men, who have a generous nature, to ball-players who, when they catch the ball thrown by another, do not hold on to it or pass it to unskilled players, but to those who are able to return the pass.

(Schol. *Works and Days*, 355)

Even more often when ball games are mentioned in Greek or Latin literature, we are reminded of the schoolboy Kingy. The Opies are perhaps mistaken in thinking that it is indigenous to Britain. It certainly seems to have been played in Greece. In the second century AD Dio Chrysostom writes, 'Boys aim at one another with their ball, and the one who is hit is the loser'. Many centuries later, Eustathius in his commentary on Homer wrote about the game Episkuros, of which he obviously had no personal experience, 'They used to chase one another by throwing a ball' (βολῇ σφαῖρας ἀλλήλους ἐξεδίωκον).[45]

Balls, of course, can be made in many sizes and of many materials, but in ancient as in modern times they tended to fall into two groups. There was the small hand-ball, like those used today in cricket, baseball, hockey and tennis, and there was the much larger ball, like the football. In origin the latter was probably the inflated bladder of an ox or pig. The medical writer Galen describes how Greek children used to blow up a pig's bladder and then try to improve its shape by warming it in the ashes of a fire, rubbing it, and then repeating the process. They accompanied this with a traditional song. Unhappily Galen did not record the words, but he says, 'The whole song is an exhortation to the ball to grow bigger'. The shape of the ball used today in Rugby and American football betrays this origin. The great weakness of such a bladder is its liability to burst; whether the Greeks and Romans ever guarded against this by enclosing it in a leather case we do not know. The small ball was stuffed with hair or feathers, and sometimes the large ball also. The case was made in panels, called leaves. We are indebted for this information to a metrical riddle, to which the solution is 'A ball':

> I am exceedingly hairy, but leaves cover my hair, unless a hole appears somewhere.
>
> (*Anthologia Palatina* XIV, 62)

Plato reveals that to make the ball more attractive to children the panels were sometimes of different colours. A single couplet has survived of a Latin poet, otherwise unknown, which gives instructions for making a ball:

> Do not hesitate to stuff it with the hair of a swift-running stag, until it weighs an ounce over two pounds.
>
> (Dorcatius; quoted by Isidorus, *Etymologiae* XVIII, 69)

This must clearly have been a large ball and a heavy one too. By Roman times, different balls had been produced for different games. Martial reveals the Latin names of five of them, *pila, follis, paganica, trigonalis* and *harpastum*; the last of these, a word of Greek origin, was also used of the game played with it. Suetonius adds *folliculus,* and Isidorus *arenata*; the Romans also used the Greek word *sphaera* (σφαῖρα) for a ball.[46]

Inevitably the characteristics of a ball have a great influence on the nature of the games played with it. Play can be enjoyable with balls which are far from perfect, but for the development of the highest skill the ball must be exactly spherical, and there must be uniformity of bounce. Ancient craftsmanship could no doubt ensure the former; the latter must have been much more difficult to secure, and this probably did much to shape the games which emerged. Nothing has contributed more to the development of modern games than the discovery and exploitation of rubber and its substitutes.

Improvement in balls and the development of organization account for some of the differences between ancient and modern ball games. An observer today is even more conscious of the gap caused by the lack of a serious spirit of contention in such games in antiquity. This is surprising. The Greeks introduced competition into spheres from which it would have been far better absent, such as music and drama. Contention (ἀγών) was the very basis of their athletics. Yet in ball games winning and losing seem to have been of minor importance; the words 'victory' and 'defeat' do not appear in connection with ball games before the Christian era, and only rarely then. This was probably the reason why these games never became a great spectator attraction. A few interested people might gather round a game to watch it— the Romans called such a ring of onlookers a crown (*corona*) —but there is no evidence that ball games were ever played in the places which afforded accommodation for large crowds, such as theatres, stadia or race-courses. The spectators seem to have been less interested in the result of the games than in the skill of the players, who had the same appeal for them as jugglers have for us. When Martial sends a poem to a friend, wishing him success in his games, he does not express a hope that he will win all his matches, but writes:

Sic palmam tibi de trigone nudo
unctae det favor arbiter coronae
nec laudet Polybi magis sinistras.

[When you are stripped and playing Trigon, may the approving judgment of the ring of players looking on assign the palm to you, and not give higher praise to Polybus' left-handers.]

(VII, lxxii.9)

Ambidexterity was obviously highly esteemed.

Whether or not ball-play originated on the seashore, that is where it makes its first appearance in Western literature. In the *Odyssey*, Nausicaa, the daughter of Alcinous, King of Phaeacia, goes with her attendants down to the seashore to do the palace laundry at the mouth of a stream. While they are waiting for the washing to dry in the sun, the girls amuse themselves:

They threw off their veils and played with a ball; Nausicaa led their song.

(*Odyssey* VI, 100)

The mention of the song suggests a very simple catching game, accompanied, as children's games often are, by singing a traditional rhyme.

When the washing is dry, they fold it and pile it into the waggon to take back to the palace. At this point

Nausicaa hurled the ball at one of her maids. She missed the girl and threw it into a deep pool. They all shrieked to high heaven.

This is tantalizing. The poet, of course, wants for his plot only the loud shriek to awaken Odysseus, who is sleeping nearby; he is not concerned with describing the game. He does not even tell us whether it was a shriek of laughter or of dismay at losing the ball. Nor is the purpose of Nausicaa's action clear. She may have been merely tossing the ball to the girl to carry home. But the language is strangely vigorous for this. Homer does not use the simple dative, 'to the girl', but a preposition (μετὰ) which has the fundamental force of 'in pursuit of'. The girl did not miss the ball; the ball missed her. It did not simply fall into the pool; the picture of Nausicaa throwing it is repeated. All this would be explained if we could believe that Homer had at some time seen girls playing Kingy—or as it would be in this case, Queenie.

The only other ball-play in Homer also takes place at the court of Phaeacia, during the after-dinner entertainment given by Alcinous for Odysseus.

> The king ordered Halius and Laodamas to dance by them-selves, for they were unrivalled. They took up a beautiful purple ball which the craftsman Polybus had made for them. One of them, bending backwards, kept throwing it up towards the cloudy heavens; the other, leaping up, would catch it easily before his feet touched the ground again. When they had given proof of their skill with the high-thrown ball, they danced on the generous earth, passing the ball quickly to one another, while the other young men, standing by the ringside [κατ' ἀγῶνα], beat time, and a loud noise arose from their stamping.'
>
> (*Odyssey* VIII, 370)

We have here a rare instance of the word '*agōn*' occurring in connection with ball-play. But it is clear that there is no question of winning and losing. What is described is a ballet *pas de deux* or a combined act by two jugglers. Such a perfor-mance demands cooperation rather than contention.

Literature has little to tell us about ball games from Homer to the time of Alexander the Great. There is a story, based on not very good evidence, that the dramatist Sophocles was a skilled player and that he created a sensation by his represent-ation of the ball game when he was acting the part of Nausicaa on the stage. Plato in one of the letters attributed to him sends greetings to his 'fellow ball-players' (συσφαιρισταῖς), and elsewhere he reveals that in children's play the one who dropped a catch fell out of the game and was called 'donkey' (ὄνος). He also appears to have been the first to use the metaphor of participants in an argument skilfully keeping the conversational ball in the air. In the *Euthydemus* he speaks of Dionysodorus 'catching up the argument like a ball'. The image is copied by several later writers, and these comparisons, trite as they are, help to extend our picture of Greek ball-play. Plutarch, insisting that the role of those listening to lectures should not be purely passive, remarks, 'Ball-players have to learn how to catch the ball as well as how to throw it', and again, 'As in ball-play the player taking a pass has to move in rhythm with the one giving it, so in argument there is a rhythm shared by the speaker and the listener.' Epictetus, humbly pleading lack of skill in argument, insists that dialogue, like ball games, needs rhythm, skill, speed and experience: 'In a game, even if I hold out my tunic to catch the ball, I miss it, whereas if I throw it, the expert catches it every time.' Epictetus' method of catching is one which even today the laws of cricket find it necessary to ban. There is other evidence of a pleasant informality in these games among Greeks and Romans alike. Plutarch records that on one occasion the Macedonian king Antigonus was delighted to see his soldiers throwing a ball about though they were still wearing breastplates and helmets.[47]

The career of Alexander the Great completely changed the face of the ancient world. A very minor aspect of the change was probably a stimulus to ball games. Alexander himself had been a fine runner in his youth, but he gave up athletics because other competitors allowed him to win. Instead he took to ball-play. He appears to have employed a professional *sphairistes*, Aristonicus of Carystus. Athenaeus tells us with a certain disapproval that the Athenians conferred citizenship on this man, and the inscription which recorded the decree granting the honour has survived. An anecdote related by Plutarch shows us the king at play. Alexander used to bestow lavish gifts on his friends, but it was noticed that there was one of them, Serapion, to whom he gave nothing. It came to Serapion's ears that the reason for this was that he never asked the king for anything. One day at play he threw catches to everyone except Alexander, and when the king complained, he replied, 'You never asked me for a catch'.[48]

Alexander was much exposed to flattery, and the sincerest form of flattery is imitation. There is no doubt that ball games received a great impetus as the result of the king's enthusiasm for them. A generation after Alexander we have the first mention in Greek literature of a *sphairisterion*, a place specially dedicated to ball-play. Theophrastus says that it is one of the characteristics of the social climber that he is sure to own a small palaestra with a sphairisterion, which he is only too ready to lend to his friends. Inscriptions of the same century found at Delos and Delphi attest the existence at each place of a sphairisterion belonging to the complex of athletics buildings. One inscription from Delphi is particularly interesting. It records expenditure on the 'digging up, levelling and smoothing' of the sphairisterion, and the construction of a small wall in it. Another item is the cost of 'black earth' for the ball court, contrasting with the white sand bought for the stadium. This court was clearly not paved with stone but had a floor of smooth beaten earth.[49]

The Romans took the sphairisterion from the Greeks, latinizing the word into sphaeristerium. There were sphaeristeria attached to the great public baths, and every wealthy Roman had a private one. The younger Pliny, not a notably sporting type, had one in each of the two elaborate country houses which he describes in his letters. In his Laurentian villa the sphaeristerium was on the seashore, facing the evening sun. In his Tuscan house the ball-court was built over the dressing-room of the baths, and Pliny adds that it was large enough for games of several kinds to be going on at the same time, each with its circle of onlookers. Statius mentions a ball-court in Rome warmed by a hypocaust, apparently for winter play. In Sicily a father and son endowed the city of Centuripae with a public sphaeristerium to commemorate their joint tenure of the office of *duoviri*. As we should expect in view of the Mediterranean climate, all ball-courts seem to have been open to the sky.[50]

Though they were lukewarm about Greek athletics, the Romans appear to have adopted Greek ball-play with enthusiasm, especially as a means of keeping fit for the wealthy. When Cicero is extolling the rhetorical ability of the orator P. Mucius, he finds it worth mentioning that he was an equally fine ball-player. In the famous description of his journey to Brundisium, Horace tells us that at Capua Maecenas went off after dinner to play a ball game, while he and Virgil went to bed, 'For ball-play is no friend to the short-sighted and dyspeptic'. After being defeated in the elections for the consulship in 52 BC, Cato tried to show his unconcern by going off to play a ball game in the Campus Martius. Vespasian used to keep fit in the sphaeristerium. Macrobius has an anecdote which reveals that the Emperor Caligula, too, was a ball-player:

C. Caesar gave orders that gifts of a hundred thousand sesterces should be made to each of the men who played the ball game with him, but only fifty thousand to L. Caccilius. 'What?', said Caecilius, 'Do I play one-handed?'

(*Saturnalia* II, vi.5)

On another occasion, it was an emperor who scored the point in a similar incident. Galba, one of those who wore the purple in the 'Year of the Four Emperors', was playing with a man who showed little keenness in chasing the ball. 'Do you think you are a "Caesar's candidate"?', he asked. (An imperial nominee for office, of course, did not need to make any effort to secure election.)[51]

Our knowledge of what went on in these courts is scanty and confused. The only direct statements about them—as distinct from mere allusions—are made by encyclopaedists and etymologists, much more interested in words than in sport. Pollux in the second century AD gives a list of terms

connected with ball games and defines a few of them.
Ourania is jumping in the air to make a catch. Aporrhaxis is
bouncing a ball and counting the bounces (*Pl.* 48). Most
interesting is his account of the game Episkuros:

> This is played by teams of equal numbers standing opposite
> one another. They mark out a line between them with
> stone chips; this is the *skuros* on which the ball is placed.
> They then mark out two other lines, one behind each
> team. The team which secures possession of the ball
> throws it over their opponents, who then try to get hold
> of the ball and throw it back, until one side pushes the
> other over the line behind them. The game might be
> called a Ball Battle.
>
> (IX, 104)

Pollux does not describe the ball used for Episkuros. It must
surely have been big and light; the distances to which a hard
hand-ball could be thrown would have necessitated a playing
area of a size difficult to find in Greece. The only other term
which Pollux defines is *phaininda*. 'This is used when a
player shows the ball to one man and throws it to another.'[52]

A thousand years after Pollux, Eustathius, Bishop of
Thessalonica, wrote among other things a vast commentary
on Homer, compiled from earlier authorities. In his notes
on the two passages in the *Odyssey* where ball-play is
mentioned, he makes some statements similar to those of
Pollux and probably derived from him, but with variations
which may be due to lapse of memory or to additional
information in his possession:

> *Ourania* is throwing the ball up towards the sky. . . . They
> use *Aporrhaxis* when they throw the ball violently not
> against a wall but on the ground, so that it bounces up
> again. *Episkuros* was used when several players joined in a
> game; for this reason it was also called *Epikoinos* [Team
> game]. *Ephebiké* [Young men's] was the same game. It was
> called *Episkuros* because the players stood on a line of
> chippings called the *skuros* and chased one another by

throwing a ball. They used the term *phaininda* when they showed the ball to one man and threw it to another. The ancients derived the word from *phenakizein* [to cheat], but this was an error.

(1601, 30 on *Odyssey* VIII, 372ff)

The mention of getting a ball across a line in Episkuros has proved fatal to modern writers on sport. Even the latest edition of Liddell and Scott's *Lexicon* defines the word as 'a game resembling Rugby Football'. But Rugby football, like any other kind of football, is based on kicking the ball; there is not the slightest evidence, either in Pollux or in Eustathius, our only two authorities for the game, that kicking played any part in it.

The most interesting point in Eustathius' account of ball games is his statement that in Aporrhaxis the ball was bounced *not against a wall* but on the ground. It is obvious that Eustathius or the author from whom he was borrowing knew a game in which the ball was bounced against a wall. This action is fundamental to Fives, Real Tennis, Rackets and Squash, and it is possible that of all modern ball games these have the longest pedigree.

Eustathius elsewhere repeats from Plato the statement that a boy who dropped a catch was called 'the donkey', but adds that a boy who never dropped a catch (ἀναμάρτητος) was called 'the king'. He also says, 'Athenaeus tells us that the game called Phaininda involved throwing and running away.' This is not found in the surviving work of Athenaeus; it suggests a game on the lines of Kingy. But Athenaeus offers some characteristically scrappy information about ball games:

In Homer the dances are sometimes performed by acrobats, at others they consist of ball-play. Agallis, the woman scholar of Corcyra, attributes the invention of ball games to Nausicaa, naturally enough favouring her fellow countrywoman.[53] But Dicaearchus attributes it to the Sicyonians, Hippasus to the Lacedaemonians as the

originators of all forms of physical exercise. Nausicaa is the
only Homeric heroine presented as a ball-player. Other
celebrated players were Demoteles, brother of Theocritus
the Chian philosopher, and Chaerephanes. . . . What is
called the *folliculus* appears to have been a kind of small
ball. Its inventor was Atticus of Naples, the trainer of
Pompey the Great. The game called Harpastum—because
that is the kind of ball used in it—was formerly called
Phaininda. It is the game I like best of all.

Competitive ball games involve much exertion and
fatigue, and are a great test of strength because of the
twisting of the neck. Antiphanes has a line, 'Oh! My poor
neck', and he describes Phaininda in this passage:

> He caught the ball and passed it triumphantly to one
> player, while he dodged another, knocked it out of
> another's hands and picked up yet another player,
> shouting all the time, 'out', 'a long one', 'past him',
> 'over him', 'a low one', 'a high one', 'put down a short
> return'.

The game was called Phaininda from the throwing
(*aphesis*) of the ball by the players, or else, as Jobas the
Moor maintains, because its inventor was the trainer
Phaenestius. Antiphanes mentions this man, 'You were
going to play Phaininda in Phaenestius' palaestra'. Ball-
players used to pay attention to rhythmic movement.
Damoxenus has this:

> A boy of about sixteen or seventeen was playing a ball
> game. He came from Cos, an island which seems to
> produce god-like youngsters. Whenever he glanced at
> us spectators, as he caught or threw the ball, we all
> exclaimed, 'What rhythm, what grace, what control!'
> Whatever he did or said seemed a miracle of beauty. I
> have never seen or heard of so handsome a creature.

Ctesibius the philosopher from Chalcis used to enjoy ball
games, and many of King Antigonus' friends used to

strip to play with him. Timocrates of Sparta wrote a book on ball games.

(Deipnosophistai I, 14)

In this hotch-potch of ill-assorted items, Athenaeus is, as usual, concerned mainly with the past; the two authors of comedy he quotes, Antiphanes and Damoxenus, belonged to the fourth and third centuries BC. The passage of Antiphanes suits well a game in which a player, standing between two lines of opponents, tries to intercept the catches they throw to one another. This accounts for the name Harpastum, 'Snatch'. The *phaininda* tactic would obviously be used in such a game. It is simply 'selling the dummy'; a player feints to throw in one direction, and when the interceptor moves to conform, he throws it to someone else. The trick is called by other authors *ephetinda* and *phennis*. Some of the terms used by Antiphanes might suggest that tackling or body-checking was allowed—'twisting the neck'—'dodged another'—'knocked it out of his hands'—and especially 'picked up another player'. But they are consistent with a less violent interpretation. A sudden movement to take a catch coming unexpectedly may cause neck-twisting. A player trying to avoid the interceptor as he throws his pass necessarily dodges. The next phrase may mean, 'knocked the ball away from the other's reach', and the fallen player may have slipped when turning abruptly.

In spite of his professed enthusiasm for Harpastum, Athenaeus does not appear to have rated ball games very highly. He quotes the Athenians' award of their citizenship to Alexander's *sphairistēs* as evidence that 'In later days the Greeks valued the vulgar skills above cultural ideas'.[54]

An anonymous Latin poem of the first century AD gives a brief but vivid picture of a game which is almost certainly the same Harpastum. The poem is a fulsome panegyric on Calpurnius Piso. After eulogizing his hero's skill in fencing, the author goes on:

Your agility is no less when you are returning the flying

ball, or just saving it as it is about to touch the ground, or sending it back with an unexpected movement when it appears to have gone past you. Spectators remain spellbound, and numbers of other players leave their own games and stand, still sweating, to watch you play.

(*Laus Pisonis*, 185ff)

Here again, as in Damoxenus' description of the young Coan, there is no mention of the number of games won; the emphasis is not on victory but on the grace, skill and agility of the players.

No single source contributes more to our picture of ancient ball games than the Roman satirist Martial, who wrote at about the same time as the author of the *Laus Pisonis*. One short poem was composed to be sent to a friend with a gift of a warm cloak. Martial says that the cloak will be useful 'if you have been grasping at the warming *trigon* or the dusty *harpastum*, or sending out passes with the feathery weight of the soft *follis*'. This seems to imply three different games played with different balls. But the same game can be played with different kinds of balls; baseball is an obvious example, and the fundamental difference between rackets and squash lies in the ball. The use of a soft ball in a game slows down the pace. Martial hints at this in three short poems which he wrote to accompany gifts of three different balls. Of one he says:

This *paganica*, filled with hard-wearing feathers, is less flabby than a *follis* and less hard than a *pila*.

(XIV, xlv)

The *trigonalis* is made to address its recipient:

If you know how to drive me [*expulsare*] with swift left-handers, I am yours. You cannot? Then, you rabbit, give up the game.

(XIV, xlvi)

The game of Trigon may have been Harpastum played by three—the smallest possible number—or it may have been a

game in which three men stood at the corners of a triangle
and gave and received catches at the same time with three
balls. Martial's *expulsare* suggests hitting the ball rather than
throwing it.[55]

In the third epigram the *follis* also is made to speak:

> Keep away from me, young men; mature age suits me. A
> *follis* is for children and old men to play with.
>
> (XIV, xlvii)

Another of Martial's poems gives us a glimpse of the scene
in a sphaeristerium attached to public baths:

> Stop play; the bell of the hot bath is ringing. You want to
> go on? Then you will have to take a cold bath before you
> go home.
>
> (XIV, clxiii)

He paints brief pictures of two unattractive characters in the
ball-court. There is the sycophantic hanger-on Menogenes,
from whom there is no escape:

> He will grab the hot Trigon ball with right or left hand, so
> that he can often put down his catches to your score. Even
> after he has bathed and changed, he will pick the *follis* out
> of the dust and throw it back to you.
>
> (XII, lxxxii)

Still less pleasant is the young pervert in the couplet on the
Harpastum ball:

> The prancing pansy snatches at this ball in Antaeus' dusty
> court, trying to make his neck muscular by this useless
> exercise.
>
> (XIV, xlviii)

Finally there is a lively glance at a man who has taken up
games in his old age:

> No lover has ever been so smitten by passion for a new
> mistress as Laurus by his craze for the ball game. In his
> prime he was a first-class performer at the game of love;

but now that he has given that up, he is a real tiger in the ball-court.

(X, lxxxvi)

(*Prima pila est* must have been a colloquial term of the sphaeristerium whose meaning has been lost. It was probably based on the military term *primipilaris*. My rendering of 'a real tiger' is a sheer guess with no authority; it merely attempts to give the general sense in a sporting metaphor.)

One of our most important sources of evidence for ancient ball games is a medical treatise by Galen, a Greek who, a generation after Martial, was court physician to the Emperor Marcus Aurelius. The work, *Exercise with the Small Ball*, is short but somewhat repetitive. Although it is not a descriptive account of ball games, some hints can be gleaned from it. The author starts by recommending ball-play as being not only beneficial but pleasant; it is cheaper and less time-consuming than such sports as hunting, and so is kindly to a man's other interests. It exercises all parts of the body, vigorously or gently according to requirements:

When the players have taken up position opposite one another, they use every effort to prevent the man in the middle from intercepting the ball [ἀποκωλύοντες ὑφαρπάσαι τὸν μεταξὺ διαπονῶσι]. This is the most vigorous exercise possible; it combines much twisting of the neck and many conforming movements like those in wrestling [ἀντιλήψεσι παλαιστικαῖς]; the head and neck, the ribs, chest and abdomen are strengthened by the quick turns and the necessity of looking up and down, by the pushing, the footwork needed to secure a firm stance [ἀπώσεσι καὶ ἀποστηρίξεσι], and other nimble movements. By it the loins and legs which are the foundation of the stance are brought into training for moving forward strongly or jumping sideways.

(*De parvae pilae exercitu*, 2)

The picture of the game is fairly clear, a man between two

rows of players, trying to intercept the passes which they exchange, The Greek word used for intercepting (ὑφαρπάσαι) gave the game of Harpastum its name.

Galen then elaborates the beneficial effects of ball-play. It is a better all-round exercise than aimless running. In particular, it gives excellent training to the hands, which become accustomed to taking catches of all kinds. It trains the eyesight, for unless the player follows the swerving flight (ῥοπή) of the ball, he drops the catch. It improves the mental powers, as the player tries not to drop the ball, or attempts to thwart the man in the middle, or to intercept a pass, if he is in that position himself. Intellectual study by itself emaciates the body, but if allied with exercise and pleasant rivalry it eventually brings health to the body and intelligence to the mind.

He next considers the contribution which these games can make to military training. Ball-play, he says, teaches a man how to keep what he has or to recover what has been taken from him. It is far superior in this respect to athletics. Galen shares to the full the contempt which most of his contemporaries felt for the professional athletes of the day, especially the boxers and pankratiasts. They are fat and sluggish, he asserts, unfit for military or political service; one would sooner entrust anything important to pigs. Even running, he repeats, is less beneficial, because it does not develop all parts of the body; moreover, battles are not won by running away.

Now he returns to the all-round benefits of ball-play. It imparts command of speedy movement. It is as vigorous as you choose to make it; some of us are too old or too young for all-out effort; sometimes we want to recover slowly from exhaustion, or we are convalescing after an illness. Nothing is more gentle than ball-play, if you make it so.

You must stay in the middle and on no account depart from a moderate level of exertion; sometimes you must move quietly, sometimes stand still, but never use your

strength to the utmost. Then have a gentle massage with
oil and a warm bath.

This passage makes it clear that, as we should suppose on
general grounds, the man in the middle, the interceptor,
could 'pace the game'.

If you need more vigorous exertion, that can easily be
obtained with the small ball; so too can exercise for any
particular part of the body:

> To throw hard for a fair distance, using the legs very little
> or not at all, rests the lower parts and gives vigorous
> exercise to the upper. To throw as far as possible with a
> long, quick run, and so need few throws, exercises the
> lower parts. If there is urgency and fast movement in the
> game, but no strong tension, it increases lung-power; on
> the other hand, the mere exchange of passes and catches
> at no great speed strengthens the body. If it is done at full
> speed and with the utmost energy, it exercises both body
> and lungs and is the most vigorous of all sports. The right
> degree must be found in practice; it cannot be expressed
> in writing. Even the best exercise is useless if it is ruined by
> excess. This is a matter for the trainer in charge to decide.
>
> (*De parvae pilae exercitu*, 4)

Finally Galen points out that ball-play is much less dangerous than the events of the athletic programme. Running has
been known to cause the rupture of a blood vessel; so too has
loud shouting. This recalls Cicero's remarkable statement
that runners in the stadium shouted at the top of their voices
(See above, p. 71). Galen does not state that the running and
shouting were done at the same time, but the intrusion of
shouting into his account of athletics at this point calls for
explanation.

Horse-riding, Galen continues, has its accidents, as have
jumping and discus-throwing and practising turns round the
post (τὰ διὰ τὸ κάμπτειν γυμνάσια). As for boxers and
pankratiasts, you can see for yourself that they are all de-
formed and battered cripples.

One point about this treatise will strike the reader immediately. A modern doctor giving advice about exercise would discuss the suitability of different games to different patients, recommending tennis or football to some, croquet or bowls to others. Galen does nothing of the kind. For him ball-play is a unity, capable of great variation according to the wishes of the players. His words imply that roughly the same game was played everywhere, and he takes it for granted that his readers will all know the game he is talking about.

Ball games were not as completely free from danger as Galen suggests. In the great *Digest* of Roman Law, compiled in the sixth century A D, the following passage occurs:

> Several men were playing a ball game when one of them, trying to reach the ball, collided with a slave boy. The slave fell and broke his leg. The question was put whether the owner of the slave had a case under the Lex Aquilia against the man who had knocked him down. My decision was that he had not, since the act was accidental and not criminal.
>
> *(Digest* IX, 2.52.4)

Galen's recommendation of ball games as healthy for all ages and temperaments is borne out by a letter of the younger Pliny, in which he describes a recent visit to Spurinna. Every afternoon, he says, his host after a walk in the sun 'plays a long and vigorous ball game; for he uses this form of exercise to keep old age at bay'. Spurinna, he tells us, was in his 78th year. A very different performer was the *nouveau riche* Trimalchio, the central figure in the *Satyricon* of Petronius, who gives us a delightful if fleeting glimpse of his hero in the sphaeristerium. Trimalchio wore a red tunic and shoes, but, no doubt in deference to the emperor's enthusiasm for the Green faction in the chariot races, he played with green balls. When he dropped a catch, he did not stoop to pick up the ball; a slave stood by him with a basketful of replacements. The scorer did not count the number of catches made, but the number dropped.[56]

Here we have further evidence that a score was kept in some games. Seneca mentions the same thing when he is complaining of the noise from the adjacent baths which disturbed him in his study: 'If the court-keeper [*pilicrepus*] comes and begins to call the score, that is the last straw.' From the same period comes one of the most moving documents in the history of sport. Just before the eruption of Vesuvius overwhelmed Pompeii, a games supervisor wrote on a wall in the city the arrangements for a ball game. Hundreds of such notices appear every day on the noticeboards of schools and clubs all over the world:

Amianthus Epaphra Tertius ludant cum Hedysto
Jucundus Nolanus petat numeret Citus et Acus Amianth(o?)

Apparently the trainer first wrote:

Players	Amianthus, Epaphra, Tertius
Ball-boys	Jucundus, Nolanus
Scorer	Citus

Then either he or someone else added 'with Hedystus' to the players, and 'Acus for Amianthus' at the end. It is not clear whether Acus is to act as ball-boy for Amianthus or to keep his score, and indeed, 'act as ball-boy' is only one of several possible interpretations of *petat*. The game involved may have been Trigon, with Hedystus acting as stand-by to replace one of the first three players as required.[57]

Other fragments of plaster from the same wall in Pompeii carry the names of two of these players, and suggest a colloquial use of the word *pilicrepus*. The brief scrawls read, '*Amianthum pilicrepum*' and '*Epaphra pilicrepus non est*'. There is no doubt that the word signified a caretaker of a court who also acted as marker for the games. Amianthus might have been employed in that capacity, but there could have been no conceivable point in scribbling on the wall a statement that Epaphra was not. Such men, like old-fashioned greenkeepers and billiard markers, no doubt acquired considerable skill at the game with which they were associated, so that *pilicrepus* came to have the same connotation of ability that 'professional' sometimes has with us. Our two graffiti reveal that Amianthus was a 'tiger', but poor Epaphra emphatically was not.[58]

Our last evidence for a ball game, which may well have been Harpastum, comes from Sidonius Apollinaris, who was Bishop of Clermont in Gaul in the fifth century A D. In a letter describing a visit to a friend's house near Nemausus (Nîmes), he says that as soon as he entered the portico he saw on one side a group of gamblers at their dice, while on the other 'teams of ball-players facing one another were exchanging catches, with swift turns and agile ducking' (*sphaeristarum contrastantium paria inter rotalites catastropharum gyros duplicabantur. Epistulae* II, ix.4). In another letter he relates how one day at Lugdunum (Lyons) the congregation waiting for Mass amused themselves according to taste. Some went off to gamble with dice, but not the Bishop:

> I was the first to call for a ball game, which, as you know, is as much my constant companion as are my books. . . . I played for some time with a crowd of students, until my body felt refreshed from the sluggishness induced by my sedentary occupation. Among the onlookers was an older man, Philomatius, who had been a fine player in his youth; now with great courage he went to join the groups of players. While he stood watching, he was several times jostled by the 'middle runner' [*medius currens*]. At last he joined in the game, but he could not intercept the ball as it flew past or over him, nor could he get out of its way; he was often almost flat on his face when he ducked, and only just saved himself from a disastrous fall. So he was the first to withdraw from the violent action of the game, puffing furiously and hot all over.
>
> (*Epistulae* V, xvii)

These two passages suggest that already the Church looked with approval on ball games, possibly as an alternative to something worse. It has long been conjectured that the complicated court of Real Tennis, with its gallery, penthouse, grille and dedans, is a stylized version of a monastic cloister. The quotations from Sidonius lend support to this view.

The game played by these young Christians seems to be basically the same as the Harpastum in Athenaeus and the small ball game implied in Galen. But there is one puzzling phrase in Sidonius, 'he could neither intercept *nor avoid* the flight of the ball' (*nec intercideret nec caveret*). Norman Gardiner translates *caveret* as 'anticipate', which fits the context admirably. But the verb has the force of 'taking precautions to prevent something from happening'; it can hardly be used for 'taking steps to ensure catching the ball'. The conclusion seems inescapable that W. B. Anderson's rendering 'dodge' is the right one. This implies that one element in the game being played was throwing the ball to hit someone, as in the games mentioned by Dio Chrysostom and Eustathius and in modern Kingy. It is not difficult to imagine a game in which the players try to hit the *medius currens* and he is allowed to catch the ball and throw it away from him, just as he can hit it away in Kingy. A natural trick in the game is to throw a catch to someone who is standing near the *medius currens* and in a good position to hit him. The man in the middle tries to intercept this catch. If he fails, he has to turn quickly towards the new holder of the ball and very likely duck to avoid his throw. These movements are vividly pictured in the Latin phrases *inter rotalites catastropharum gyros* and *per catastropham saepe pronatus*. Anderson's translation, 'he would often bend low in a flying tackle and then scarcely manage to recover from his staggering swerve', though lively, introduces an element into Roman ball-play for which there is no other evidence.[59]

Modern writers on ancient ball games often find it difficult to escape from the preconceptions induced by the highly organized sport of today. Norman Gardiner is shocked by the account in Sidonius Apollinaris of how the elderly Philomatius was taken into the game and then retired from it. He comments:

> One thing is certain. If this game is Harpastum, Harpastum is not a team game. For it is impossible for a player to join in a team game and retire at his pleasure.

(*Athletics of the Ancient World*, 234)

Gardiner, perhaps happily, did not live to see the day when the timing of the sending in of a substitute was to become an important item in football tactics, but he must surely have taken part in games in circles where it is quite normal for a bystander to pick up a tennis racket or croquet mallet and take the place of a player who has been called away. There is a hint that the Romans had a traditional rule covering substitution. Whenever a ball game is played in a restricted space, it is necessary to guard against over-exuberance in those throwing or hitting the ball. Small boys playing cricket in these conditions decree that a batsman who hits the ball into a garden shall retrieve it himself, and even if he is successful his innings is terminated; the law is expressed in the succinct formula 'Over, out and fetch it'. Isidorus defines the ball called *arenata* thus:

> The *arenata* was used in the team game [*in grege*] in which, when the ball was thrown out of the circle of spectators, those standing outside the boundary [*ultra justum spatium*] could catch the ball and enter the game.

(*Etymologia* XVIII, 69)

Though most of our sources for ball-play show the ball being thrown and caught, there are indications that it was sometimes struck with the hand or a club. Artemidorus of Daldis writes:

> Ball-players play in rivalry, and whenever they receive the ball they hit it back again [ἀντικρούουσι].

(*Oneirocritica* IV, 69)

Sextus Empiricus has an interesting reference when he is dealing with the nature of Motion:

That which sets in motion does not accompany the object which is set in motion; it is separated from it, as the hand is separated from the ball which is being hit away by it [τῆς ἀποπαλλομένης σφαίρας].

(Physica II, 73)

One or two Latin words used of ball-play, repercutio by Seneca, expulsare by Martial and expulsim by Varro, lead to the same conclusion. There appears to be no certain mention of a bat in ancient literature. The Greek Anthology has a brief poem in which a young man passing out of the class of Ephebes dedicates to Hermes his uniform and trappings. He enumerates the broad-brimmed hat, the strigil and unstrung bow, the characteristic cloak and then

The 'clefts' and the ball which was always in the air [καὶ σχίζας καὶ σφαῖραν ἀείβολον].

(Anthologia Palatina VI, 282)

The word translated 'cleft'—a piece of wood split off a large block along the grain—is not a common one in Greek. Elsewhere it is used of a piece of firewood and of the shaft of a spear. The latter sense would obviously fit here. It is only the fact that the word occurs alongside the ball that suggests the possibility that it might here refer to bats or clubs used in a game. To produce a 'cleft' from a willow log is the first step in making a cricket bat.

A more probable mention of a bat or hockey stick is found in Cicero. When he is recommending different spare-time occupations for young and old, he suggests dice and knucklebones for the latter, but insists that young men should devote themselves to 'Arma, equos, hastas, clavam et pilam, natationes atque cursus'. Clavam has generally been taken closely with hastas, and explained as the wooden singlestick used as a sword by Roman soldiers in their weapon training. But the rhythm of the sentence throws clavam et pilam together as a phrase, and we should probably translate, 'Weapons, horses, spears, bat and ball, swimming and running'.[60]

The scanty literary evidence for ancient ball games is not much helped by sculpture and vase painting. The British Museum has a base (*Pl.* 48) depicting a girl playing Aporr-haxis—bouncing a ball and keeping it bouncing. A relief on a statue base in Athens (*Pl.* 46) shows a ball game being played. The base was found in the wall hastily built by the Athenians from any available material in 478 BC, immediately after the Persian war, and so must be dated before then. It may re-present a team game, in which a ball is about to be thrown between two rows of players as in a Rugby line-out, or it may be simply a game of catching and intercepting. A black-figured vase of the same period in the Ashmolean (*Pls.* 50, 51) shows a man throwing a ball to three players, each carried pick-a-back by another. Between two of the pairs is inscribed 'Call for it' (κέλευσον), which recalls the story of Alexander and Serapion. There is a similar vase in the British Museum. Modern commentators connect these vases with the term 'donkey' applied to a boy who dropped a catch, and suggest that the under-dogs carrying the other players are such donkeys; this, however, is sheer guesswork.[61]

Even more famous and more perplexing is the 'hockey' relief (*Pl.* 47) from the same source as that of the ball-players just mentioned. This is the sole certain evidence we possess of a ball game in classical antiquity in which clubs or bats were used. On the slight evidence of the relief it does not appear to have been a team game. The figures to the right and left of the central pair suggest players awaiting their turn rather than competitors taking part in the game, like hockey players near a bully. Soon after the discovery of this base, a Greek scholar, M. Oikonomos, suggested that it might throw light on a mysterious passage in a *Life* of Isocrates attributed to Plutarch. In this it is stated that in the sphairis-terion of the Arrephoroi in Athens there was a statue of the orator as a boy 'keretizōn' (κερητίζων), a word not found elsewhere in the Greek language. Oikonomos proposed for it a derivation from 'keras' (κέρας), a horn, which might well have been the term for the curved stick depicted on the relief; thus Isocrates would have been shown as a hockey player. The fact that the statue mentioned by the biographer stood in a ball-court makes the suggestion attractive and highly probable, though not completely certain. It is interesting to note that a painting in an Etruscan tomb shows an athlete holding a stick very like those in the Athenian relief, but with no ball in the picture.[62]

The earliest mention in Greek literature of a game in which a ball is hit by a club comes in the twelfth-century Byzantine historian Cinnamus. Relating how the Emperor Manuel Comnenus fell and was rolled on by his pony while playing what is obviously polo, he takes the opportunity to give a description of the game:

> The young men, divided into two teams of equal numbers, select a level piece of ground of suitable measurements. The ball is made of leather and is about the size of an apple. It is rolled into the middle of the field, and the two teams gallop towards it at full speed. Each player has in his right hand a club of a length to suit him. The club broadens out at the end into a flat curved head, fitted inside with a kind of net woven of dry gut. Each team tries to force the ball into its opponents' goal—the goals, of course, have been marked out before the game. When the ball is hit by the clubs into either goal, victory falls to that side. The game is dangerous and full of accidents, for the player must constantly bend in the saddle, twist his body, turn his horse abruptly and continually vary his pace and movements to conform with the movement of the ball.

> (*Historiae* VI, 5)

The most remarkable feature of this is the nature of the clubs, which seem more appropriate to lacrosse or tennis than to polo. This is all the more surprising because the available evidence suggests that the Persians, from whom the Greeks took the game, had long used polo sticks exactly like those used in the game today (*Pl.* 83).

Cinnamus' description contains the first mention in literature of winning a ball game, but victory in such games is recorded in a group of inscriptions a thousand years earlier. In Sparta during the Roman Imperial period there was an annual competition for teams of boys in a ball game, conducted as a knock-out competition. It is mentioned in the *Anacharsis* of Lucian, an essay devoted to a defence of the Greek way of life, especially its athletics. The work presents some difficulties of interpretation, because, while it was written in the second century AD, it is cast in the form of a dramatic dialogue between Anacharsis, a Scythian represented as a critic of the Greeks, and Solon the Athenian, who lived at the beginning of the sixth century BC. There is little doubt, however, that the Greek sporting life depicted in the work is that of Lucian's own day. At the end of it Solon, who has been defending the events of the Greek athletic programme, ironically urges Anacharsis, if he visits the rest of Greece, not to laugh at the Spartans

> when in their ball game in the theatre they fall down on top of one another in heaps and come to blows [συμπεσόντες παίωσιν ἀλλήλους].
>
> (*Anacharsis*, 38)

Happily we know something more about this game from a dozen fragmentary inscriptions of the early Christian era, found at Sparta. These make it clear that the competition was between teams drawn from '*obai*', probably the platoons into which Spartan youths were divided for military training. None of the inscriptions is complete, but one gives the names of fourteen players, so each team must have included at least that number. As several teams claim to have won 'without drawing a bye' (ἀνέφεδροι), it follows that the competition was on knock-out lines. Club officials are named, the Bideos, Aristindes, Diabetes and Presbus; of these the first was apparently a Spartan Youth Leader, parallel to the Ephebarch of other cities, and the Presbus (the 'Old Man') probably the captain. Aristindes is found no-

where else, so speculation is unlimited. The most complete of
the inscriptions runs thus:

TO GOOD FORTUNE

Patronomus:	Lysippus, son of Damaenetus, friend of the emperor and friend of his country.
Bideos:	Peducaeus, son of Epaphroditus.
Aristindes and Diabetes:	Damaenetus, son of Aristocrates, who volunteered.

This team of ball-players won the competition for the
Obai without drawing a bye. Their captain was Galen.

(Inscr. Sparta Museum, 400)[63]

The words in which Lucian describes the game, 'They
hurl themselves on one another in heaps and have a punch-
up', give exactly the impression produced on uninstructed
onlookers by Rugby or American football. It would be un-
wise, however, to deduce from this that the Spartan game
was some form of football. Greek literature appears to offer
no instance of a ball being mentioned in the same sentence as
foot or leg. Indeed there is one piece of evidence against
Greek football. Plato in the *Laws* says that men are not left-
footed or right-footed in the way that they are left-handed
or right-handed. Even in top football circles there are a few
players who are notoriously 'one-foot' men, and in the lower
echelons of the game the vast majority of players are very
much stronger with one foot than the other. So acute an
observer as Plato could not have failed to notice this had
football been played in the Athens of his day.[64]

The National Museum in Athens has a gravestone relief
depicting a naked youth standing on one foot with the other
knee raised, balancing on his thigh what appears to be a large
ball (Fig. 4). It is true that this resembles an exercise performed by modern footballers when they are practising ball
control. But we know of nothing to connect it with a game.
It seems to have more in common with juggling. Juggling

21 The remains of the *husplex* in the stadium at Priene (see pp. 28-9 for a description of its operation).

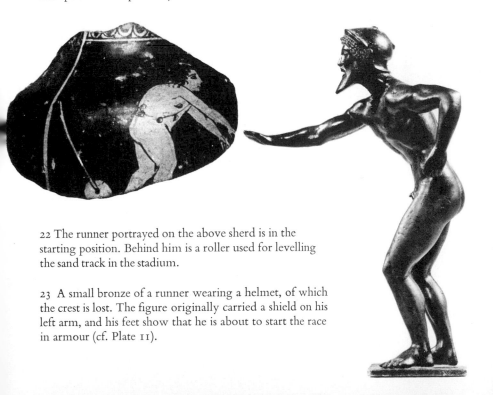

22 The runner portrayed on the above sherd is in the starting position. Behind him is a roller used for levelling the sand track in the stadium.

23 A small bronze of a runner wearing a helmet, of which the crest is lost. The figure originally carried a shield on his left arm, and his feet show that he is about to start the race in armour (cf. Plate 11).

24 The officials of a winning team handing to Artemis the torch carried in a race. Because of a mention of the relay race on horseback in honour of Artemis Bendis (see p. 181), this is usually said to be a team competing in that race, but there is no evidence in the relief to connect it in any way with horses. Fourth century BC.

25 A victorious team relaxing after a torch race. Fifth century BC.

26 A small bronze statuette of a runner holding a torch aloft.

27,28 This small fifth-century red-figure vase shows the change-over being made in a torch race. In order to win the team had to keep its torch alight to the end.

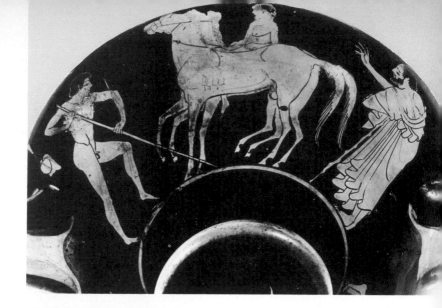

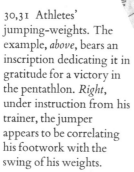

29 An unusual
representation of an
athlete pole-vaulting onto
a horse, held by another
rider.

30,31 Athletes'
jumping-weights. The
example, *above*, bears an
inscription dedicating it in
gratitude for a victory in
the pentathlon. *Right*,
under instruction from his
trainer, the jumper
appears to be correlating
his footwork with the
swing of his weights.

32,33 Javelin-throwing. *Right*, the thrower is measuring his run-up, watched by an umpire. He is holding the javelin in his left hand and the thong in his right. This is one of the most important pieces of evidence for the theory that the thong of an athletic javelin was not permanently fixed to the shaft but was attached to it for each throw by a half-hitch and fell off in flight. *Below*, the forward end of the javelin is bound in order to prevent splitting. The thrower pushes the shaft back with his free hand to keep the thong taut (cf. Plate 11).

34 It is still a matter of dispute whether this bronze statue represents Zeus hurling a thunderbolt or Poseidon throwing his trident. As it is of superhuman size, it is almost certainly a god, but the model for it must have been an athlete of magnificent physique. The forefinger of the throwing hand is cocked like that of a javelin-thrower over his loop.

35 Tarquinia, Tomb of the Olympiads. In this Etruscan wall-painting, c. 500 BC, the discus-thrower wears shorts and is depicted in the act of throwing; the bent elbow of the throwing arm is noteworthy.

36 This large amphora was a prize at the Panathenaic Games at Athens,
presumably for the pentathlon. In spite of Norman Gardiner's strictures it is
among our best pieces of evidence for the field events. It shows the bent elbow
of the discus-thrower and suggests his rotary action, it depicts clearly the
javelin-thrower's loop and it attempts to show the jumper's take-off. Late
sixth century BC.

37-40 Discus-throwers seen in a copy of Myron's famous original in bronze, a coin of Cos (note the bent elbow), a gemstone (note the discus in its carrying case), and with a javelin-thrower, jumper and flute-player.

Fig. 4 *Athlete balancing a ball on his thigh. Athens, National Museum (Conze, 1046).*

with balls is of immense antiquity. It appears in paintings in Egyptian tombs at Beni Hasan which Egyptologists date before 2000 BC. We tend to make a very clear distinction between juggling, which is for us a form of public entertainment, and ball games, which belong to sport. The Romans at least seem not to have done this. The Vatican Museum has the gravestone of one Ursus Togatus, who claims to have been the first man to play with a glass ball, winning great applause from an admiring public. From the grave he appeals to ball-court keepers (*pilicrepi*) to adorn his statue with roses and violets, and to pour libations of the choicest wines. The inscription ends thus:

> I have been beaten not once but often—I admit it myself—by my patron Verus, three times consul, whose *exodiarius* I am only too glad to be called.

> (*CIL*, VI, 9797)

Ursus was obviously a ball-court professional himself, sometimes called on to play with the aristocratic patrons of the court. But he also claims to have been an *exodiarius*, an actor in variety shows, and this, together with the mention of the glass ball, reveals that he was a juggler as well. His innocent vanity in claiming acquaintance with his consular patron enables us to date the inscription. Verus was consul for the third time in AD 126.

Ursus is not the only Roman juggler with balls known to us by name. An inscription of the second century AD is from a gravestone erected by Aelia Europē to her husband P. Aelius Secundus, whom she describes as the most eminent of all ball-jugglers (*pilario omnium eminentissimo*). We are justified in translating *pilarius* here as 'juggler' rather than 'ball-player' by a passage in Quintilian in which he is making the point that an orator should be such a master of language that the right word comes to his tongue almost without his thinking about it:

> We see the same skill in those wonderful performances on the stage by jugglers and prestidigitators [*pilariorum ac ventilatorum*], when you might well believe that the objects which they have thrown up come back of their own accord into their hands and move where they are ordered.[65]

(X, vii.11)

If Greek literature is innocent of any reference to ball and foot together, it cannot be said that Latin literature is very much more helpful. It can show two places where a ball is mentioned in connection with leg or foot, but neither passage gives a picture of a ball game in any way resembling football. The first occurs in Manilius, whose poem about astronomy and astrology occupied much of the academic effort of that erratic writer A. E. Housman. The poet describes the characteristics of those born under the influence of the constellation Lepus, the Hare. They are swift movers, good runners and nimble boxers. Then he goes on to offer the following information:

164 *Ille pilam celeri fugientem reddere planta*
165 *et pedibus pensare manus et ludere fulcro,*   MS *fulto*
167 *ille potens turba perfundere membra pilarum*
    per totumque vagas corpus disponere palmas,
    ut teneat tantos orbes sibique ipse reludat
    et velut edoctos iubeat volitare per ipsum.

[This man is skilled at returning the flying ball with a swift movement of the sole of his foot, at balancing hand against foot and playing from a firm base. Another can cover his limbs with a host of balls, and apparently grow hands all over his body, so that he can control all that number of balls and play a game against himself, and make them skip over his body like obedient pupils (*Pl.* 48)].

(V, 164ff)

The last four lines give a lively picture of a juggler. In his interpretation of the first two, where we most need guidance, Housman is at his most exasperating. No one will quarrel with his explanation of the first, '*non manu sed solo pedis opposito repercutere*', 'to drive back the ball not with the hand but by applying the sole of the foot to it', but he cannot resist the temptation to follow this with a schoolboy jibe at his rival editor Salmatius: 'If I were Salmatius, I should ask what kind of game or exercise this movement belongs to. Being a mere mortal, I am content to interpret what the author wrote.' Many will think that if Salmatius had asked the question he would have been performing one of the elementary duties of an editor. Housman then adds to the confusion by insisting that *reddere planta, pedibus pensare manus* and *ludere fulcro* all refer to the same thing. It is far more probable that the last two phrases indicate the swift footwork necessary in many ball games in order to bring the body into a balanced position for making a catch or a stroke. By mentioning this, Manilius shows that he had considerable practical knowledge of such games. Housman does not appear to have shared this with his author. No man with any real feeling for games could have written the lines:

> The goal stands up, the keeper
>   Stands up to keep the goal.
>   ('Is My Team Ploughing?' from *A Shropshire Lad*)

If we accept Housman's rendering of the first line, as we surely must, we must risk his contempt by asking with Salmatius what kind of game is involved, and particularly why the sole of the foot should be specified. In modern football the use of the sole is not unknown. A player working the ball closely may roll it with the flat of his foot, or near goal he may make a desperate lunge at a low cross almost out of his reach and try to stab it into the net with the sole. But neither movement is fundamental to the game, and it is impossible to believe that Manilius would have used this language if he had had in mind anything resembling modern football. The best explanation of the first line is that in the game in which the object was to hit a player with the ball, he was allowed to knock it away from him not only with the hand but also with the sole of the foot.

It is possible that this line gives us the clue to why the Greeks and Romans did not play football. Norman Gardiner writes:

> Shall we one day discover a representation of Greek boys playing football? . . . The Greeks and Romans had an air-filled ball, the 'follis', and they surely must have discovered how conveniently it could be propelled by the foot.
>
> (*Athletics of the Ancient World*, 238)

But the true method of propelling the ball with the foot is by no means a natural movement. We have only to watch a small child or a woman kicking a ball to see that they use the point of the foot, which allows little power or accuracy. Fifty years ago, though the correct method of using the top of the instep had long been discovered, the tradition that the ball was kicked with the toe still governed the construction of football boots; they had their toes reinforced to a concrete hardness which today would be considered excessive in industrial protective footgear. Many old players will remember the revolutionary change when these bulbous excrescences were replaced by lighter models which at last took into account the way the game had been played for generations. The Greeks and Romans played their games with bare feet. If they kicked an air-filled bladder with the point of the foot, toe-nails must soon have punctured it. If they did the same with Dorcatius' hair-stuffed two-pounder, they would not have been likely to repeat the experience. It is true that many Africans today play football barefoot with great skill, but the modern method of kicking with the instep had been developed long before the game was introduced into their countries.

The thrust forward with the sole of the foot implied in Manilius' line is a useful movement in spheres other than ball games. It is one way of pushing open a swing door or of smashing the panels of a locked one; it is often the best way of knocking down an obstacle. In fighting, a stab with the flat of the foot at an adversary's groin is much more effective than an upward kick, which dangerously exposes the shin of the kicker. The Greeks were no doubt accustomed to using this stab movement not only in combat but also in sport, in the pankration, and possibly also in boxing. It would have been much more natural, therefore, for them to use it in a ball game than to kick with the point of the foot; but it is not a method which is capable of being developed into any form of football proper.[66]

The other relevant passage is even more perplexing. It comes in the *Etymology* compiled in the seventh century AD by Isidorus, Bishop of Seville. (It is a curious coincidence that three bishops should have contributed to our knowledge of ancient ball games.) We have already considered two passages from him, but in order to assess his value as an authority it will be convenient to quote the whole of his entry under the heading *Pila* (a ball):

Pila is appropriately so called because it is stuffed with hair [*pili*]. It is also called *sfera* because it is carried [*ferendo*] or struck [*feriendo*]. Dorcatius has this about its nature and weight: 'Do not hesitate to stuff it with the hair of a swift-running stag, until it weighs an ounce over two pounds.' Among the kinds of ball are the *trigonaria* and the *arenata*. The *trigonaria* is so called because it is used in the game for three players. The *arenata* was used in the team game in which, when the ball was thrown out of the circle of spectators, those standing outside the boundary could catch the ball and enter the game. The term 'elbow game' [*cubitalem lusum*] is used when two opponents strike the ball at close quarters with their elbows almost linked. A player is said to 'give the calf' when by pushing forward his leg he serves the ball for his fellow-players to strike [*Suram dicitur dare qui pilam crure prolato feriendam conlusoribus praebet*].

(*Etymologia* XVIII, 69)

This is a strange ragbag of sense and nonsense. The derivation of *sfera*—a late spelling of *sphaera*, the latinized form of the ordinary Greek word for a ball—from *fero* or *ferio* is absurd. The couplet from Dorcatius, as we have seen, is a useful addition to our knowledge of ancient balls, and his account of Arenata reveals a convention in games played in the sphaeristerium not mentioned in any other source. 'Elbow play' is otherwise unknown. Probably it was not the name of a separate game with its own rules, but a technique used in any ball game, parallel with 'volleying at the net' in tennis. The last sentence is the most tantalizing. If we disregard the mention of legs, the language accurately describes 'service' in such court games as tennis, rackets or fives; in the early history of these games, service was simply a way of bringing the ball into play and not a method of scoring aces, as it has become in lawn tennis. But it is not easy to see how this could be done 'by pushing forward the leg', still less why the calf of the leg should be used in the technical term. Moreover, the sentence admits of other renderings, 'when, with one leg pushed forward, he serves the ball', 'when he serves the ball for his fellow-players to strike by pushing forward a leg' or 'for his fellow-players to strike with one leg pushed forward'. There is the further possibility that the authority from whom Isidorus was copying wrote not '*Suram dare*' but '*Curam dare*'; that a player about to serve called out '*Cura*', 'Look out', where a modern player calls 'Service', and that the phrase '*Curam dare*' originated in this practice. It is sometimes thought that the game of Tennis may owe its name to '*Tenez*' called by the server in the same way. Probably it is wisest to admit defeat by the utter illogicality of a sporting idiom; one could scarcely construct a game of Roman football on the basis of 'giving the calf'.

If then we are to use some parallel in our own day to form a picture of the technical details and social position of ball games in antiquity, we must free our minds of all preconceptions formed in them by European Cups, World Series, Test Matches, Wimbledon Championships, League Tables and International Associations, and think rather of a small group of businessmen going off to a set of tennis or a round of golf or to some other game of which they have never read the rules, but of which they picked up the general principles from older players when they first took up the game.

CHAPTER IV

SWIMMING AND ROWING

IT SEEMS TO HAVE BEEN TAKEN FOR GRANTED among the Greeks that everyone should be able to swim, as might be expected of a people whose lives were so bound up with the sea. The Greek phrase for the most elementary fundamentals of education—our 'Three Rs'—was 'The alphabet and swimming' (γράμματα καὶ νήχεσθαι). Some recorded incidents in history show that many of them were expert in the water. The most famous of these is related by Thucydides. During the Peloponnesian War, when a body of Spartans was blockaded on the island of Sphacteria in the bay of Pylos, they were furnished with supplies by men from the mainland who swam under water, towing skins filled with food light enough to float. A similar incident occurred earlier, when the Persian fleet which accompanied Xerxes' invasion was lying at anchor off Mount Pelion. Greeks swam under water and cut the anchor cables, with the result that many ships were thrown on the rocks and wrecked. The earliest author to record this is the epigrammatist Apollonides in the first century A D; he attributes the feat to one Scyllus. This man appears under the name Scyllias in Herodotus, who had heard many stories about him but records only the garbled legend that when he deserted from Xerxes' forces he swam ten miles under water to join the Greek fleet; reasonably enough, Herodotus suggests that he probably made the journey by boat. Pausanias, calling him Scyllis, tells the story of the anchor cables, and adds that he was helped in the enterprise by his daughter Hydna, whom he had taught to dive. Pausanias saw statues of Scyllis and Hydna at Delphi, erected in their honour by the Amphictyonic council, and this supports the tradition of their feat. The text of Pausanias at this point includes the surprising statement that in order to be able to dive a girl must be *virgo intacta*.[67]

Sponges were an important commodity in the Greek world, and diving for them provided a livelihood for many Aegean islanders. The depth to which they descended is indicated by Aristotle's statement that they often suffered from burst eardrums. He describes some of the precautions they took against this; some slit their ears and nostrils; others tied sponges over their ears; others filled their ears with olive oil. A good description of this diving for sponges is given by Oppian in his poem about fishing. He insists that it is the most unpleasant and dangerous of occupations; the divers have to be sparing in eating and drinking, and must train their breathing as carefully as any singer preparing his voice for a competition. Then he goes on:

> A man ties a long rope round his waist, and in his left hand he holds a heavy lead weight, while in the right he grasps a sharp sickle; his mouth is filled with olive oil. Standing in the bows of the boat he gazes at the waves of the sea, thinking of his heavy task and the dread water. His friends encourage him and urge him on to his job, as if he were a runner on his mark at the start of a race. Summoning up his courage, he jumps into the eddies, and as he leaps, the weight of the grey lead drags him down. When he comes to the bottom, he spits out the oil, and its gleam mixes with the water and shines brightly, like a beacon fire glowing in the darkness of the night. There he sees the sponges growing in the crevices of the rocks. . . . At once he darts at them and cuts them with the sickle in his right hand, just like a man mowing; then without delay he shakes the rope, signalling to his friends to pull him up quickly.

> (*Halieutica* V, 634ff)

The skill of Greek underwater swimmers in coming up for

air without disturbing the surface of the sea can be judged from a chance remark of Libanius:

> A diver can remain hidden from watchers on shore as long as he likes.
>
> (*Orationes* XII, 63)

It was embodied in Greek proverbial language; of a problem requiring deep thought for its solution they said, 'It needs a diver from Delos'. This was no doubt why Bacchylides, writing an ode to be sung in Delos in honour of Apollo, chose a legend about Theseus accepting a challenge from Minos to prove his descent from Poseidon by diving to re- trieve a gold ring from the bottom of the sea. Homer too pays his tribute to these island divers. In one of the battles of the *Iliad*, Patroclus hurls a stone at Cebriones, Hector's squire, and sends him flying headlong from his cháriot. Then he taunts him:

> Heavens, what a nimble man! How smoothly he takes a header! If he were on the fish-haunted sea, he could support a large family by diving from a boat and bringing up oys ers, even in a storm. Apparently there are divers even among the Trojans.[68]
>
> (*Iliad* XVI, 745)

Further evidence of ancient skill in diving appears in Plutarch's story of the trick which Cleopatra played on Antony. It is translated thus by North:

> On a time he went to angle for Fish, and when he could take none, he was as angry as he could, because Cleopatra stood by. Wherefore he secretly commanded the Fisher- men, that when he cast in his Line, they should straight dive under the water, and put a Fish on his Hook which they had taken before: and so snatched up his Angling- rod, and brought up a Fish twice or thrice. Cleopatra found it straight, yet she seemed not to see it, but wondered at his excellent fishing: but when she was alone by her self among her owne People, she told them how it was, and

bade them the next morning to be on the water to see the
fishing. A number of People came to the Haven, and got
into the fisher-boates to see this fishing. Antonius then
threw in his Line, and Cleopatra straight commanded one
of her men to dive under water before Antonius men, and
to put some old Salt-fish upon his baite, like unto those
that are brought out of the Countrey of PONT. When he
had hung the Fish on his Hooke, Antonius thinking he had
taken a Fish indeed, snatched up his Line presently. Then
they all fell a laughing: Cleopatra also laughing said unto
him: Leave us (my Lord) Aegyptians (which dwell in the
Countrey of PHARUS and CANOBUS) your Angling-
rod: this is not thy Profession, thou must hunt after con-
quering of Realmes and Countreys.

Shakespeare did not miss the opportunity which this anecdote
offered (*Pl.* 57).[69]

Herodotus says that the disparity in the casualties at the
battle of Salamis was partly due to the fact that most of the
Greeks could swim, while few in the Persian fleet could do
so. Thucydides relates that when the Syracusans tried to
safeguard their fleet in the Great Harbour by a stockade of
piles driven into the sea-bed, Athenian divers sawed off the
stakes under water. In spite of this technical skill, however,
there is hardly anything in Greek literature to suggest that
the Greeks looked on swimming as something to be done for
pleasure or as a sport. Pausanias records that swimming races
were held in honour of Dionysus at Hermione in the Peloponnese. A great boxer, Tisander of Naxos in Sicily, four
times winner at Olympia in the sixth century B C, is said by
Philostratus to have used long-distance swimming as part of
his training. In the fifth century A D, Nonnus, the last of the
Greek epic poets, introduced two swimming races into his
Dionysiaca; each was the outcome of a challenge to a friend,
and the second ended in a fatal accident.[70]

The Greek medical writers are anything but enthusiastic
about the value of swimming. Their objection appears to be

based on the risk of being chilled by the coldness of the sea, but Antyllus does not recommend it even in warm water:

> If you must bathe, grease yourself with olive oil and warm yourself by brisk rubbing, and then plunge suddenly into the water.

(Quoted by Oribasius VI, 27)

This reads like a warning to a friend about to take a holiday in Iceland rather than advice to dwellers in the sunny Aegean. But the attitude it embodies is graphically confirmed by a small bronze now in Boston (*Pl.* 55), which evokes a sympathetic fellow-feeling in many of us.

Possibly because of the accidents of literary survival, the picture from Rome is different and much more like our own experience. Horace in the *Odes* shows us the young aristocrats of his day delighting in river bathing. His Enipeus has no rival in swimming downstream; Hebrus, beloved of Neobule, after his exercise 'bathes his oil-smeared shoulders in the waters of the river', while Lydia is reproached because her Sybaris now fears even to touch the tawny Tiber. In the *Satires*, Horace recommends those suffering from insomnia to swim across the Tiber three times. Ovid, languishing on the shores of the Black Sea, thinks longingly of his friends in Rome, bathing in the waters of Aqua Virgo. In the best of all 'boy on a dolphin' stories from antiquity, the younger Pliny gives a description of a beach scene at Hippo in North Africa which could stand for any holiday resort today:

> There people of all ages enjoy fishing, boating and swimming, especially boys, who have leisure for such delights. They compete to be able to boast of having swum the greatest distance out to sea; the winner is the one who has left the shore and his fellows farthest behind him.

(*Epistulae* IX, 33)

This account is pleasantly illustrated by a splendid Roman

mosaic in the Bardo Museum in Tunis, showing a bather having his toe nipped by a crab—still a favourite subject for comic postcards sold at the seaside (*Pl. 56*). Yet Latin literature is even more barren than Greek of any references to swimming races. Horace's mention of Enipeus as unrivalled in swimming may hint at them, but Pausanias' statement about the matches at Hermione appears to be the only firm evidence for organized swimming events in antiquity.[71]

When we read in Horace of Hebrus' well-oiled shoulders as he bathes, we are reminded of Antyllus' injunction. But Hebrus has been taking exercise before his plunge into the river, and for that he would naturally have anointed himself. We do not know whether Greek and Roman swimmers normally oiled themselves for a bathe. In the pages of Ovid, Hero, anxiously awaiting Leander who is going to swim the Dardanelles to visit her, pictures to herself what is happening on the other side of the straits. 'Do you suppose', she asks her nurse, 'that at this moment he is taking off his clothes, and covering his body with rich oil?' (*Pallade iam pingui tingere membra putes?*) But this may have been a device of the poet to indicate an unusually long swim; even today Channel swimmers grease themselves.[72]

All this suggests that the ability to swim was general among Romans. During his campaign in Egypt, Julius Caesar on one occasion swam two hundred yards, holding some important papers above the surface in his left hand and dragging his cloak behind him with his teeth to prevent it from falling into the hands of the enemy. Augustus personally taught his grandsons 'Letters and swimming and other rudiments' (*litteras et natare aliaque rudimenta.* The phrase recalls the Greek 'Letters and swimming'.) Earlier, Cato the Elder had been equally careful in the education of his son, teaching him not only to throw the javelin, fence, ride and box, but also to swim in the swiftest and roughest parts of a river. Caesar's facility in the water contrasts strangely with Alexander the Great, who once, when his troops were held up by a deep river, lamented that he had never learnt to swim. And

Suetonius records with surprise that the Emperor Gaius (Caligula), for all his other accomplishments, was unable to swim.[73]

In early days, swimmers used sea and rivers, and long continued to do so. Horace's young Romans swam in the Tiber. Pliny has an interesting account of a tributary of the Tiber, the Clitumnus. Its source was a large pool, on whose banks stood a temple of the River God and shrines of other deities. At the point where the river flowed out of the pool, it was crossed by a bridge; bathing was allowed in the river below the bridge, but not in the pool above it, which was considered sacred water, a suitable receptacle for coins thrown in as offerings to the gods. As wealth grew, these natural swimming facilities were supplemented by artificial swimming pools. Republican Rome had one outside one of the southern gates of the city near the Via Appia. The grammarian Festus tells us that in his day, the second century AD, it no longer existed, but he quotes an interesting reference to it from the satirist Lucilius, who wrote some three centuries earlier: 'To judge from his battered face, he is a boxer, who haunts the swimming pool.' This suggests that Tisander may not have been the only boxer in antiquity to use swimming as part of his training. Every Greek and Roman city had its public baths, but in discussing these we are confronted with an ambiguity to which we have a parallel in our own language. We distinguish in English between a bath and a bathe, but while in speech we can make it clear whether a man bathing is taking a bath or a bathe, the written word leaves the matter doubtful. And an Englishman in a strange town in his own country would be by no means sure what went on in the Town Baths. They might contain an elaborate swimming pool or merely make good the shortage of private bathrooms. So too in Greek and Latin, if the ordinary word for public baths is used (βαλανεῖον, balneum), there is no knowing whether swimming facilities are included; it is only when the specific term for a swimming pool occurs (κολυμβήθρα, piscina) that we can be certain. Thus when Pliny tells us of the bathing in the Clitumnus, he adds that the authorities of a neighbouring town, who were responsible for administering the site, had built there a hotel and a public bath (*balineum publice praebent*). It is not clear whether this building was simply for washing, or whether it included a swimming pool, which in view of the very strong current of the river would have been a welcome amenity. Because of this ambiguity it is not possible to say when the first indoor swimming pools were constructed. The one solid piece of evidence we have is the statement of Dio Cassius that Maecenas was the first to build a warm-water swimming pool in Rome. Unheated pools presumably existed earlier. Excavation has revealed many such pools of the Roman Imperial period. There is also an unheated one in the north-west corner of the site at Olympia. At Gafsa in Tunisia, at Pammukale in Asia Minor and at Bath in Britain there are Roman pools still supplied with water from natural warm springs, but normally the water had to be artificially heated.[74]

The luxury of these warm-water establishments came to be generally expected, and there were protests when the highest standards were not maintained. The satirist Nicarchus in the first century AD has an epigram about Onesimus, the father of a young son, going to the Baths. If he waits for the water to be warm, says Nicarchus, the baby will be the father of three by the time he returns. Another epigram in the *Anthology* is a cry from the heart of an anonymous poet who takes the same chilly view of bathing as Antyllus, the second-century Greek medical writer whose attitude we noticed earlier:

Who put a wall round the river, bathman? Who gave the lying name of 'Bath' to this stream? Aeolus son of Hippotas, that favourite of the immortal gods as Homer calls him, took the winds from their home and brought them here. And what are these two planks doing under our feet? They are not there to protect us from the heat but from the snow. This place is the haunt of Shiver and Numb.

Put up a notice, 'Bathe here in midsummer, for the North Wind blows inside'.

(Anthologia Palatina IX, 617)

As the word for 'midsummer' is Egyptian, the epigram was probably written in Egypt in the Ptolemaic or Roman period. It is not clear whether the bath was literally an open air pool with a stream or a diverted channel of the Nile flowing through it, or whether the poet is denouncing in exaggerated terms a covered pool which claimed to be warmed.[75]

In the last days of the Western Roman Empire, the poet Rutilius Namatianus, describing the enclosed harbour of Cività Vecchia, compares it to a swimming bath at Cumae in the Bay of Naples:

> It is as calm as the water imprisoned in the bath at Cumae, which supports the supple arms of swimmers in their alternating swing.

(De Reditu Suo, 247)

This seems to imply an open-air sea-water pool.

It was not only public Baths which included swimming pools. Pliny had a warmed pool in his Laurentian villa, from which the swimmers could look out to sea. He says that there was no need for a cold pool here because the sea was near at hand. But his Tuscan villa, where there was neither sea nor suitable river available, had two pools, warm and cold. Each villa, of course, had also the usual elaborate provision of baths for hygienic purposes.[76]

It is no easier to discover the technical details of the swimming that went on in these baths than it is to learn those of any other ancient sport; the evidence has to be assembled from the oddest sources. Our most complete account of swimming in antiquity comes in Manilius' poem on Astronomy. He tells us that those born under Delphinus are likely to be good swimmers:

> *Sic, venit ex illo quisquis, volitabit in undis,*
> 423 *nunc alterna ferens in lentos bracchia tractus,*

424 *et plausa resonabit aqua, nunc aequore mersas*
diducet palmas furtiva biremis in ipso,
nunc in aquas rectus veniet passuque natabit
et vada mentitus reddet super aequora campum;
aut immota ferens in tergus membra latusque
non onerabit aquas summisque accumbet in undis
pendebitque super, totus sine remige velum.
431 *illis in ponto iucundum est quaerere pontum,*
corporaque immergunt undis, ipsumque sub antris
Nerea et aequoreas conantur visere nymphas,
exportantque maris praedas et rapta profundo
naufragia atque imas avidi scrutantur harenas.[77]

[Thus, whoever comes under that constellation will shoot through the waves like a bird. At one moment he will ply his arms alternately in smooth swings, and will make the water resound as he smacks it. At another he will keep his hands under the water and sweep them apart, like a sculler with his sculls unseen. At another he will go upright into the waves and swim by walking, appearing to turn the sea into solid land. Or he will keep his arms motionless behind his back or by his side and float on the water, seeming not to impose any weight on it, and he will project slightly above the surface like a sailing ship without oars. Others find pleasure in seeking a world below the sea and plunge into the waves, trying to visit Nereus and his sea nymphs; they carry off the booty of the ocean, take possession of wrecked ships in the depths, and greedily explore the sandy bottom of the deep.]

(*Astronomica* V, 422ff)

Here we have unmistakably the two fundamental styles of swimming, the breast stroke and the overarm crawl or free style. The swimmer also displays floating, treading water or 'dog-paddling'—'swimming by walking'—and underwater swimming, including salvage from wrecks; submarine archaeology is not so recent as we might suppose.

The only other author in antiquity who certainly refers to the breast stroke is Nonnus. In the turgid language of his Homeric pastiche he describes Semele swimming:

> The maiden cut through the water by plying her hands like oars [χεῖρας ἐρετμώσασα]. With practised skill she kept her head unwetted, raising it high above the foam and dipping her neck only to the hairline; spreading wide her breast to the waves, she pushed the water behind her with alternate thrusts of her feet [ποσσὶν ἀμοιβαίοισιν].
>
> (*Dionysiaca* VII, 185)

In the accounts of the two swimming matches in his epic, one between Bacchus and Ampelus in the river Pactolus, the other between Carpus and Calamus in the Maeander, Nonnus' words again suggest the breast stroke. In both, the arms are used like oars (χεῖρας ἐρέσσων and ἐρεσσομένων παλαμάων). Bacchus 'throws his naked breast against the current' (XI, 48); Calamus 'stretches his neck above the surface' (XI, 421). But the leg actions which Nonnus attributes to Semele—the 'alternate thrusts of her feet'—and to Calamus, 'waggling his feet' (πόδας δονέων), are incompatible with the modern breast stroke, though the latter phrase fits very well the leg action of the crawl. It would be foolish, however, to base any theory of ancient swimming on Nonnus. Whatever virtues he may have possessed as a writer, accuracy of observation was not one of them.

Though there appears to be no specific mention of the back stroke in ancient literature, such skilful swimmers as the Greeks and Romans are not likely to have left it undiscovered. Manilius' swimmer when floating was obviously on his back, and there is a hint in Ovid. The poet in exile pleads to a friend that he does not need advice about how he could have avoided his sad fate, but practical help in escaping from it, and he uses this image:

> *Brachia da lasso potius prendenda natanti,*
> *nec pigeat mento supposuisse manum.*

[Rather hold out an arm for a tired swimmer to grasp, and do not be ashamed of having put a supporting hand under his chin.]

(*Epistulae ex Ponto* II, vi.13)

The last phrase recalls pictures of life-saving drill, with the victim's chin supported by the life-saver swimming on his back. Ovid has also a brief description of Arethusa bathing which suggests a general all-round ease and facility in the water and a considerable repertory of different strokes:

> *Nudaque mergor aquis, quas dum ferioque trahoque*
> *mille modis labens excussaque brachia iacto.*

[I plunged naked into the pool, and gliding through it in a thousand ways I struck the water and drew it backwards, I raised my arms and tossed them in the air.]

(*Metamorphoses* V, 595)

Statius, who in matters of sport is one of the most knowledgeable of all ancient writers, has a brief description of a swimmer unmistakably doing the crawl. Among the prizes for the chariot race in the *Thebaid* is a cloak embroidered with a picture of Leander swimming the Hellespont:

> *In latus ire manu mutaturusque videtur*
> *bracchia, nec siccum speres in stamine crinem.*

[He is seen with one hand coming in to his side, and he is about to change arms; you would not for a moment believe that his hair in the embroidered picture is dry.]

(*Thebaid* VI, 544)

The action described is that at the moment when the forward arm is just starting its stroke, while the other, having completed its stroke, has been brought in to the side and is about to be taken forward for the next.

The passages which have been interpreted as describing the breast stroke might be thought to refer equally well to the butterfly. Yet it is difficult to believe that the Greeks and

Romans, who appear not to have been much interested in swimming races, would have practised so ugly and unnatural an exercise. The Greeks especially would surely never have endured the sight of those bouncing bottoms. The constant recurrence in Latin, whenever swimming is mentioned, of the words *iactare* and *alterna*, which indicate raising the arms alternately above the surface of the water, makes it certain that the normal stroke was some form of crawl. (*Pl.* 58).

Those learning to swim were helped, as they are today, by some kind of lifebelt or support. There is no direct evidence that they used inflated bladders after the manner of Elizabethan boys, but there is no reason why they should not have done so. As we have seen, they used such bladders as balls, and soldiers used inflated animal skins to help them in crossing rivers. But such skins would be too cumbersome to give the beginner any assistance, and bladders are liable to burst suddenly and leave the novice helpless; there are more satisfactory patterns. Horace's father, warning his young son that sooner or later he would have to face life standing on his own legs, used the metaphor, 'You will swim without cork' (*nabis sine cortice*). Plautus reveals a different material:

> When boys are learning to swim, they put on floats made of bamboo, so that they shall not feel themselves in difficulties but swim and move their arms more easily.
>
> (*Aulularia,* 595)

In Homer, Odysseus, a strong swimmer, welcomes the help of the headscarf of the sea-goddess Ino Leucothea in a storm, binding it on 'under his breast' to act as a lifebelt.[78]

Such slight evidence as exists suggests that the ability to swim was no less widespread among women than among men in antiquity. Nausicaa and her maidens bathed in the river while they were waiting for the palace laundry to dry, but Homer does not tell us whether or not they swam. Pausanias implies only that Hydna's skill in diving and underwater swimming was exceptional and due to special training by her father, not that her ability to swim was out of the ordinary. The evidence from Latin literature is a little less scanty. According to tradition, in the early days of Rome when the Etruscans were besieging the city and Horatius Cocles held the bridge, a number of young Roman girls, kept as hostages by the Etruscans, escaped under the leadership of Cloelia by swimming the Tiber. Centuries later, when the Emperor Nero tried to murder his mother by having her ship scuttled as she was sailing across the Bay of Naples by night, Agrippina foiled the plot of her amiable son by striking out for the shore through the darkness until she was picked up by a fishing boat. None of the authors who relate these incidents suggest that there was anything in the least unusual in a woman being able to swim. Ovid, it is true, says to young women in his *Art of Love,*

> The cold water of the Aqua Virgo does not tempt you, and Tiber does not carry you along in his calm stream.
>
> (*Ars Amatoria* III, 383)

But he is urging them to affect a feminine helplessness in order to attract virile young lovers. Propertius gives us a different picture. Parted from his Cynthia, he wonders what she is doing far away in Baiae, and hopes that she is boating or bathing rather than lying on the sand listening to the passionate whispers of one of his rivals. His words imply swimming:

> *Aut teneat clausam tenui Teuthrantis in unda*
> *alternae facilis cedere lympha manu.*
> [May the water of Teuthras' calm sea, yielding readily to your hands as you ply them alternately, hold you prisoner.][79]
>
> (I, xi.11)

Whatever may have happened in sea and river, in public Baths men and women were segregated. The male epigrammatists of the *Greek Anthology* are very arch and coy on the subject of women's Baths, and this in itself strongly suggests that at any rate in covered swimming pools, mixed bathing was frowned upon in antiquity. It was a black mark against the Emperor Domitian that he swam with common prostitutes (*inter vulgatissimas meretrices*).[80]

Swimming is not a spectacular sport, and it did not much lend itself to inclusion in those grandiose shows, so beloved of the Romans, when a theatre or arena was flooded to allow the performance of mock sea battles. But Martial reveals that when the Colosseum was opened at Rome in A D 80, among the attractions offered was a representation of Leander swimming the Hellespont:

> Do not be surprised, Leander, that the sea spared you; it was Caesar's sea.
>
> (*Liber Spectacularum*, 25)

The other aquatic sports of today, rowing and sailing, receive even less attention in Greek and Latin literature than does swimming. We have seen mention of pleasure boating in Propertius, and Pliny, in the same letter in which he describes swimming in the Clitumnus, speaks of boating for pleasure on the river. But although both Greek and Latin have several words for different varieties of small boat, there is no evidence of the specialized craft which sailing and rowing need for their full development. Catullus affords the only hint in antiquity of sailing races. He boasts of his *phaselus*, which he had sailed home from Asia Minor to Sirmio on Lake Garda, that she was able to pass anything afloat, either under sail or oar; this suggests informal challenges among friends.[81]

Even the largest ships in antiquity used oars as well as sail. The Greeks and Romans appear not to have achieved much skill in sailing; they could do little more than run before a reasonably favourable wind. For reasons of economy, merchant ships relied mainly on sail. Warships used sail in transit, but under sail they were far too slow and unmanoeuvrable for battle. As soon as an engagement was imminent, masts were lowered and sails stowed away. Victory depended largely on the skilful manoeuvring of the ships, and for this reason the rowers were very highly trained. Racing formed part of this training. Xenophon tells us how Iphicrates, perhaps the finest military commander Athens ever possessed, employed races to add interest and stimulus to the training of his crews. On a voyage round the Peloponnese in 372 BC, when he was expecting to engage the Spartan fleet any day, he used to send his ships out to sea before every meal, draw them up in line, and set them to race to the shore, with the prospect of having first go at the rations as sufficient prize. A century earlier, a similar race had been held off Abydos to encourage keenness in the crews of Xerxes' fleet; Herodotus records that it was won by a Phoenician ship from Sidon. Just before his death, Alexander promoted boat races (ἀγῶνες τῶν ἐρετῶν) at Babylon. We hear on one occasion of trireme races being included in funeral celebrations, as athletic events often were; this was in Cyprus, where in 374 BC Nicocles thus honoured his father Euagoras, prince of Salamis.[82]

At some places these regattas were clearly held as regularly as athletic meetings. Pausanias records boat races at Hermione, along with the swimming races. Augustus included them in his festival of Actia, no doubt because Actium was primarily a naval victory. At Athens, trireme races were part of the Panathenaic celebrations; an inscription of the fourth century BC, recording the prizes at the festival, ends with the item,

Prizes for the ship race [νεῶν ἁμίλλης] 300 drachmae to the winning 'tribe', plus 200 for a feast [καὶ εἰς ἑστίασιν].
(IG, II/III², 2311 = Syll.³, 1055)

It is pleasant to find that the Bump Supper has so long a pedigree. These are probably the races at the Peiraeus, to which the comic dramatist Plato refers when he says that the monument of Themistocles looked out on 'the contest of the ships' (ἅμιλλα τῶν νεῶν). Other races were held by the Athenians at Sunium; an anonymous litigant, for whom

Lysias wrote a speech, claims that his victory there with his trireme cost him 15 minae, equivalent in purchasing power to several hundred pounds today.[83]

Late Greek writers tried to give a spurious antiquity to boat races, as to many other things, by inventing legends about them in the Heroic Age. Philostratus has a story of how Palamedes persuaded Agamemnon, when plague was raging during the Trojan War, to hold boat races, because the air out at sea was healthier. Dio Chrysostom, putting the origin of the Isthmian Games far too early, says that a race for ships was included at their first celebration and was won by the Argo, rowed by the Argonauts, who lived even before the siege of Troy. The only possible hint of evidence from the Heroic Age itself comes when Homer makes Alcinous include skill with ships among the sports of the Phaeacians.[84]

No parallel exists today to the ships used in these races— large sea-going vessels powered by oars in several banks, the arrangement of which is still a matter of high controversy. Perhaps the best picture of them is given in the irreverent words of a modern poet:

> Just imagine a crew of a hundred or two
>   Shoved three deep in a kind of a barge,
> Like a cargo of kegs, with no room for their legs,
>   And oars inconveniently large.[85]

> (R. H. Foster)

Although the historic records of ancient rowing are so meagre, boat-racing evoked one masterpiece of sporting literature—the event in the Funeral Games in Virgil's *Aeneid*. This race provides a minor literary mystery. So many of the ancient epics include Funeral Games that we are tempted to suppose that the prestige of Homer made them inevitable in every example of the *genre*. In fact, the only epic which has survived from the centuries between Homer and Virgil, the *Argonautica* of Apollonius Rhodius, has none, although

Apollonius' native Rhodes had a fine athletic tradition and he of all poets might have been expected to include them. Virgil returns to the Homeric precedent and imitates his master closely in his descriptions of the foot race and boxing match. Yet, although Homer had lavished more care on his account of the chariot race than on any other event, Virgil here abandons him completely and substitutes a boat race for the chariots of the *Iliad*. We have it on the authority of Hyginus that he was the first poet to write of such an event. Probably Virgil's motive in all this was a desire to please Augustus, whose encouragement of Greek athletics we have seen, and who had included boat races in his own Actian festival.[86]

The race is described with considerable spirit, and the reader is left with the impression that the poet had himself witnessed such events with enthusiasm but without much technical knowledge. Four ships take part, drawn from the fleet which had brought Aeneas and his companions from Troy to Sicily on their way to found Rome. They are the *Shark*, commanded by Mnestheus, the *Chimaera*, whose captain is Gyas, the *Centaur* under Sergestus, and Cloanthus' *Scylla*. The course is 'out and home' from the shore, rounding a rock out at sea. It is not known whether this was normal for boat-racing in Virgil's time, or whether he is imitating the course for the chariot race in the *Iliad*. On the whole, as Homer is not looking over his shoulder as he writes this episode, it seems more probable that it was contemporary practice.

After the draw for stations, the ships take up their positions for the start. The captains, standing at the stern near their helmsmen, are resplendent in purple and gold. The crews wear crowns of white poplar, partly no doubt as festive headgear and partly for protection against the sun; their naked shoulders gleam with olive oil. As they await the signal, they experience the same emotions as every crew in every age at the start of a race:

Their fluttering hearts are drained of their strength by
shuddering panic mingled with keen anxiety to win.

(Aeneid V, 137)

Then the trumpet sounds and they are off; all is foam and
spray, shouting and clamour. At this point Virgil shows by
an apt simile that he could have described a chariot race with
equal *élan*:

> Not so speedily do the chariots dash out onto the track as
> they leave the starting-traps for the race; not so eagerly do
> the drivers shake their waving reins as they give the horses
> their heads or strain forward over their teams to lash them
> on.

(144–7)

Now the ships are well into the first leg of the course, and
it is soon clear that *Chimaera* and *Scylla* are the fastest boats.
The poet wisely concentrates on the tactics of the turn, on
which so much depends in any course of this shape. At first
sight it might appear that the point for the steersman to aim
at is the right-hand edge of the rock, × in Fig. 5, but with
oar-propelled boats this is not so. The essence of steering
such a boat is to use the rudder as little and as gently as
possible, and to call on the rowers on the outside of the turn
—the starboard side in this case—for extra effort to bring the
boat round. If the helmsman aims at point ×, he cannot
begin his turn until he is clear of the rock, and he is then
tempted to use his rudder violently and so upset the rhythm
of his crew. The proper course is to take water out to the
right on the first leg in order to be able to begin the change
of course early and pass the rock at the peak of the turn. This
is what Menoites, the steersman of Gyas' *Chimaera*, starts to
do. Here we can see why we are justified in believing that
Virgil had seen such races without understanding the tactics
involved; he attributes Menoites' course to a desire to avoid
wrecking his ship on the rock. Gyas sees Cloanthus in the
Scylla taking the apparently shorter course to port of his own

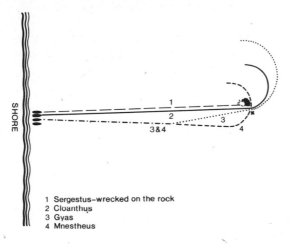

1 Sergestus—wrecked on the rock
2 Cloanthus
3 Gyas
4 Mnestheus

Fig. 5 *Virgil's boat race.*

ship, and shouts to Menoites to do the same, but the experienced helmsman refuses to obey. Every coach of an Eight
must at some time during a race have longed to throw the
cox overboard and take his place. Fortunately he is helpless,
but not so Gyas. He does just that to Menoites, takes the tiller
himself and steers for the inner line, while the deposed
Menoites swims to the rock and sits there, dripping and
spitting out water to the great amusement of the spectators.

Meanwhile the two slower ships are coming up behind.
Sergestus steers his *Centaur* on the inner line with fatal results;
she crashes on the rock. Mnestheus, forced to swing wider,
makes the best turn of all, and this puts his *Shark* in contention
again with the leaders. Gyas is proving himself a poor helmsman; Mnestheus soon passes him and closes on Cloanthus.
All seems prepared for a splendid finish, and then Virgil
spoils everything. He makes the result of the race depend on
the intervention of a god in response to Cloanthus' prayer.
That the issue of a race should be decided by such heavenly
interference is thoroughly repugnant to religious belief and
sporting instinct alike. For us, religion and morality are
inextricably interwoven; if God intervened in a sporting
event, he would, being the embodiment of perfect justice

and goodness, have to do so on behalf of the competitor who was morally the best man. The slightest acquaintance with the sporting scene shows that this does not happen. So while everyone recognizes the important part which chance or luck plays in games, even the most fervent believer will not accept that success in them is evidence of special divine favour to the winner. The spectacle of a Latin American footballer devoutly falling on his knees and crossing himself after scoring a goal in the World Cup is apt rather to evoke mild amusement than to strengthen religious faith.

The ancients were not hampered by any such notions of gods as necessarily embodiments of moral qualities, and divine intervention is a commonplace in epic descriptions of games. In popular legend their gods were anything but moral beings, and so there was nothing unnatural in the greatest of scoundrels enlisting the help of one of them in a sporting encounter. If he could do so, his cleverness was a cause for admiration rather than reprobation. But we must not allow Virgil's blunder at the end of his race to blind us to the merits of the early part of his description.

If it is surprising that Virgil was the first ancient writer to describe a boat race, it is even more surprising in view of his success that he was apparently also the last. Almost every subsequent epic poet imitated him by including Funeral Games—indeed it might be argued that it was Virgil rather than Homer who made them an indispensable part of epic—but none followed him in describing a boat race. Valerius Flaccus, it is true, imitating Apollonius Rhodius, has a vivid account of Heracles achieving the ambition of every oarsman by breaking his oar in the middle of a stroke when he was rowing in the *Argo*; he fell over backwards, knocking down Talaus, Eribotes and Amphion, and finished with his head on Iphitus' thwart. But this was not in a race. For the next boat race in fiction, it would seem, the world had to wait for the brief description of the Cambridge Mays in Fitzgerald's *Euphranor* in 1851.[87]

CHAPTER V

HOOP-BOWLING

THE STRANGEST ATHLETIC EXERCISE of the Greeks and Romans was the bowling of hoops. Sixty years ago, before our streets became filled with car traffic, every child had a hoop, and the hoop season took its place in the annual rota along with the top season, the marbles season, the conkers season and others; small girls propelled a wooden hoop with a stick, small boys an iron hoop with a hook. But in modern times it has never been regarded as a pursuit for adults. There is, however, sparse but unmistakable evidence that both Greeks and Romans took it seriously as a sport. The Romans latinized a Greek word for a hoop, *trochus,* so it is reasonable to assume that they adopted the sport itself from Greece. Unfortunately the word was used in Greek—though not in Latin—for many other things, a cart-wheel, a potter's wheel, a water-wheel, a round cake, the disc of the sun, the circuit of a city wall or of a race course, the ring of a horse's bridle, a ring in a ship's rigging and a kind of fish. In some passages, therefore, it is not easy to decide the precise significance of the word. When, for instance, the medical writings of the fifth and fourth centuries BC which are ascribed to Hippocrates recommend an exercise which they call '*trochoi*', there is much dispute about what is meant. We are told that it is a cure for biliousness, that it soon makes a man breathless, that it is quick, and that it is less likely to make the body slow and thickset than is long-distance running; it is contrasted with running in the stadium or xystus. This last statement renders unlikely the traditional translation of *trochoi* in these passages as 'running on a circular track'. There is no evidence for such tracks, and even if they existed, it is difficult to believe that running on them would be a different exercise from running in a stadium. The Hippocratic evidence suggests some form of brisk exercise, and is perfectly compatible with the description of hoop-bowling given many centuries later by Antyllus.[88]

Greek children certainly played with hoops. At the first appearance of Medea's ill-fated sons in Euripides' play they are coming 'fresh from their hoop-bowling'. Dio Chrysostom uses them to illustrate a point. Some atheists, he says, will not even accept the idea of a Creator who made the Universe and then left it to look after itself, 'as children set their hoops in motion and then let them roll from their own impetus'. Sextus Empiricus takes the view that we should expect when he writes that children love ball-play and bowling hoops, but when they grow up they choose other pursuits. Yet in spite of this last assertion, there is no doubt that hoop-bowling, no less than ball games, appealed to adults too. The best evidence for this in the classical period comes not from literature but from art. The Ashmolean Museum has a charming vase of about 500 BC, depicting a youth, of the same age as the young athletes often portrayed in similar paintings, who is bowling a hoop. He is not primarily engaged in athletic exercise, for he is obviously bringing food home from market, carefully covered by a cloth weighted at the corners. Even more significant is the gravestone of Panaetius, now in the Athens Museum, with a relief showing the young man bowling a rather larger hoop (Pl. 52). Such gravestones often depicted the athletic activities of the youths they commemorated, and this example seems to confirm hoop-bowling as an established sporting activity of the time.[89]

After the fourth century BC there is a wide gap in the evidence from Greek sources for hoops. Theophrastus, it is true, says that it is a characteristic of the Stupid Man to compel his children to wrestle and *trochazein* until they are exhausted, but the ambiguity of the word leaves it doubtful whether he made them bowl their hoops or simply 'run

quickly'. However, the sum total of our information is so
small that it would be wrong to assume that this gap in the
evidence implies a cessation of the activity.[90]

An inscription from the Greek city of Priene in Asia Minor
records a decree in honour of a wealthy magistrate, Aulus
Aemilius Sextus Zosimus, who had conferred great bene-
factions on his fellow citizens. The name shows that the decree belongs to the period when Asia was a Roman province.
Among his other civic activities, Zosimus had been 'gym-
nasiarch for the young men', and in this capacity, during
athletic festivals, he had 'provided olive oil for all from sun-
rise throughout the day until the first hour of night'. He had
also endowed the city with a gold trophy for boxing, and
had provided the gymnasium with a punch-ball, hoops and
balls (κώρυκον καὶ κρίκους . . . ἔτι δὲ σφαίρας), hoping to
produce tough bodies (σῶμα ἄοκνον) in the young. This
suggests that hoops were in no way regarded as effeminate.[91]

Our most impressive references to hoop-bowling come
in the Latin literature of the century following the foundation of the Empire, and as the Romans clearly took the sport
from the Greeks, this makes it certain that it was still pursued
at this time in Greece. Ovid, contrasting tough young men
with their female counterparts, includes hoops among
javelins, weapons and horsemanship as appropriate to the
former; and in exile at Tomi he thinks of his friends in Rome
training horses and enjoying weapon drill, ball-play and
hoop-bowling. Horace, on the other hand, laments that the
young Romans of his time are becoming degenerate; they
neglect horses and hunting and are 'more skilled at playing
with the Greek hoop'. His words, however, show that an
element of skill was involved, and elsewhere he brings this
out even more clearly:

A man who does not understand games and is unskilled
with ball or hoop keeps quiet, for fear that the crowds of
spectators standing round will burst out laughing.

(Ars Poetica, 379)

This implies also that hoop-bowling had some interest for
onlookers. Ovid's view of the hoop as suited to virile young
men is borne out by a reference in the *Sayings of Cato*. In their
existing form these *Dicta*, which were immensely popular
in the Middle Ages, date from the Christian era, much later
than either of the two famous men in history who bore the
name Cato, but their general tenor is in no way incompatible
with the stern character of those figures. Among such
tersely expressed moral advice as 'Love your wife', 'Instruct
your children' and 'Fight for your country' comes 'Play with
the hoop; keep off betting' (*Trocho lude; aleam fuge*). The
austere context makes it certain that play with the hoop was
not generally looked on by the Romans as effeminate or
luxurious.[92]

Propertius, describing the masculine pursuits of Spartan
girls, reveals that in antiquity the hook was used as well as
the stick to bowl a hoop;

> *Increpat et versi clavis adunca trochi.*
> [The hooked 'key' clangs on the rolling hoop.]
> > (III, xiv.6)

Increpat will bring back a long-forgotten sound to many an
elderly ear.

Martial has two epigrams about hoops. The first (XIV,
168) tells us that children used the iron tyre of a wheel as a
hoop, just as today in the Greek islands they use a barrel hoop
for the same purpose. The second shows that hoops were
fitted with jangling rings to give warning of their approach
in crowded streets:

> *Garrulus in laxo cur anulus orbe vagatur?*
> *Cedat ut argutis obvia turba trochis.*
> [Why do tinkling rings wander round the large rim? So
> that the crowd who block the path may make way for the
> clanging hoops.]
> > (XIV, 169)

The note in the Loeb edition of Martial makes unnecessary

difficulty about these rings. 'How the hoop was able to run is obscure. Perhaps loose rings were supported in position by the *clavis*, or hook for trundling the hoop. Or perhaps the rings were attached to the inner circumference.' Martial's word 'wander' makes it certain that they were not attached to the hoop but simply strung on it. A combination of friction and the weight of the rings would ensure that as soon as the hoop was set in motion the rings would cluster in the quadrant between the driving hook and the point of contact of the hoop with the ground, where they would keep up a very satisfactory jingling. Sixty years ago the windows of some seaside shops used to display wooden hoops with spokes fitted with bells; they were regarded with contempt by all right-minded children.[93]

We may well wonder whether the Greeks and Romans had devised a game which made hoops more deserving of adult attention than the mere bowling of them. R. M. Ballantyne, who spent some years in Canada, describes in *The Dog Crusoe* such a game played by the North American Indians; one young man bowled a small hoop, while another, running alongside, tried to throw a dart through it without stopping it. But there is no hint of any such game in antiquity. Nor is there anything to suggest that the ancient hoop was a hula hoop, which certainly requires some skill and affords good exercise. At the conclusion of the banquet in Xenophon's *Symposium* Socrates calls the attention of his fellow-guests to the floor show provided by their host:

'I see the girl standing ready and an attendant bringing her hoops.' Another girl played a tune for her on her pipe; the attendant stood beside the dancer and handed hoops up to her one after another until she had twelve. She grasped them as she continued to dance, and tossed them up spinning, calculating carefully how high she must throw them to be able to catch them in time with the rhythm of her dance.

(*Symposium* II, 7)

The fact that Xenophon describes the performance in this way shows that it was not the ordinary exercise with hoops of the young men of his day.

Fortunately we possess one piece of evidence which gives the clue to what this exercise may have been. In the fourth century AD Oribasius, court physician to the Roman Emperor Julian, wrote a medical treatise which was mainly a compilation, with due acknowledgments, of the work of earlier writers. Among these was one Antyllus, of whom hardly anything is known except that he probably lived about two centuries before Oribasius. He was clearly much interested in the medical aspects of sport, and the majority of his work which has survived deals with the effect on health of various games and athletic exercises. Like all Greek writers, he tantalizingly takes it for granted that all his readers will be well acquainted with the pursuits he mentions, and for this reason his writings do not reveal as much about the technical details of athletic events as we might have hoped. Here and there, however, he does throw useful light on some disputed subject, as for instance hoop-bowling (which he calls κρικηλασία). He recommends it on many grounds. It relaxes tight muscles and makes stiff parts supple because of the quick turns and twistings of the body which it involves; it strengthens the sinews, tones up enervated bodies and calms excited minds. The hoop, he says, should be less in diameter than a man's height, reaching about to his chest; it should be bowled not simply in a straight line but 'wandering' (πεπλανημένως). The 'driver' (ἐλατήρ) should be of iron with a wooden handle (this exactly describes the hook of fifty years ago). He too mentions the jingling rings on the hoop which we have encountered in Martial, and adds that some people think them superfluous; Antyllus, however, disagrees and finds the sound pleasant. Then comes the illuminating passage:

At first bowl the hoop straight, but when the body has warmed up and begun to perspire, then is the time to jump

and run through the hoop [διεκπηδᾶν τε καὶ διατρέχειν].
At the conclusion of the exercise, drive the hoop straight
again, to relax the tension produced by the exertion. The
best time for it is just before a meal or a bath, as with other
strenuous exercise.

(Quoted by Oribasius VI, 26)

From more than half a century ago, memory penitently
recalls a small boy exasperating his elder sister by constantly
trying without much success to run through her large
wooden hoop while it was in full flight, quite unaware that
he was practising an athletic exercise of young men two
thousand years before.

Perhaps the closest analogy in the modern world of sport
to the place of hoop-bowling in antiquity is furnished by
skipping. We think of skipping as primarily an amusement
of small girls, but it has often been used as part of the training
programme of athletes, boxers and footballers. These are
usually content with its simpler manifestations, but well-
trained schoolgirls sometimes show us that skipping is
capable of great diversity, can be developed to a very high
degree of skill, and can afford considerable aesthetic satis-
faction. The Greeks and Romans appear to have found
similar possibilities in hoop-bowling, and one of them used
its aesthetic potential in a surprising way. Ovid always
imagined that he was banished because the authorities in
Rome believed that his *Art of Love* corrupted the morals of
the citizens. In exile he devoted a long poem to a defence of
this work, in the course of which he pointed out that other
poets had written with impunity on various spare-time
occupations, dicing and backgammon, the application of
cosmetics and the giving of parties. In the middle of this
section comes the intriguing couplet:

Ecce, canit formas alius iactusque pilarum,
hic artem nandi praecipit, ille trochi.
[One poet sings of the different kinds of balls and how they

are thrown; another instructs on skill in swimming, a third on skill in hoop-bowling.]

(*Tristia* II, 485)

Blameless subjects indeed! Perhaps when we are mourning the missing masterpieces of Greek and Latin literature, we may spare a sigh for the loss of that poem by an unknown Roman author, *On Bowling a Hoop*.[94]

For ancient hoop-bowling of a rather different kind there survives only a single piece of evidence. The early Byzantine emperors built themselves a great palace in Constantinople and adorned it with superb mosaics. The Mosaic Museum of Istanbul now occupies the site and preserves the mosaics, some of them still in their original position on the floors. One of these depicts a number of boys running a race with hoops (*Pl.* 54). It is clearly intended as a caricature of the chariot races in the hippodrome; the *metae* with their triple obelisks are unmistakable, and the competitors wear green or blue tunics, with obvious reference to the Green and Blue factions of the charioteers. Each boy is driving a pair of spoked hoops not much more than a foot in diameter, using a method still occasionally seen today. Children find a small wheel, often from a discarded pram, equip it with an axle which projects a few inches on each side, and propel and guide it with a stick pressing against this axle. This is easy enough, but to control two hoops at the same time, one with each hand, as the boys in the mosaic are doing, would demand a considerable degree of skill. Whether such comic races were ever held as popular entertainment in the hippodrome, or whether the artist was drawing purely on his imagination, we cannot tell. The surrounding mosaics do not help. Some of them depict ordinary scenes of everyday life, a fisherman, a mare suckling her foal, peasants milking a goat or feeding a donkey, a child driving geese; others are entirely fanciful, a winged unicorn, Pan carrying the infant Bacchus on his shoulders, a gryphon eating a lizard, and a monkey in the full accoutrements of a human fowler catching birds in a date palm. There is no knowing to which class the hoop-bowlers belong. Until further evidence is forthcoming, it is wiser to assume no more than that there we see one of the children's games of the time.[95]

The tendency to detect a sexual significance in anything and everything has not spared even the humble hoop. Some Greek vases depict winged putti holding or bowling a hoop. These led one savant to comment: 'La signification érotique du trochus est indiquée par la présence de cet objet dans les mains d'Éros, soit seul, soit avec la colombe, avec le coq ou avec le dauphin.' We are so accustomed to thinking of this passion for sexual symbolism as a mark of the anthropologists and psychologists of our own day that it is surprising to find that these words were written in 1854.[96]

CHAPTER VI

WEIGHT-LIFTING

IN THE MUSEUM AT OLYMPIA is a block of sandstone, roughly
rectangular, 27 in. × 15 in. × 13 in., and waterwashed so
that all edges and corners are rounded (*Pl.* 53). Its weight is
288 lb. (143 kg.). Cut on one of its two largest sides is an
inscription in the form of a spiral starting from inside which
runs

Βύβων τἠτέρῃ χερὶ ὑπερκέφαλα μ'ὑπερεβάλετο ὁ Φ . . .
[Bubon threw me over his head with one hand.]
(Inscr. *Ol.*, 717 = *Syll.*³, 1071)

The last few letters have been lost, so that the end is uncertain;
most probably it gave the name of Bubon's father, Phorys
or Pholas. The inscription is assigned by epigraphists to the
middle of the sixth century B C.

On the island of Santorin near the ruins of the ancient city
of Thera is a large volcanic rock weighing 966 lb. (480 kg.),
which bears a very similar inscription. This too is spiral, and
it reads

Εὐμάστας με ἄηρεν ἀπὸ χθονὸς ὁ Κριτοβούλου.
[Eumastas son of Kritoboulos lifted me from the
ground.]

(*IG*, XII³, 449)

These two inscriptions have been treated by scholars with
as much solemnity as if they were on a par with the many
others which record the victories of athletes in the great
Games of Greece; some have even imagined that they constitute evidence for regular weight-lifting competitions

among the Greeks. No doubt then as at all times men challenged one another to such feats of strength. Aelian has an anecdote about an incident of this kind. The great wrestler Milo of Croton met a peasant named Titormus who had gained a local reputation for exceptional bodily strength, and challenged him to a trial. Titormus, modestly declaring that he was not particularly strong, led him to a river-bed, where he found a huge boulder. Taking off his cloak, he first rocked the stone backwards and forwards once or twice; then he raised it onto his knees, next onto his shoulders, carried it for about fifteen yards and threw it down. Milo could hardly move it. This is a pleasant enough story of the expert confounded, but we must not use it as proof of regularly organized weight-lifting competitions among the Greeks, for which there is no evidence whatever.[97]

Not surprisingly, the attempts to reconcile the two inscriptions with the facts of real life have produced a large mass of literature, not all of it very clear or very intelligent. By far the best modern discussion is by L. Moretti, who concludes, 'We may therefore be sure, either that in fact they lifted weights less heavy and more manageable than the inscribed stones which have come down to us and then had the record cut on larger and heavier stones, or that their statements are merely boasting, without any connection with feats actually performed.' It is true that the weight of the Bubon stone is below that lifted above the head by the greatest modern weight-lifters. But these men use two hands, and the weight is carefully disposed with equal parts at the ends of a bar offering the best possible grip. Even if we granted that Bubon's feat was just within the bounds of possibility, however, we cannot believe that Eumastas ever lifted a stone weighing over eight hundredweight.[98]

A curious feature of the discussion about Bubon's inscription is that none of the authors mention a peculiarity of the stone which catches the eye at once and which is probably responsible for the whole mystery. In one of the long narrow sides is cut what at first sight appears to be a carrying handle.

A rough hemisphere has been hollowed out here, leaving a cross-piece of stone uncut. It is in fact an unfinished cleat for a rope—unfinished because the hole through the cross-piece was never cut. Stone cleats of this kind were fairly common in the ancient world. Anyone who keeps his eyes open as he travels in the Mediterranean will see plenty of examples. Such cleats are found in the fortress of Eurualos and at Akrai west of Syracuse, cut into vertical stone walls to tether horses. The simplest way to make a cleat in stone is to bore diagonally behind the angle of a corner; the divisions between the stalls in the stables at Tebessa in North Africa and the horse-troughs at Utica afford examples of this method. These cleats in a corner-stone survive in the restored Crusader fortress at Acre; whether they were cut in the Crusader period or are in stones recovered from Ptolemais it is impossible to say. In the rock tombs of Beni Hasan in Egypt there are cleats cut in the floor; the tombs are dated by Egyptologists at *c.* 2050 BC, but they were opened in antiquity, as Greek graffiti on the walls show, and they have been used as shelters for animals. But not all these cleats were used for tethering animals. One in the theatre of Cillium (Kasserine) in Tunisia may have held the cords supporting the awning. Homer records their use for another purpose. When Odysseus and his companions left Phaeacia, 'They untied their cables from the pierced stone'. Such a 'pierced stone' still holds ships' cables at Bol in the Dalmatian island of Brač, and very similar stones are built into the town wall of Dubrovnik facing the harbour, now too high to serve their proper function.[99]

At first sight it might appear that to cut a cleat in stone was an unduly laborious method of doing a very simple job. We must remember, however, that in the Mediterranean world the ground is often too hard to hammer a peg into, or too sandy to hold it against any strain. The stone-cut cleat might take a long time to make, but it had the merits of efficiency and durability.

Though there can be no doubt that this was the purpose

planned for the hollow cut in Bubon's stone, it was never completed. But this is not apparent unless the stone is examined closely. At a cursory glance it looks as if it had been equipped with a handle enabling it to be lifted by one hand. But even if the hole had been cut and the handle provided, there would still be a very good reason, apart from the weight of the stone, for believing that Bubon's feat was never performed—the existence of the Thera inscription. There can be little doubt that Hiller von Gaertringen was right in suggesting that the Thera inscription was derived from Bubon's, and the feat recorded on the Thera stone is frankly impossible.[100]

If then we reject the literal interpretation of the Bubon inscription, as we must, there is only one purpose it can have served, that of satire. The joke may have been simply at Bubon's expense, but it is possible that it had also a wider significance. There was a practice in the Greek world of dedicating in temples objects which had played a part in great events. At Olympia may still be seen a helmet dedicated by a Miltiades, possibly the one worn at Marathon by the most famous bearer of that name. Herodotus records that the fittings of the bridges by which Xerxes crossed the Hellespont were carried off by the Greeks to adorn their temples. The epigrams of the *Anthology* show that in Hellenistic times the temples must have resembled junk-shops, with their deposits of children's hair and toys, hunters' spears, fishermen's nets, housewives' distaffs, travellers' hats, ships' rudders and other relics of an active life. In the sixth century BC athletes had already begun to mark with appropriate inscriptions the discuses and jumping-weights with which they had won their victories and to dedicate them in this way. The British Museum has such a discus from Cephallenia, and jumping-weights with dedications have been found at Olympia and Eleusis (*Pl.* 30). It is probable that at first this practice was not universally approved; significantly the earliest known attack on athletes from the literary world— that of Xenophanes—belongs to this period. We ourselves view with equanimity in Westminster Abbey the helmet and shield with which Henry V fought at Agincourt, but there would be unfavourable comment if it were proposed to dedicate in the same shrine a pair of football boots which had helped to win the World Cup. The most powerful weapon against such practices is ridicule.[101]

If these suggestions are granted, it becomes possible to see an explanation of the puzzle of the inscriptions. At some time in the dim past a peasant started to cut a cleat in a large stone at Olympia to tether his donkey. Then in the sixth century a satirically minded wag, who disapproved of the pretentious inscriptions of athletes, saw in the stone with its apparent handle an opportunity to parody these epigraphic claims and at the same time to poke a little fun at Bubon. What Bubon had done to deserve this we do not know; he may have been an athlete too much given to talking about his own feats or he may have been simply a very small man. The joke was obviously appreciated. Among the crowds who came from all over the Greek world to the Olympic Games was a man from Thera who thought it worth imitating at the expense of Eumastas when he returned home. In two respects he improved on his model. He chose a larger stone, and he put his inscription in the form of a hexameter, like many which record the genuine achievements of athletes of the time.

This unknown Theran was not the only humorist to imitate the satire of the Bubon stone. Some years ago there was discovered, built into a wall in the valley of the Kladeus about two miles from Olympia, a rectangular stone about 8 in. thick, 13 in. wide and 16 in. long, bearing the words

Ῥιπίρ ἐγω ΞενϜαρέ[ου]

Epigraphists date this inscription to the same period as Bubon's. The word ῥιπίς usually means a fan for winnowing or blowing up a fire, and this has led one German scholar to make the unlikely suggestion that the stone was part of a blacksmith's bellows. It seems more probable that ῥιπίρ is connected with ῥίπτω, and that the inscription means, 'I am the throwing-stone of Xenareus'. The weight of the stone is not recorded, but its dimensions indicate a weight of about 100 lb. This could certainly be thrown a short distance, but it is said that the surface of the block—limestone with many shells incorporated—is far too rough for it to have been used in this way. The most probable explanation is that the inscription was the work of someone who had seen the Bubon stone and was simply imitating it with the same satiric intent.[102]

Another stone-carrying feat by a Greek deserves mention. From the medical centre at the shrine of Asklepios at Epidaurus have come a number of inscriptions recording cures effected there. Among them is the following:

Hermodicus of Lampsacus; bodily weakness. The god cured this man as he slept, and ordered him when he came away to carry into the temple the largest stone he could. He carried the stone which now stands in front of the shrine.

(*IG*, IV, 951, 107)

By a fortunate chance the stone has survived; it bears this metrical inscription:

Hermodicus of Lampsacus
As proof of Thy merit, Asklepios, I dedicated this stone which I lifted myself, plain for all to see,
Clear evidence of Thy skill; for, before I came into Thy hands and the hands of Thy servants, I lay sick of a foul disease,
Congestion of the lungs and utter bodily weakness; but Thou, Healer, persuadedst me to pick up this stone and to live completely cured.

(*IG*, IV, 954)

The stone weighs 674 lb. (334 kg.).

It is perhaps unfortunate that of the nineteen cures recorded in the first of these two inscriptions the opening one is the claim of a lady named Kleo to have been pregnant for five years before being safely delivered of a healthy boy in the divine clinic. The scepticism which this naturally engenders is not justified in most of the cases of the inscription. There is one, for instance, which is of particular interest to students of Greek athletics. Agestratus suffered from insomnia caused by headaches. He slept in the shrine and dreamed that Asklepios cured his headache as he slept, set him on his feet naked and gave him a lesson in the pankration. At daybreak he found himself cured, and not long afterwards he won the pankration at the Nemean Games. In modern times several outstanding athletes have been weakly creatures in their early years. The constant mention of dreams in the accounts of cures at Epidauros suggests that hypnosis figured largely in the treatment given there, and it is possible that Hermo-dicus was persuaded under hypnotism that he really had carried the stone into the temple. The incident, in fact, belongs rather to medical than to athletic history.

While there is no evidence for ancient contests in weight-lifting, there are some signs that it was used as part of training for other sports, as it is today. The chief source is Epictetus. Among the ardours of training he includes, 'Carrying round a leather roof, a mortar and a pestle'. This mysterious passage is rendered a little less obscure a few pages later, when he is insisting that some training exercises, though painful, are beneficial:

> The trainer is acting rightly when he says, 'Lift that pestle with both hands'; and the heavier the pestle is, the more good it does me.

(III, xx.10)

'Leather roof', 'mortar' and 'pestle' clearly belong to the difficult territory of sporting slang. The traditional shape of a pestle (Fig. 6) might suggest that Greek athletes used a weight in the shape of an over-sized dumb-bell, fundamen-tally the same as that used in modern weight-lifting. The 'mortar' would then be a circular weight with side handles. This was apparently raised above the head to a position as dangerous to the lifter as the one with which we are familiar today. It produced a proverbial expression corresponding to our 'Sword of Damocles'. In the fourth century AD, the Greek philosopher Libanius, writing to a friend about his health, complains that his nephritis threatens him 'like a "mortar" over my head, as the saying goes'. So our last piece of evidence supports our earliest—the Bubon inscription—in establishing that the supreme test of Greek weight-lifting was the ability to raise the weight above the head.[103]

What the 'leather roof' may have been is beyond conjecture; in sporting colloquialisms logic is no guide. Three thousand years from now, posterity may well know what a

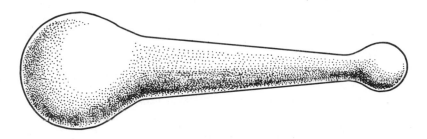

Fig. 6 *A pestle.*

twentieth-century bucket is, but the knowledge will not help them in the least to understand what a twentieth-century oarsman is doing when he is bucketing.

A gravestone survives from Salona in Dalmatia, the birthplace of the Emperor Diocletian, with this inscription:

M. Pomponius Zosimus, a timber merchant, erected this during his lifetime for himself, for his beloved daughter Pomponia Semna who died before him, and for the excellent Pomponius Secundinus who also predeceased him. He played with stones of these weights, 40, 50 and 100 pounds [*Hic lapide lusit ponderibus his*, XXXX,L,C].
(*CIL*, III, supp., 12924)

In pounds avoirdupois the weights would be 30, 37½ and 75. It is not clear whether it was Zosimus or Secundinus who 'played with stones' (or 'performed with stones'), probably the latter. Nothing is known of this pursuit from any other source. The facts given preclude any possibility that the reference is to a weight-lifting competition; some kind of juggling performance appears more probable. We are reminded that Cinquevalli, in addition to his feats with billiard balls, used to throw up a cannon ball and catch it on the back of his neck.

A nineteenth-century scholar, Gatti, in a note on the Salona inscription, called attention to a passage written about AD 400 by Jerome in his commentary on the Old Testament:

> In the cities of Palestine there is an ancient custom, kept up to this day throughout the whole of Judaea, that in the villages, towns and strongholds, round stones are set out with which young men take exercise. They lift them according to their individual powers, some up to their knees, others to their middle, others as high as their shoulders or head. A few raise the weight above the head, straightening their arms [*rectis iunctisque manibus*], thus showing off their great strength.
>
> (*Ad Zechariam*, c. 3)

This is the clearest evidence we have of anything approaching competition in weight-lifting in the ancient world.

There is even a hint in Juvenal that the fashionable Roman women of his day included weight-lifting in the exercises which they undertook:

> It is at night that she goes to the baths, at night that she gives orders for her oil-flasks and other impedimenta to be taken there; she loves to sweat among the noise and bustle. When her arms fall to her sides, worn out by the heavy weights, the skilful masseur presses his fingers into her body, and makes her bottom resound with his loud smack.
>
> (VI, 419)

CHARIOT-RACING

CHAPTER VII

GREEK RACING: EARLY DAYS

FROM THE BEGINNING OF THEIR RECORDED HISTORY, the Greeks and Romans made use of horses, but their employment was not as widespread as, for instance, in Britain in the eighteenth century, before the appearance of mechanical transport, when the horse, ridden or driven, provided almost all land communication and much of the power for work on the farm. For agricultural work the Greeks preferred the strong ox, and for local travel, as they still do, the mule or donkey. The Old Testament reminds us that in antiquity the horse was regarded primarily as a weapon of war. The words of Job are unforgettable:

> He mocketh at fear and is not affrighted; neither turneth he back from the sword. The quiver rattleth against him, the glittering spear and the shield. . . . He saith among the trumpets, Ha, ha; and he smelleth the battle afar off, the thunder of the captains, and the shouting.
>
> (XXXIX, 22ff)

Among the Greeks and Romans its other functions were in sport—hunting and racing.

There are several reasons for this. The chief superiority of the horse over donkey or mule is its greater speed. Even when the horse is ridden, this can only be fully exploited on a reasonably good surface, and the same applies still more to wheeled traffic. Greek roads rarely provided such a surface. On the rough tracks of the Mediterranean countryside, which then as now were often the stony beds of mountain torrents, the sure-footed donkey has the advantage. The first people in the ancient world to use the horse effectively for long-distance communication were the Persians with their Royal Road from Susa to Sardis, 1,600 miles in length with stables of post horses at regular intervals. The Greeks never attempted anything on this scale, and it was not until the Romans covered their empire with an enormous mileage of fine roads that the horse came into its own for this purpose in the West. Another advantage of the ass and mule is that they are far more tolerant of hardship and a poor diet than are horses. For pulling a plough or farm waggon the ox was clearly superior, if only in sheer strength; the heavy shire horse was not yet developed. Moreover the Greeks and Romans never discovered the device which makes a horse an efficient instrument of traction—the collar. Oxen can be harnessed reasonably effectively for heavy work by the yoke; but the horse needs a collar to enable the weight to be taken by the bone structure of the shoulders. In antiquity the horse pulled by means of a band across its chest, which inevitably constricted its breathing. When four horses were drawing a light racing chariot with a single driver on a flat and fairly level course, the pressure on the band must have been slight, but not so in the heavy work of a farm. For maximum efficiency the opening in the horse-collar must be pear-shaped, and it is possible that its invention was delayed by the problem of getting such a collar over the horse's head. The solution is simplicity itself, but in the history of human progress it is often the simplest problems which have taken longest to solve.

Although the horse was regarded primarily as an instrument of war, cavalry were not a very important arm in ancient warfare. Until the declining years of the Roman Empire of the West, no efficient saddle had been produced and stirrups were unknown. Under these conditions, riders must have achieved a remarkable degree of proficiency in balance and grip, but even the finest bareback seat is an inadequate foundation for resisting the shocks inevitable when using sword or lance in battle. Cavalry were never a serious threat to well-drilled infantry unless they could attack unprotected flanks or rear. Apart from reconnaissance duties, they were used on the wings of ancient armies chiefly to protect them from enemy cavalry; they came into their own in the pursuit of a routed force. It is true that Alexander the Great, who had been trained as a leader of cavalry, planned his battles to allow him to deliver the final blow with a cavalry charge, just as Napoleon, a gunnery officer, often made artillery the decisive arm in his battles. But Alexander delayed his charge until his infantry had opened a flank somewhere in the enemy's line; his victories do not invalidate the general principle that in ancient warfare it was the infantry—the Greek hoplite, the Macedonian phalanx, the Roman legion—which dominated the battlefield. With the invention of saddle and stirrups and the development of defensive armour for horse as well as rider, supremacy passed to heavy cavalry and remained with it until late in the Middle Ages, when the counter was found in the long-bow and gunpowder.

Although cavalrymen may not have played an important part in warfare, they had a significant place in the social, political and economic scene in Greece and Rome. In early years, when military service was obligatory on every citizen, a man who could afford to do so was expected to bring his horse to serve with him; only in this way could cavalry be provided. Thus both in Greece and Rome the word for cavalry (ἱππεῖς, *equites*, generally translated 'Knights') came to be applied to a class defined by qualifications of wealth, who had responsibilities and rights beyond those of poorer citizens. In this way the horse early acquired a certain position as a status symbol which it has never entirely lost.

In the Greek society of the second millenium BC depicted in the poems of Homer, the horse figures mainly in connection with war. It is true that in the *Odyssey*, when Telemachus goes from Pylos to visit Menelaus at Sparta, he is sent by Nestor in a car drawn by swift horses—Mycenean

roads appear to have been better than those of later Greece
—but when Menelaus presents his visitor with three horses
and a chariot to take back to Ithaca, he refuses the gift on the
ground that horses were useless on the island. And when
Nausicaa takes the palace washing down to the seashore, the
waggon is drawn by mules. The warriors in the *Iliad* never
ride horses. They are carried to battle in chariots drawn by
two horses; sometimes they hurl a javelin from the car, but
generally they dismount for the fight, while the charioteer
holds the car in readiness for the hero to re-embark and be
carried swiftly away to safety. These were the chariots which
competed in the race which was the first event in the Funeral
Games of Patroclus. Homer was obviously much more
interested in it than in any of the other contests of the Games,
and his description of it has the distinction that it inaugurates
three thousand years of sporting literature.[104]

Five warriors competed. Eumelus drove a pair of mares;
Diomedes' chariot was drawn by two Trojan stallions which
he had captured from Aeneas. Menelaus had a mixed pair,
a mare, Aethe, which he borrowed from his brother Agamemnon, and his own stallion, Podarges. Antilochus drove
the Pylian horses of his aged father Nestor, and had to listen
to a great deal of advice about racing from the same source.
The fifth competitor was the Cretan Meriones. Homer gives
no indication of the length of the course. It was a simple out-
and-home, with a left-handed turn round a post which was
only just in sight from the starting line. This post was a dead
tree, whose trunk still stood to a height of six feet, supported
by two white stones which made it conspicuous. Achilles,
acting as marshal of the race, pointed it out to the competitors,
and stationed the aged Phoenix near it as umpire to ensure
that all the chariots made the turn in accordance with the
rules. The drivers could take their own line over the plain,
but on the return leg there was one point where winter rains
had so broken up the surface that there was reasonable going
for only one chariot at a time. The spectators clustered round
the starting line which was also the finish.

The charioteers draw lots for station, come into line and are sent off. The poet shows considerable skill in not attempting to describe the whole of the race but selecting a few decisive incidents. He has already depicted the difficulties of the turn round the post in the advice which Nestor gave to his son before the start, so he takes up the story at the point where the chariots have made the turn and are just setting out on the homeward run. At this stage, Eumelus shoots out into a lead, closely followed by Diomedes. Now Homer disappoints the reader. We all recognize the important part which sheer luck plays in sport. Homer and his imitators ascribe these accidents to the direct intervention of a god or goddess. Today a race is sometimes lost because a jockey drops his whip. We may perhaps not protest when Homer makes Apollo knock Diomedes' whip out of his hand, but when Athene picks up the whip and restores it to him and then goes on to wreck Eumelus' chariot, the modern reader is apt to ask whether this is a description of a sporting event or of a private war in heaven. With this divine aid Diomedes has only to swerve round the wreckage of Eumelus' car to be left with an impregnable lead.

The interest of the race now lies in the struggle for second place between Menelaus and Antilochus; it has already become obvious that Meriones and his horses are out of their class in this field. Antilochus realizes that Menelaus' team have the legs of his own and can be beaten only by a trick. He calls on his stallions not to allow the mare Aethe to beat them, and adds an unpleasant threat that if they fail, Nestor will cut their throats. By these means he brings his chariot up close behind Menelaus just as they are approaching the place where there is passage for only one at a time. Menelaus yells to him to stay back: 'You will have plenty of time to pass me where the track is wider. If you carry on like this you will wreck us both.' Antilochus pretends not to hear, and comes up alongside. For the distance of a discus throw they run neck and neck. Then the older man, who has more sense than to risk his life for second place in a race, reins back, calling out as

Antilochus goes past him that there will be an objection. Though his sudden check has cost him a lot of ground, he pulls his team together and sets out in pursuit.

Now Homer shifts the scene to the spectators at the finishing line. In the middle stages of the race most of them have lost sight of the chariots in the cloud of dust, but Idomeneus has climbed up to a point where he has a better view. He saw Eumelus leading at the turn, and now, as the competitors come into sight again, he is surprised to see no sign of him. He calls down to the other spectators that Diomedes is now in the lead. For no reason at all, Ajax denies this, and says that he is prepared to bet that the leading driver is Eumelus. A violent argument develops in the silly way familiar among crowds at sporting events in all ages. Ajax and Idomeneus are about to come to blows when Achilles intervenes and tells them to stop behaving like children; the matter in dispute will inevitably be decided in a few minutes.

In spite of his long lead, Diomedes drives his team hard right to the finish, and he has already dismounted when the second chariot crosses the line. Menelaus just fails to make good the ground he lost at the narrow point; in a few more strides he would have passed Antilochus, but he is beaten by a bare length. Meriones finishes a poor fourth. Eumelus has succeeded in catching his mares, and he now arrives on foot, driving them and dragging his wrecked chariot behind him. He presents so sorry an appearance that Achilles takes pity on his bad luck and proposes that he should be given the second prize. This brings a strong protest from Antilochus, who has the impudence to suggest, with a reference to Apollo and Athene, that Eumelus crashed because he did not pray enough. He bluntly tells Achilles to find some other prize for Eumelus. Achilles, taking a kindlier view of Antilochus than the modern reader is likely to do, adopts this course; but before the second prize can be handed to Antilochus, Menelaus puts in his objection. Antilochus now realizes that he has not a leg to stand on, and meekly withdraws his claim to the prize. Menelaus, however, magnanimously refuses to accept the sacrifice, and expresses himself content with third. Meriones takes the fourth. The fifth prize which is now vacant—Eumelus having been otherwise rewarded at Antilochus' insistence—is handed to Nestor as a memento of the occasion. This gives the old hero the excuse for a speech of thanks, in which he relates how in his youth he competed in Funeral Games at Buprasion and won the boxing, wrestling, running and javelin, losing only the chariot race. He attributes this defeat to the fact that the winning chariot was driven by the sons of Aktor, one of whom managed the reins while the other plied the whip. This passage in Homer puzzled the ancient commentators, because no racing chariot ever carried two drivers; they arrived at the solution that Aktor's sons must have been Siamese twins.

The Greeks believed that mares were speedier than stallions, and in Homer's description of the Games it is conceded that Eumelus' team were the best pair in the race and but for the accident would have won. Antilochus' plea to his stallions not to endure the shame of being defeated by the mare Aethe is simply based on the normal Greek assumption of masculine superiority in the world generally.

Elsewhere in the *Iliad* we have a hint that already in Mycenean times there may have been chariot races at Olympia. In another speech of reminiscence, Nestor tells of an insult offered to his father Neleus. He had sent four racehorses with their chariot to rich Elis to compete in a race for the prize of a tripod, but Augeas, the king of Elis, seized the horses and sent the unhappy driver back home without his team. Augeas appears to have been a negligent horse-owner. He never had his stables mucked out, and their condition became such that the task of cleaning them was one of the traditional Twelve Labours of Heracles; it could be performed only by diverting the river Alpheus to flow through them.[105]

We can never be perfectly certain whether Homer in his epics is using traditional material and so depicting the Mycenean scene of the thirteenth century B C, or drawing on his experience of his own age some five or six centuries later. There can be no doubt, however, that a race for four-horse chariots (which it will be convenient to call by the Roman name *quadrigae*) was early introduced into the historic Olympic Games. The date given by Pausanias is 680 BC; thirty-two years later came the race for ridden horses. It appears to have been felt that these two made an inadequate equestrian programme, and at the beginning of the fifth century two other races were added, one for mule-carts in 500, and in 496 an event which remains mysterious. Pausanias, our sole authority, calles it *Kalpē* and describes it thus:

> It was a race for mares; in the last lap the riders jumped off and finished the course running alongside their mounts and holding them by their bridles, as in the modern races for the 'Anabatai'. But the modern event differs from the *Kalpē* in that the riders now wear different distinguishing marks, and the horses today are stallions.
>
> (V, ix.2)

Kalpē is usually translated 'Trotting race'. Slight evidence from cognate words does suggest that fundamentally it meant one of the horse's paces, and as it could be no faster than a man could run, 'trot' or 'canter' seems the most likely. Although the event formed part of the Olympic programme for half a century, nothing more is known of it (*Pl.* 60).[106]

To a modern reader a race for mule-carts seems as out of place in the Olympic Games as it would be at Royal Ascot. It is true that mules do not enjoy a high reputation in Britain, largely because those who have any experience of them gained it in wartime under conditions in which no animal is seen at its best. But undeniably the mule does not possess either the cosy chumminess of a donkey who is behaving himself or the splendour of the horse. The Greeks seem to have felt some reservations about the event. Aristotle has a significant anecdote:

> A man who had won a victory with his mule team commissioned the poet Simonides to celebrate his achievement,

but offered him too small a fee. Simonides refused to compose an ode on the ground that mules were no subject for poetry. But when the owner stepped up his offer, Simonides produced a poem which included the line 'Hail, daughters of horses swift as the wind'. He had conveniently forgotten that they were equally the daughters of asses.

(*Rhetoric* III, 2.14)

Pindar's patrons must have been sufficiently generous, for two of his thirteen Olympian odes celebrate victories in this mule race. Curiously, in both of them the poet calls attention to the dangers of the event. Mules may have been more difficult to control than horses, but a mule-waggon can hardly have travelled as fast as a *quadriga*, and speed is the great source of danger. Pindar was probably trying to find some merit in a race which was already regarded with a certain contempt. Yet it attracted distinguished competitors. Hiero, the wealthy tyrant of Syracuse, whose horses won the *quadriga* race at Olympia in 468 BC, and whose ridden horse Pherenicus won him two more Olympic crowns, gained a victory with a team of mules. It is not known to have been at Olympia, but it must have been at an important meeting, because Pindar celebrated it in an ode. Hiero had given the mules to the victorious charioteer as a reward for his efforts, but had not given him the cart. Pindar, who was as sensitive as Simonides about pay, hinted in his poem that this was rather mean treatment of the driver. The ode has not come down to us, but it was sufficiently well known for Aristophanes to be able to parody it in his *Birds*, and it is to this parody and to the ancient commentators on it that we owe our knowledge of the incident (*Pls.* 64, 67).[107]

Even such aristocratic patronage, however, could not confer a real *cachet* on the mule race. Pausanias says that it had neither ancient tradition nor dignity (εὐπρέπεια) to recommend it, and in 444 BC, together with the *Kalpē*, it was abandoned. This reduced the equestrian programme at Olympia once again to two events. In 408 it was modestly

extended to include a race for two-horse chariots or *bigae*
(*Pls.* 62, 63, 68). It is surprising that this event, with all the
prestige of the race in Homer's *Iliad* behind it, had to wait so
long for admission. Thereafter the authorities at Olympia
took a logical step to improve their festival. For centuries the
athletic contests had been duplicated, with classes for boys
as well as men in each event. Division by age was now applied
to horses. In 384 a race was instituted for *quadrigae* drawn by
colts, but a further two centuries were to elapse before
corresponding colts' classes were introduced for *bigae* in 264
and for ridden mounts in 256. Certainly no one could accuse
Olympia of hasty innovation; the programme of the Games
was now complete, but it had taken five centuries to arrive at
that consummation. Pausanias tells us that the same events
were introduced into the Pythian Games in the same gradual
way at intervals between 582 and 310 BC. We have no such
evidence of dates for the Isthmian and Nemean festivals, but
there is no reason to believe that the equestrian programmes
there differed in any important way from the Olympic.
Elsewhere in Greece the race-card was longer. An inscription
recording a meeting in Athens about 165 BC has details of
twenty-five events, including open classes and others confined to Athenian citizens. At this festival the open race for
ridden colts was won by the eldest son of Ptolemy V of
Egypt, who was later to become Ptolemy VI Philometor;
he was the great-great-great uncle of Cleopatra.[108]

CHAPTER VIII

THE GREEK HIPPODROME

OUR EVIDENCE FOR GREEK EQUESTRIAN SPORT is even scantier than for athletics, but there is sufficient to show that all important athletic festivals included horse races and that local meetings were held all over the Greek world. One of the most interesting of these pieces of evidence is an inscription now in the museum at Sparta, recording the achievements of a Spartan, Damonon, and his son Enymachratidas in the middle of the fifth century B C. Damonon proudly claims that he bred all his horses with his own stallion and brood mares, and that he always rode or drove them himself. He records 43 victories in his *quadriga* and 18 with ridden horses. His son was a runner as well as a rider. His 20 athletic victories covered all distances; three times he won all three races, 200 yards, 400 yards and long-distance race, on the same day, and at one of these meetings his father also won the chariot and the horse races. On another day, Enymachratidas won three races on foot and the horse race. In a pompous prefix to the inscription, Damonon claims these achievements as a record 'such as no one of the present generation ever equalled'. This was no doubt true, but it is noticeable that none of the victories was gained at a festival of any importance. Most of the nine meetings at which Damonon and his son won year after year are otherwise unknown; where they can be identified they are all in the south Peloponnese near Sparta. In every sport in every age there are those who contrive to shine by carefully avoiding competition with their equals or superiors in skill. Damonon and his son obviously belonged to this not very admirable class.[109]

These local meetings must be borne in mind when we try to picture the racecourses or hippodromes on which Greek horse-racing took place. We must dismiss from our minds any resemblance to our own railed courses or to the Roman Circus. Much misconception has been caused by modern authorities who have tried to depict the hippodrome at Olympia, for instance, in terms of Roman racecourses. The largest of the latter, the Circus Maximus at Rome, was constructed to accommodate twelve chariots. Pausanias' description of the racecourse at Olympia makes it clear that at least sixty chariots could race there at a time, and Pindar reveals that in a single race at Delphi forty chariots crashed. Greece was far too poor a country for the large areas required for such races to be permanently sequestrated for racing purposes. Our nearest modern parallel to a Greek hippodrome is the course marked out for the point-to-point races of a local hunt on land which at all other times of the year is used for ordinary agricultural purposes. The Greeks, of course, had no jumps, since there were—and are—no hedges or walls dividing fields; different holdings were marked only by small boundary stones. Any flat stretch, as soon as the crops were taken off and the exposed soil baked by the summer sun, would afford adequate going for horses or chariots, provided it was not crossed by watercourses or irrigation channels. The only preparation needed to convert such a stretch for racing was the removal of any large stones and the provision of two turning-posts. The Greek hippodrome had no *spina* or barrier down the centre to separate the up and down lanes as was normal in a Roman Circus. A description of a chariot race in Sophocles' *Electra* includes a head-on crash which such a barrier, had it existed, would have rendered impossible.[110]

That hippodromes were ordinary agricultural land is proved by an inscription from Delos which records the leases of farms on the island. In it the hippodrome figures as one of the farms. Anyone who knows Delos will realize that its hippodrome, wherever it may have been, can hardly have been perfectly flat; several modern racecourses in our own country show that a slight slope is no drawback to a track, and for spectators may be a positive advantage.[111]

Like our racecourses, Greek hippodromes varied in size according to the land available. Unfortunately the only one unaffected by modification in Roman times which we can identify with certainty is not a characteristic example. It is on Mount Lycaeus in Arcadia, where athletic and equestrian festivals were held in honour of Zeus Lycaeus. While most hippodromes were in the plains, this one is on an alp among the mountains at a height of nearly 4,000 feet. The site, shut in by mountain slopes, allowed a track of 300 yards long by 150 at the widest point. Excavation has revealed no trace of a starting-gate for horses, but a sill with grooves for runners' feet half-way along its length shows that after ceasing to be used for horse-racing it was adapted as a stadium. Pausanias makes it clear that chariot-racing there had been abandoned long before his day.[112]

At Olympia the length of the track was three stades—600 yards. The Panathenaic hippodrome, which like the modern Athenian racecourse was situated in the low-lying ground between the city and the Peiraeus, was eight stades long, the longest known. This permitted races of a single length 'without a turn' (ἀκάμπιος) to be run, the distance being slightly greater than our six-furlong scampers. Similar single-length races are also attested on Delos; they were the only ones in which the starting line was not also the finish. Another race at Athens and Delos was the diaulos, out-and-home like that in Homer. But most races were over a considerably greater distance. Pindar reveals that at Olympia the races for chariots and mule-carts were over twelve 'courses' (δωδεκάδρομοι). It is not certain whether these were lengths or laps; the latter is more likely.[113]

The only Greek hippodrome of which we have a description from antiquity is that at Olympia. Pausanias gives this account:

As one passes out of the Stadium at the point where the Hellanodikai sit, one comes to the hippodrome and the starting-gate [aphesis] for the horses. This starting-gate looks like the forepart of a ship, with the projecting bows pointing towards the track. The prow is widest where it is nearest the Stoa of Agnaptos; at the very tip of the projection is a bronze dolphin on a pole. Each wing of the gate, with the stalls built into it, is more than 400 feet long. The entrants for the equestrian events draw lots for the stalls; the barrier in front of the chariots and ridden horses consists of a cord passing through the stalls. For each Olympiad a plinth of unbaked brick is built at about the middle point of the prow, and on this plinth is a bronze eagle with its wings fully extended. The starter works the mechanism on the plinth; when it is set in motion, it causes the eagle to jump up so that it becomes visible to the spectators, while the dolphin falls to the ground. The traps at each end—those which are nearest the Stoa of Agnaptos—open first, and so the horses standing in them get away first. As they run, they come alongside those who have drawn the second station, and then the traps of this station open. The same thing happens in turn for all the horses until, opposite the projecting point of the prow, they are on level terms with one another; after this point comes the proof of the skill of the charioteers and the speed of their horses. The original inventor of the gate was Kleoitas; he was obviously proud of his invention, for on a statue in Athens he inscribed the epigram:

> The work of Kleoitas, son of Aristokles, who first invented the starting-gate for horses at Olympia.

They say that after the time of Kleoitas, Aristeides introduced some further refinements into the mechanism.

One side of the hippodrome is longer than the other; the longer side is a bank. Near the entrance through the bank stands Taraxippus, the terror of horses. It looks like a round altar, and as the horses pass this point they are

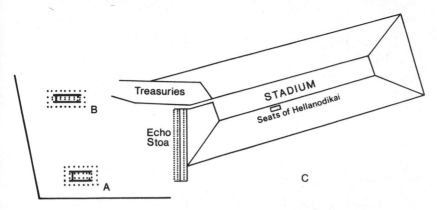

Fig. 7 *Sketch-plan of Olympia, showing the Temple of Zeus (A), the Temple of Hera (B) and the site of the hippodrome.*

seized by a sudden panic and the chariots are thrown into chaotic disorder; this is the place where crashes occur and drivers are injured. So charioteers offer sacrifices to Taraxippus and pray that he will be kind to them. . . . On one turning-post is a bronze statue of Hippodameia holding a ribbon which she is about to bind on Pelops as a token of victory. The other side of the hippodrome is not an embankment but a low hill.

(VI, xx.10ff)

This description is characteristic of Pausanias; it contains a large number of details assembled with little hint of their relative importance or of the connection between them. At least it fixes quite certainly the site of the hippodrome, southeast of the stadium (Fig. 7). The strangest statement is that one side was longer than the other. This makes it clear that there can have been no regular enclosure round the racecourse. It is explained by the further statement that the longer side was an artificial mound and the shorter a low hill. The plain in which the hippodrome lay is bounded on the south side by the river Alpheus, and the nearest hills in that direction are far away across the river-bed and cannot possibly include the hill mentioned by Pausanias. His low hill must therefore be the eastern extension of the hill of Kronos which overshadows the Altis and the stadium from the north. This afforded a good view for spectators at the west end of the course, near the start and finish, but did not extend as far as the eastern end. On the south side of the hippodrome an artificial mound for spectators was constructed between the course and the Alpheus, extending the whole length of the track, and this south side could therefore be described as longer than the north. Floods and changes in the bed of the river have swept away all traces of this mound.

The most interesting feature in Pausanias' account is the starting-gate, which appears to have been unique in the Greek racing world. When he wrote, in the second century A D, gates had been used in Roman Circuses for many hundreds of years, and most of his readers must have been familiar with them. Comparison with the Roman pattern would have made his description much easier to understand, yet he does not mention them. Nor does he draw any parallel with the starting-gate for athletes used in every Greek stadium, though it served fundamentally the same purpose as the traps for horses. Only one other reference to the gate in the hippodrome at Olympia is known; it occurs in an inscription from Pergamum recording the Olympic victory of an Attalus of the royal house in a chariot race, and the word used for the gate, *husplex*, is the ordinary term for the starting-gate for runners in the stadium.[114]

The purpose of any gate is to ensure a fair start. Horses are excitable creatures before a race, and it is never easy to bring them into line, whether they are ridden or harnessed to chariots. The obvious solution is a straight line of traps across the course, in the manner that is being increasingly used in modern racing. But neither Greeks nor Romans adopted this. The shape of their courses, with the abrupt turn round a post, introduced into the problem an element unknown on modern tracks. It was highly important to secure the inside position for the first turn, and this meant that a lead in the first few yards of the race might be decisive. The importance of this early lead was greatest in the Roman Circus, where the *spina* made it necessary for all chariots to

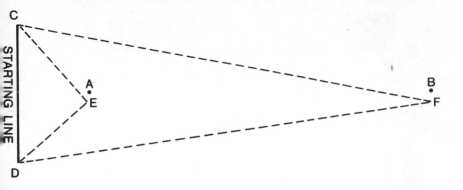

Fig. 8 *The Greek hippodrome.*

pass to the right of the nearer post (E, Fig. 8), but even in the
Greek hippodrome, where drivers were aiming at a point to
the right of the farther post (F, Fig. 8), those at the ends of
the starting line felt at a disadvantage compared with those
in the middle. To obviate this, the Roman solution was to
stagger the start in space by laying out the stalls on a concave
curve with its centre opposite the point on which the chariots
converged (Fig. 9). The solution at Olympia was to stagger
the start time, each driver being given a flying start on his
inside neighbour. The 'ship's prow' lay-out of the traps made
it impossible for a charioteer to take advantage of the flying
start to cut across the front of his inside rival (Fig. 10). It is not
difficult to see how the device could have been worked. The
cords across the front of the traps in the two halves of the
gate would be pulled in by a single central capstan (Fig. 11).
The dolphin and eagle were not an essential part of the
mechanism; they signalled to spectators at the far end of the
course—more than a quarter of a mile from the gate—that
'They're off'. From other sources we learn that a trumpet
played an important part in the start. If we combine this with
Pausanias' account, we can form a coherent picture of what
happened.

The horses were marshalled in the space between the Stoa
of Agnaptos and the gate, and then led into the traps from the
rear; with fifty or more chariots, this must have taken a

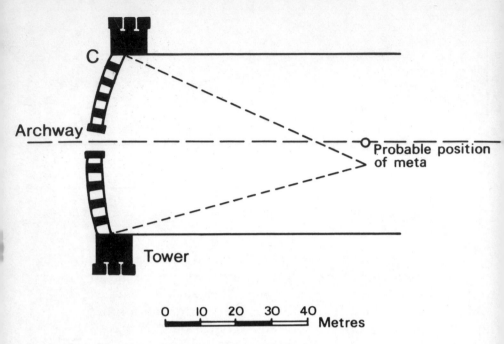

Metres

Fig. 9 *The* carceres *at Jerash (after E. B. Müller and A. H. Detweiler).*
Fig. 10 *The starting-gate at Olympia.*

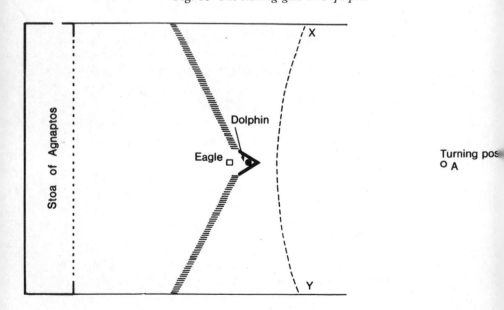

41 The scene on this late sixth-century BC vase could just conceivably be a vigorous dance, but the women's arm action and the whole lay-out of the vase suggest a race for women, since both correspond exactly with those of undoubted men's races on contemporary vases.

42 A small archaic bronze of a girl runner. She lifts the hem of her short 'gym-slip' the better to assist her running.

43 A bronze strigil (variously described as Etruscan or Hellenistic). The handle is a finely modelled girl athlete who scrapes herself with a strigil whilst placing the victor's crown upon her head. It was probably a prize at a sports meeting.

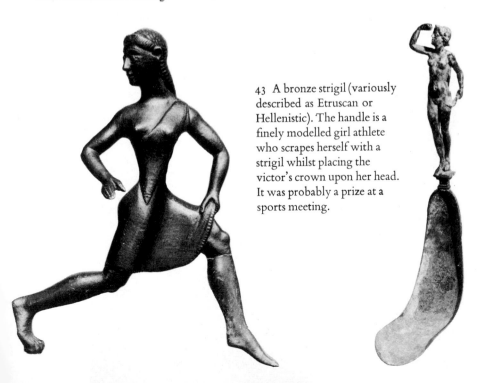

49 A small terracotta of a juggler that perfectly illustrates Manilius' description (p. 107).

48 A scene on a red-figure hydria showing a girl playing Aporrhaxis, a game entailing the continuous bouncing of a ball (pp. 86, 101).

50,51 This catching game is depicted on several surviving vases, but is otherwise unknown. It has been suggested that the boy who was called 'donkey' because he had dropped a catch had to carry another boy on his back in this version of the game, but there is no evidence for this.

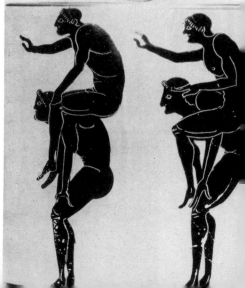

52 Relief from an Attic gravestone showing a boy bowling his hoop.

53 Bubon's stone. This large stone, weighing 288 lb, has a rough hemisphere hollowed out on the back, actually an unfinished cleat for a rope, but looking at first glance like a handle, a circumstance which obviously prompted the satirical inscription seen here on its face (see pp. 142–6).

54 A mosaic from the Great Palace in Constantinople, showing several boys, each driving a pair of spoked hoops; the scene is clearly intended as a caricature of the chariot races in the hippodrome.

55 A fifth-century BC bronze, apparently of a reluctant swimmer. Marks on the back of the figure, however, suggest that the boy may have been carrying another on his back for the ball game depicted in Plates 50 and 51. If this is so the sculptor has accidentally achieved a masterpiece of suggestion in another direction!

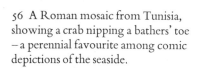

56 A Roman mosaic from Tunisia, showing a crab nipping a bathers' toe – a perennial favourite among comic depictions of the seaside.

57,58 Two representations of
diving. *Right*, a graphic bronze
statuette showing the diver about to
plunge. *Below*, a red-figure vase of
c. 500 BC, signed by Andocides,
showing a group of women bathing.
One appears to be oiling herself,
another does the crawl, and a third
is poised to dive.

59 One of the masterpieces of the ancient world, the bronze boy jockey salvaged from the sea near Artemisium exhibits the perfect balance and control required by his calling (p. 183).

60 A fifth-century coin of Himera (Sicily). It represents the *Kalpē* (p. 158) or a similar event, and is evidence of the enthusiasm for equestrian sport among the rulers of the Sicilian cities at this time.

61 Panathenaic amphora of *c.* 500 BC, a prize in the Games at Athens, presumably for the race for ridden horses (pp. 156, 179).

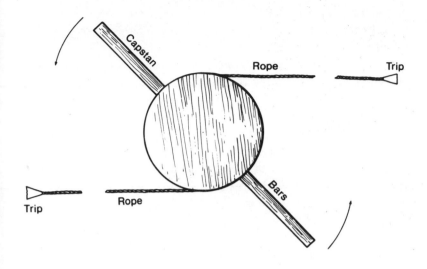

Fig. 11 *A possible trip mechanism for the chariot starting-gate at Olympia.*

considerable time. When all were in, a trumpet call indicated
to the drivers that the start was imminent. The starter pulled
his lever, the dolphin fell and the eagle rose, and the attendants began to turn the capstan. The rope barrier across the
stalls started to be withdrawn and the chariots to emerge,
first those at the extremities of the line and then the others in
turn. The result of the staggering was that when the final pair,
those in the centre, came out of the traps, the chariots formed
a concave line (X–Y, Fig. 10), and now, in Pausanias' words,
'they were on level terms with one another'. To prevent
premature crashes at this stage, it must have been obligatory
on all charioteers to drive straight forward until all had
started. Then the trumpet sounded again, the drivers could
'break', and as Pausanias says, 'after this point came the
proof of the skill of the charioteers and the speed of their
horses'. There is one piece of evidence for a rule which for-
bade drivers' swerving in front of their opponents. In
Aristophanes' *Clouds*, Pheidippides, dreaming that he is

driving in a chariot race, calls out in his sleep: 'You're cheating, Philo, stick to your own lane' (ἔλαυνε τὸν σαυτοῦ δρόμον).¹¹⁵

The part played by trumpeters was so important that from 396 BC a competition for them was included in the Olympic Games. Later in that century a trumpeter from Megara, Herodorus, won the event at ten successive Olympiads. This interesting figure was only just over five feet tall, but he was a prodigious eater and drinker and could play two trumpets at the same time. He did not confine his efforts to the sports arena. The success of Demetrius Poliorcetes in his siege of Argos in 303 BC was due to the inspiration which the trumpeting of Herodorus exercised on the troops.¹¹⁶

Pausanias' account of the 'Taraxippus' at the different hippodromes has caused much discussion. He conscientiously lists the many legendary heroes whose ghosts at Olympia were supposed to frighten the horses, and adds that there was a similar phenomenon at Isthmia, also thought to be caused by a ghost. At Nemea, he says, there was no hero to excite the panic, but a red rock overlooking one of the turning-posts had the same effect. In typically Greek fashion he suggests a scientific explanation for what happened at Nemea, that light reflected from the red rock looked like fire and so startled the horses. When he comes to the hippodrome at Delphi, whose location is now lost among the olive groves in the valley below the main site, he remarks with a certain wry scepticism that there was no Taraxippus there, but accidents were no less numerous than elsewhere. In modern times there have been many attempts to find a rational explanation for the panic of the horses at Olympia, such as dazzling flashes caused by reflection or long shadows in the early morning sun. In fact there is no mystery about it. Horses have an uncanny ability to detect fear or nervousness in their riders or drivers, and they react to it with similar emotions. The Taraxippus was just before the first turn in the race. Even after 600 yards the runners would have been fairly well bunched, and the emotions of the riders or charioteers must have been those of a jockey in the Grand National approaching Becher's on the first circuit.[117]

None of the chariots used in Greek or Roman racing has survived, but vase-paintings suggest that they did not differ in any important respect from the Egyptian examples found in Tutankhamen's tomb and now in the museum at Cairo. For obvious reasons they were of the lightest possible construction, and the standard of craftsmanship must have been superb to enable them to stand up to the strains imposed by the tight turns and the jolting on rough courses. The ancients do not appear to have discovered the valuable principle of 'dish' in the design of wheels, which helps to resist the violent outward thrust of the axle on the hub of the wheel at the turn. In some vase-paintings depicting chariots head-on, there is a slight suggestion of dish, but it is the wrong way round. Homer reminds us how severe the jolting could be on an uneven course. 'At one moment the chariots were rolling on the ground, at the next they were bouncing high in the air.' To enable drivers to maintain a steady foothold in these conditions, clogs were fitted to the floorboards of the chariots, like those into which oarsmen fit their feet on the stretchers of racing boats.[118]

The two horses of a *biga* were harnessed abreast under a yoke at the end of a central pole. Neither the Greeks nor the Romans appear ever to have driven horses tandem. The four horses of the *quadriga* also ran abreast. The centre pair were under the yoke; the outer were linked to the yoke but drew the chariot by traces. For the Greeks, the most important member of the team was the off-side trace-horse because of its key position in the left-handed turns; 'right trace-horse' was used metaphorically in Greek for an outstanding human performer in any sphere, just as 'top-notcher' used to be employed in English. In Roman racing, however, the most experienced horses were harnessed as the centre pair under the yoke (*iugales*) (*Pls.* 62, 63, 65, 68).

Though the Romans did not drive horses tandem, they did give the word to the English language through University slang. In the eighteenth century, horsemanship was the chief leisure occupation of undergraduates, all of whom knew more Latin than most of their kind today. When they adopted the fashion of harnessing one horse in front of another, they said that they were driving *tandem*, 'at length'.

The leatherwork of the ancient bridle was very similar to our own, with brow-band, cheek-strap, nose-band and throat-lash. The bit was sometimes a plain bar, sometimes a simple linked snaffle (*Pls.* 67, 70). Evidence for the use of the curb by Greeks or Romans is somewhat dubious; to control mettlesome horses they employed bits of varying degrees of barbed ferocity. It is not certainly known whether there was any attempt to link reins. A late Roman sarcophagus has a relief of putti driving chariots, in which a single rein passes across the muzzles of all four horses, but this hardly constitutes evidence. The one detail about which all accounts of ancient chariot races agree is the furious use of the whip by the drivers. This makes it certain that the team could be controlled with one hand, at any rate in the straight. But it is difficult to believe that four horses abreast could possibly be brought round a tight turn with a single hand on the reins.[119]

CHAPTER IX

LATER GREEK RACING

IN THE EQUESTRIAN EVENTS at Greek festivals the prizes were the same as for athletics. At the great 'crown' meetings they were wreaths of olive, laurel, pine or wild celery; at Athens jars of olive oil were given, at Pellene woollen cloaks. After the time of Alexander money prizes became common at the newly instituted festivals, but these can never have made horse-racing anything but a rich man's sport. The list of Olympic winners of these events known to us, not a long one, includes some of the most famous figures of the ancient world, in the early days kings of Sparta and Cyrene and tyrants of the great cities of Greece and Sicily, Myron and Cleisthenes of Sicyon, Gelon of Gela, Hiero of Syracuse, and Theron and Empedocles of Acragas, the latter the grand-father of the philosopher of the same name. Others were members of the wealthiest and most powerful families at Athens, Alcmaeon, Miltiades, Callias and Alcibiades, who in 416 BC ran seven teams in the *quadriga* race at Olympia and took first, second and fourth places. Another prominent Athenian victor was Cimon, the father of Miltiades; he won at three successive Olympiads with the same team of four mares, who were buried in a grave near their owner's.[120]

The interest of the wealthy tyrants of Sicily in racing continued into the fourth century. In 388 BC Dionysius of Syracuse sent several *quadrigae* to Olympia, together with rhapsodes to recite his poems and marquees of cloth of gold adorned with richly embroidered hangings to accommodate the performances. The chariots duly competed, but some ran out and others crashed. The ship carrying them back to Sicily was wrecked; the sailors attributed the disaster to the badness of Dionysius' verses.[121]

Soon after Alcibiades' sweeping of the board in the *quadrigae*, a prince of the royal house of Macedon won the same event, and in the middle of the next century Philip of Macedon won three races at different Olympiads. According to tradition, he received news of the first victory—with a ridden horse in 356—on the day on which his son Alexander was born. Alexander himself was too busy during his short life to have time for organizing a racing stable, but several of the successor kings appear in victor lists. An Attalus of Pergamum, who won in 276 with a team of colts, is the only known Olympic victor among them, but several Attalids and Ptolemies appear in Athenian lists. Early in the first century BC, Mithridates Eupator of Pontus, the last of a number of kings of the same name, was a keen charioteer. An inscription from Chios records that he practically swept the board in the equestrian events at a meeting in the island —the only exception was a race won by a woman owner named Eucleia—and Plutarch tells us that the king poisoned a rival driver, Alcaeus of Sardis, who beat him in a race. For about a century before the beginning of the Christian era the equestrian events at Olympia, and probably the whole festival, were under a cloud. Almost the only recorded victors with horses at the time were local owners from Elis. Then at the end of that period a famous name appears as victor with a *quadriga*, the future Emperor Tiberius, and some twenty years later his adopted son Germanicus Caesar won the same event; obviously for such distinguished competitors the rule requiring pure Greek blood at Olympia was waived.[122]

The antics of the Emperor Nero at Olympia and elsewhere will demand separate treatment. From the three centuries after his day to the end of the Olympic Games, scarcely any names of equestrian victors are recorded. Clearly the completely different organization of racing in the Roman world had stolen all the glory from the great Greek hippodromes.

Lucius Minicius Natalis, proconsul of Africa, who won with
his *quadriga* in AD 129, is a rare exception. Rather more than
a century later comes the last record of an Olympic victory
in these events. Titus Domitius Prometheus was an *anti-
kosmetēs* at Athens, a deputy director of youth clubs. In his
inscription he proudly claims that with his *quadriga* he had
won once at Olympia, once at Isthmia, once at Nemea and
twice in the Pythian Games. In addition he had won sixty
crowns at other meetings 'at which a crown was the only
prize'. It is the sad cry of a man who had bravely tried in the
utterly professional world of horse-racing to keep the spirit
of amateurism alive. Across the centuries Titus Domitius
reaches out a hand to Mr Avery Brundage.[123]

The feat of Cimon in the sixth century BC of winning at
three Olympiads with the same team had been achieved
earlier in the same century by Euagoras of Sparta, who also
accorded his mares an ostentatious tomb. We have thus two
instances of teams of mares being at their prime over a
period of at least nine years. If we bear in mind the distance
of the races, certainly not less than three miles and probably
considerably more, it is clear that in spite of the absence of
obstacles, Greek chariot races had more in common with
our steeplechasing than with our flat racing. Another interesting point is that these mares can hardly have been used for
breeding; there must have been a greater separation between
racecourse and stud than with us.[124]

Since the expense of horse-racing was so great, it is not
surprising that from an early time joint ownership was permitted. The first known instance was at Olympia in 672 BC,
when the winning *quadriga* was entered by the city of Dyspontium. The winner of the horse-race in 480 was owned
by the city of Argos, and eight years later the same city won
the event again. In 420 BC a remarkable scene was witnessed
in the hippodrome at Olympia. Lichas, a wealthy Spartan
whose father had twice won the *quadriga* race there, had a
formidable team with which he hoped to repeat his father's
success, but in that year the authorities were not accepting

entries from Sparta, because the city had failed to pay a fine inflicted on it for a breach of the Olympic truce. Accordingly Lichas leased his team to the city of Thebes. When it won, he did not wait for the official proclamation of the name of the victor, but advanced into the hippodrome himself, to show who was the real owner, and bound the ribbons of victory on the charioteer. For this offence the Stewards had him flogged; much in the administration of Olympia is open to criticism, but at least the officials did their best to see that the rules were kept.[125]

The latest evidence for such public ownership is an inscription from Corinth, recording the victory in a race for colts' *bigae* of a chariot entered by Antinoe, a city on the banks of the Nile, founded by Hadrian in memory of his favourite Antinous. The inscription cannot be earlier than the middle of the second century A D.[126]

Most owners bred horses on their country estates but they also bought in good animals from outside, and no doubt many a farmer who could not afford to race bred horses for the track. In Roman times Pliny recommended the breeding of horses for chariot-racing as the most profitable form of stock-farming. There must always have been a ready market for mounts for cavalry and for hunting, and a farmer could always hope for a stroke of luck to produce a promising colt for the racecourse. The ancients well understood the importance of heredity in breeding; they also appear to have believed that the sire is more influential than the dam in transmitting racing quality to the offspring. Although records of pedigree were kept, there is no evidence of any restriction such as that imposed by the existence of the Stud Book.[127]

From the earliest times owners were allowed to employ substitutes to drive for them in race meetings. The first evidence we have of the practice is an inscription recording a victory of a member of the celebrated Athenian family of the Alcmaeonidae at the Panathenaic Games in the middle of the sixth century B C; the charioteer is named. Sometimes an owner drove himself, or a young member of his family. Pindar reveals that when Xenocrates, brother of Theron the tyrant of Acragas, won the *quadriga* race in the Pythian Games of 490 BC, the charioteer was his son Thrasybulus. In another Ode the poet celebrates a victory by Hiero of Syracuse, probably in a festival at Thebes:

> With crowns that gleam afar Hiero has adorned Syracuse, the haunt of Artemis, with whose aid he guided his richly-harnessed horses with gentle hands.
>
> (Pythian II, 5)

This must surely mean that Hiero drove himself, though he can no longer have been a young man at the time. Pindar rarely shows any profound knowledge of the technicalities of athletics or horse-racing, but at least he can claim that this is the only passage in ancient sporting literature which hints at the importance of light hands for rider or driver.[128]

In his *Clouds*, Aristophanes gives us a picture of a young man, Pheidippides, mad on horse-racing, who is ruining his father by his wild expenditure on thoroughbreds and chariots, and who dreams in his sleep that he is driving in a race. Pheidippides was obviously intended by his creator to remind the audience of Alcibiades, and we would give a great deal to know whether in the chief event at Olympia in 416 BC Alcibiades drove one of the seven teams he entered, and if he did, whether his judgment of horseflesh enabled him to pick the winning team to drive himself.

While there is good evidence for these amateur charioteers drawn from the same social class as the wealthy owners, it is not certainly known whether stable hands, most of whom would be slaves, were used as drivers in the golden age of Olympia, as they assuredly were in Roman racing. Undoubtedly they were so employed in Greece in Hellenistic and Roman times; beyond a peradventure, the little jockey from Artemisium (*Pl.* 59) is a professional.

The use of substitute drivers meant that from early times in Greece the owner of a horse or chariot could be a woman;

this was the only way in which women could participate in the great Games. The first woman victor at Olympia was Cynisca, a member of one of the royal houses of Sparta, who won the *quadriga* race at the beginning of the fourth century B C. She celebrated this and a second victory in the same event by erecting a monumental group at Olympia, the base of which with its inscription has survived. Rather more than a century later, Belistiche, the mistress of Ptolemy Philadelphus king of Egypt, won the colts' *quadriga* race at the Olympiad of 268 B C, and at the next festival she won the event for colts' *bigae*, run in that year for the first time. During the first century B C, when the fortunes of the Olympic Games were at a low ebb, six members of the same family of Eleians are recorded to have won victories in equestrian events, and two of them are women. One of the last known winners of a chariot race at Olympia was a woman, Kasia of Elis, in the middle of the second century A D.[129]

A particularly interesting piece of evidence about women in chariot-racing comes in the well-known inscription from Delphi recording the victories of three girl athletes from Tralles in the first century A D. One of the girls, Hedea, who won prizes for running at Nemea and for music at Athens, claims that at Isthmia she won 'wearing armour in a chariot' (ἐνόπλιον ἅρματι). This must be understood in connection with races for war-horses recorded at Athens and with the races for war chariots about which Pheidippides talked in his sleep in the *Clouds*. These references are puzzling, because after Homeric times the Greeks did not use chariots in war; but there is a possible explanation. One of the Athenian inscriptions shows that the prizes for these events were less valuable than those for thoroughbreds (ἵπποι λάμπροι or πομπικοί). It is a reasonable assumption that these races were for working cavalry horses; there is a parallel today in our steeplechases for 'bona fide hunters'. When chariots were drawn by them they were called war chariots, and to make the event more spectacular the drivers were dressed as warriors. The wording of the inscription implies that Hedea drove her war chariot herself. At the beginning of the Christian era, women were becoming emancipated throughout the whole of the Roman empire.[130]

The event for ridden horses, the staple fare of the modern race-goer, aroused far less interest than chariot-racing, and the Romans omitted it altogether from their programme. Literature affords only one description in fiction of such a race, and it is not very exciting. In the fourth century AD, Quintus of Smyrna wrote a sequel to the *Iliad* in slavish imitation of Homer's language, metre and methods. To match the Funeral Games for Patroclus in his model he included a description of the Funeral Games for Achilles, and in them the chariot race is immediately succeeded by a horse race:

In another part of the plain men harnessed their riding horses and brought them to the course. Taking their ox-hide whips in their hands they all leaped onto their mounts, which were foaming at the mouth as they champed their bits and pawed at the ground, longing for the start. They set off at full gallop as they darted away, eager for the race, and then rushed on, raising an endless cloud of dust over the plain with their flying hooves. Each rider kept shouting to his horse, with one hand ceaselessly plying his whip and with the other constantly shaking the jingling bridle round his horse's jaws. The steeds thundered on. From the crowd rose an unbroken roar, as the riders flew on over the level plain.

And now the swift Argive mount of Sthenelus would have won easily, if he had not swerved from the course and gone racing across the fields. Skilled though his rider was, he was not strong enough to turn him back, for the horse was new to racing. He was well bred, of the stock of the swift Arion, that divine horse by the West Wind out of a Harpy; this made Arion the swiftest of all horses, and with his flying hooves he could outstrip the speedy blasts of his sire. Adrastus had received him as a gift from

the immortal gods, and from his stock came Sthenelus'
mount, whom Diomedes had given him at sacred Troy.
Sthenelus, relying on his speed, had entered him in the
race, expecting to gain great glory for himself among the
champion riders, but he had no joy in this contest for
Achilles' relics. Speedy though his horse was, he came in
second, and Agamemnon beat him by better riding. The
crowd applauded the winner, and they had cheers too for
Sthenelus and his horse, so high-spirited that time and
time again he swerved from the straight course.

(Posthomerica IV, 545ff)

The literature of sport presents many difficulties, not least
that of matching the speed of a race with the pace of the
description. It cannot be said that Quintus, with this dull
mixture of cliché, padding and repetition, has solved any of
the problems.

Much more useful is an anecdote related by Pausanias
about a mare named Aura (Breeze), owned by Pheidolon of
Corinth, who ran at Olympia towards the end of the sixth
century BC:

Early in the race she unshipped her jockey, but in spite of
this went on running without interfering with the other
horses, did the turns round the posts, and when she heard
the trumpet quickened her pace and passed the judges
first. Then, realizing that she had won, she stopped.
Pheidolon was proclaimed the winner, and he was
allowed to dedicate a statue of his mare.

(VI, xiii.9)

Pheidolon's sons inherited their father's enthusiasm for
racing, and with a stallion named Lycus (Wolf) they won
at Olympia in 508 BC and at the Isthmian Games. The story
about Aura provides the evidence for the use of the trumpet,
like the bell in modern athletics, to signal the start of the last
lap. It also shows that the Greeks were not in the least concerned with the weight carried by a horse in a race. But the

phrase 'without interfering with the other horses' suggests that there may have been rules forbidding crossing, bumping and boring (*Pl.* 61).[131]

Just as we have equestrian competitions such as show jumping and Pony Club gymkhanas as well as our formal race meetings, so the Greeks had events for horses alongside those in the regular festivals. Chief among these were torch races on horseback, relay races in which a torch took the place of our baton. Such races on foot were common enough all over Greece; a torch race on horses is first heard of in the opening pages of Plato's *Republic*, where the scene is being set for the dialogue. Socrates had gone to the Peiraeus to celebrate a festival of Bendis and was returning to Athens when he was stopped by friends and invited to their house. One of them put forward a special inducement for him to remain:

> 'Don't you know,' said Adeimantus, 'that later in the day there is to be a torch race on horseback in honour of the goddess?' 'On horseback?' I said, 'That is a new idea. Do you mean that they will carry torches and hand them on in relays as they race on their horses?' 'That is right,' said Polemarchus.
>
> (*Republic*, 328a)

The new idea evidently caught on, for such races are attested by an inscription of three centuries later at the Panathenaic festival at Athens, and at the beginning of the Christian era at Larissa in Thessaly. And although the *Kalpē* may have been abandoned at Olympia, events which involved dismounting from horse or chariot or transferring from one horse to another during a race persisted for many centuries. The competitors in these events were usually called 'dismounters' (ἀποβάται), but Pausanias' name for them, 'mounters' (ἀναβάται), suggests that they had to remount while the horses were still running. We should like to know more about them (*Pl.* 60).[132]

Victors in the equestrian events at the great festivals, like winning athletes, were allowed to erect commemorative monuments. For the chariot races these usually took the form of a group comprising horses, chariot, charioteer and sometimes the owner as well. None of these has survived complete, but at Delphi there is a famous bronze statue of a charioteer from such a group (Pl. 71). It was dedicated by Polyzalus of Gela, brother of Hiero of Syracuse, and is a reminder of the part which these wealthy Sicilians were playing in sport in the first half of the fifth century B C. In accordance with the conventions of the sculpture of the period, which avoided any attempt to represent violent action, the driver is depicted at rest, either before the start or after the finish of a race. He wears the long tunic which seems to us a strange costume for energetic exercise, but which was the standard dress of Greek and Roman charioteers for centuries. The figure has something of the aloofness of the best Greek art of the time; the tendency to idealization, however, has not been carried to the point of producing an icy nullity. There is character in the face, due partly to the fact that the two sides of it are by no means symmetrical.

A quartet of bronze horses from a similar monument now adorn the façade of the Cathedral of San Marco in Venice (Pl. 73). They were taken to Venice from Constantinople when that unfortunate city was sacked by the Crusaders in 1204. In 1797 Napoleon carried them off to Paris, but they were returned after Waterloo. These wanderings of the horses are well authenticated. It is sometimes stated in guide-books that they originally stood in Alexandria, were removed to Rome after the death of Cleopatra and then taken by Constantine to adorn his new capital. These early travels appear to be based on nothing better than guesswork. Apart from the superb vigour of the horses as a work of art, they afford useful evidence of the details of harness of the period.

The depicting of this harness is an example of the tendency to greater realism which distinguishes sculpture of the fourth century from earlier work. Another development was that sculptors set themselves increasingly harder problems to solve, such as that of representing movement and action in their very static medium. In 1935 an outstanding example of such an attempt was recovered from the sea near Artemisium, the bronze jockey now in the National Museum at Athens (*Pl. 59*). The subject had one great advantage for an artist trying to depict speed. No matter how fast his horse is galloping, a horseman must be able to sit still on it. The boy jockey gives a remarkable impression of perfect balance and control, yet his unseen horse is obviously travelling at full tilt; there is no doubting the boy's utter determination to win. A large fragment of a bronze horse, comprising the head and one foreleg, was dredged up at the same time as the jockey, but they cannot have belonged to one another. Apart from other considerations, there is no attempt to depict harness on the horse's head, and it is impossible to believe that the unknown sculptor who lavished such care on the straps which hold the jockey's spurs would have dodged the challenge of the horse's harness.[133]

In the great age of Greece there appears to have been less excitement among spectators about equestrian events than about athletics. Certainly there is no evidence of the frenzied crowd hysteria about chariot-racing which we shall encounter in the Roman world. This was perhaps due to class consciousness, a feeling among the masses that the horse events were the preserve of the wealthy, whereas in athletics all men started equal. Although Alcibiades brought Athens the glory of an Olympic victory with his *quadrigae*, his racing interests tended to be held against him by his political opponents. But there is no doubting the enthusiasm of the wealthy owners. Pheidippides in the *Clouds* may be a caricature, but accident has preserved a moving testimony to the love of horses in real life. A tombstone of the fifth century BC, discovered near the sanctuary of Hera outside Argos, commemorates Hyssematas, an Argive who was killed in battle; his wife Kossina records that she erected it near the hippodrome in which he had won his victories. Hyssematas had exercised his skill on that wide Argive plain where centuries earlier Agamemnon and Diomedes had trained their teams.[134]

CHAPTER X

THE ROMAN CIRCUS

SUPERFICIALLY, ROMAN CHARIOT-RACING seems to differ little from Greek. The chariots used were of the same pattern, usually drawn in both countries by two or four horses; the course in Rome as in Greece was up-and-down, entailing the same turn round the posts at each end of it; in the Roman Circus as at Olympia the chariots started from traps. But there were important differences in the organization of racing, and these ultimately go back to a gulf between Greek and Roman conceptions of sport.

(Our 'circus' is the same word as the Latin *Circus*; it is used for an entertainment originally purely equestrian but now much more varied, still performed in a *circus* or ring. In this book, to avoid ambiguity, the Roman racecourse will be spelt with a capital, Circus.)

In its earliest origin in Greece, sport, whether athletic or equestrian, was based on the idea that it was for the enjoyment and benefit of the competitors, and it was assumed that the participants would pay for their pleasure, just as they would pay for any other enjoyment in life. If spectators enjoyed watching the competitors, well and good, but that was incidental. As time went on, provision was made for them. In the Roman imperial era, lavish seating was installed in many Greek stadia, but at Olympia at least, such provision was kept to the minimum; to the end, no seats were provided for spectators, only bare banks. It is true that even before Greece became part of the Roman empire, athletics had become almost wholly professional and were mounted solely for the entertainment of spectators, but the change to this situation from the earlier scene where all the leading competitors were wealthy amateurs took place so gradually that there was never a point at which the organization of the great Games was altered to meet the changed circumstances, and the distinction between amateur and professional appears never to have become a subject of controversy. In the modern world the change from a sporting scene dominated by amateurs to one where in most games the players at top level are performers paid to entertain spectators has occurred in less than a century, and this has produced tensions of which we are only too well aware. These tensions persist because no one will admit that the 'sport' provided as public entertainment for spectators is an entirely different thing from sport arranged for the enjoyment of the participants.

The Romans were never in danger of suffering from any such tensions. From early in their recorded history, chariot-racing, along with athletic meetings, gladiatorial combats and fights with wild animals, was provided as public entertainment. In Republican times, these shows were given by politicians anxious to capture votes; under the Empire they continued to be presented by magistrates, because to do so had become one of the established duties of their office, or by the emperor to keep the people quiet. No doubt in early centuries wealthy amateurs played an important part in Roman chariot-racing as in Greek. One branch of the great Claudian clan which produced the emperors from Tiberius to Nero bore the family name Quadrigarius, which suggests that an ancestor in the remote past had shown skill in handling a team. But in the Imperial period, the great age of Roman chariot-racing and the only one of which we have any substantial evidence, the amateur played as little part as the amateur rider does on the modern Turf.

Whether the Romans took chariot-racing from the Greeks or the Etruscans is uncertain; it is in any case an academic point, since the Etruscans probably took it from the Greeks. According to tradition, the great Roman racecourse, the Circus Maximus, was first laid out in the legendary age of the kings by one of the Tarquins, who were Etruscan. The site chosen indicates that the convenience of spectators was the first consideration. It was a valley between the Palatine and Aventine hills, whose lower slopes afforded accommodation for the greatest possible number of onlookers. The Circus was reconstructed by Julius Caesar, and in the middle of the first century A D, according to the elder Pliny, it held a quarter of a million (*Pls.* 74, 75). Even this proved inadequate, for the younger Pliny congratulates the Emperor Trajan on adding seating for a further five thousand, giving everyone as good a view of the racing as the emperor himself, and also a good view of the emperor. Time has not dealt kindly with the Circus Maximus. In the nineteenth century Rome planted her gasworks in it, and although the gasometers have been cleared away, the inevitable result has been that while we know a good deal about it from literary sources, archaeology has been able to add little. Fortunately at the beginning of the fourth century the Emperor Maxentius built another Circus outside the city walls near the Via Appia, and this has survived in a much better state of preservation (*Pls.* 80, 81). The emperor's motive in constructing it is obscure. It is much smaller than the Circus Maximus—its track is 530 yards × 52 as against 650 × 250—and it could accommodate only a fraction of the number of spectators; perhaps its merit was that it kept unruly crowds outside the city at their moments of greatest excitement. There is no doubt, however, that its architect embodied in its design all the experience gained from centuries of racing in the Circus Maximus.

The chief difference between Greek and Roman racing lay in the number of chariots involved in a race. In Greece, as we have seen, where the only boundaries to a course were those imposed by the lie of the land, fifty or sixty could race together. The narrowness of the valley between the two hills of Rome made this impossible. The Circus Maximus provided for twelve chariots, and we know of no Circus in the Roman world which accommodated more. A second important difference was that in order to prevent head-on collisions the Romans joined the two turning-posts with a low wall called a *spina* (A–B, Fig. 12). This separated the runners on each leg from those who had turned the post in front of them. But while the *spina* solved one problem it caused another. Whereas in the Greek hippodrome with no *spina* the drivers at the start could make for a point to the right of the further post (F, Fig. 8, p. 167) and pass on either side of the near one, the Roman *spina* compelled them to converse on a point to the right of the near post (E, Fig. 12). One result of this was that the first post had to be placed further from the starting line in the Circus than was necessary in the hippodrome; the part of the track thus sacrificed (A–G, Fig. 12) was little used in the remainder of the race, and the spectators at that end had a poor view of the racing. To alleviate the difficulty, two refinements were adopted in the Circus of Maxentius; the *spina* is set askew from the main axis (B–H, Fig. 12), and with the same aim of affording a wider front of entry in the first lap, the designer has given a bulge to the row of spectators' seats at this point at the side of the Circus (*Pl.* 80).

From early times the Romans used starting traps (*carceres*) in their Circus; according to Livy, the gate was introduced in 429 BC. They probably took the idea from Olympia, for the Kleoitas who invented the gate there lived early in the fifth century BC, but the Roman pattern differed considerably from the Greek. The necessity of passing to the right of the near post (*meta*) meant that Roman charioteers were even more conscious than Greek of the disadvantage of starting from an outside trap compared with those in the middle. As at Olympia, the Romans tried to compensate for this in the design of their gate, but whereas the Greeks staggered the start in time, the Romans adopted the simpler course of staggering it in space. The stalls were laid out not in a straight line, but in an arc of a circle with its centre at the point on which the chariots converged at the start. The Circus at Jerash affords a good example (Fig. 9, p. 168). The radius of the circle there is 80 yards, and the centre is a point 8 yards to

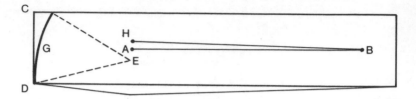

Fig. 12 *The Roman Circus.*

the right of the turning post; as a result, the stall at the left end of the gate is 6 yards in front of the one at the right end. Jerash is a small Circus with only ten stalls. In the larger Circus of Maxentius, the advantage to the chariot on the left is over 10 yards.[135]

This curving of the line may have made the start fairer, but it obviously increased the risk of crashes in the opening seconds of a race as the drivers converged on the coveted inner position. To lessen the danger, the Romans adopted a device of which we learn from a sixth-century Christian writer, Cassiodorus:

> Not far from the traps a white line is marked right across the track from side to side like a straight ruler, in order that, as the chariots race forward, the real dogfight may not start before that point; otherwise, if they tried too early to cause one another to crash, they might appear to be robbing the spectators of the most entertaining part of the spectacle.
>
> (*Variae* iii, 51.7)

The purpose of Cassiodorus' white line across the track is best understood by comparison with what happens in a half-mile race on a quarter-mile track at a modern athletics meeting. The race has to finish at the end of a straight, and so it must start at the beginning of a bend. If the runners started from a line drawn straight across the track, there would be a great deal of bumping as they made immediately for the inside position. Accordingly it is now usual to employ a staggered start with the runners in lanes to which they must

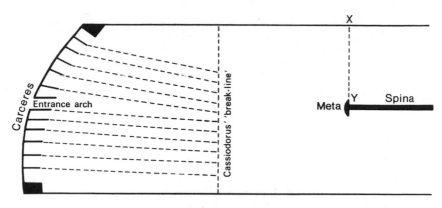

Fig. 13 *The Circus marked out for the start.*

keep round the first bend. At the end of the bend there is a white line across the track—exactly like that in Cassiodorus —which is the signal to the runners that they may now break from their lanes and take their best way home. In the same way, Roman charioteers had to keep to their own lane from the traps to the white line, with each driver free to make a dash for an early lead and its advantage at the first turn or to avoid trouble by holding back and reserving his effort for the later stages (Fig. 13). Cassiodorus clearly believes that the object of the rule was not to avert crashes altogether, but to prevent them from happening before the race had fairly started and in a part of the track (A–G, Fig. 12) which, for reasons we have seen, would otherwise be least attractive to spectators.

As on our running tracks, the lines were marked out on the track itself. The elder Pliny, enumerating the different varieties of chalk, writes, 'The cheapest kind is that with which they mark out the Circus near the winning-line'. The winning-line may have been the same as Cassiodorus' break-line or it may have been level with the *meta* (X–Y, Fig. 13). Pliny's words are equally suitable in either case, as the lanes were at the same end of the Circus as the winning-post and near it.[136]

The *spina* down the middle of the track varied in elaboration from place to place. In the smaller Circuses it was simply
a low wall or even an earth bank. In larger courses it
became an important ornamental element, carrying statues,
columns and other decorative items. Every visitor to Istanbul
sees the Serpent Column from Delphi and the two obelisks
still standing on the *spina* of the Circus of Byzantium. The
spina of the Circus Maximus at Rome once held two
Egyptian obelisks, one of which is now in the Piazza del
Popolo, the other in the Piazza di San Giovanni Laterano.
The obelisk now in the Piazza Navona once stood on the
spina of the Circus of Maxentius. When Julius Caesar reconstructed the Circus Maximus, he had a moat placed all round
the track to divide it from the spectators' seats. This was
presumably to allow it to be used for wild-beast shows. After
the Colosseum had been built especially for this purpose, the
moat was unnecessary, and its decorative functions were
transferred to the *spina*, which became a water channel.

The most important of the objects on the *spina* were the
lap counters. The earliest of these in the Circus Maximus was
a stand carrying seven large oval discs called 'eggs', one of
which was lowered at the end of each lap; Livy tells us that this
was introduced in 174 BC. In 33 BC, according to Dio Cassius,
Agrippa supplemented the eggs with another tower from
which seven bronze dolphins dived one by one into the water
channel of the *spina* as the laps were run. The earlier counter
was apparently not superseded, for many representations of
the Circus Maximus in art show both eggs and dolphins. Dio
asserts that Agrippa added the dolphins because the human
counters of the laps who lowered the eggs had sometimes
slipped up on their job, a failing only too familiar in modern
athletics and motor racing. But as the dolphins presumably
had to be worked by men no less prone to error, Agrippa's
motive would appear to have been aesthetic rather than
practical. The multiplication of the adornments of the *spina*
had one unfortunate result; they became so numerous that
they obstructed the view of spectators on the lower seats.[137]

Circuses were built in many parts of the Roman Empire, of varying degrees of elaboration according to the wealth of the cities; some of them have been examined and even more identified. One of the best surviving examples of a turning-post or *meta* is visible at Dougga in Tunisia. The Circus there, like the hippodrome of Lycaeus, is curiously situated near the top of a hill, where a long sloping ledge of rock afforded excellent accommodation for spectators. The *meta* is a well-built semi-circle about 20 feet in diameter. Strangely enough, there is no sign of a *spina*. If it had been a stone wall, since carried away for building, it is difficult to see why the *meta* should have been spared. Presumably the *spina*, if it existed at all, must have been a low earth bank which has sunk to the level of the surrounding track. At Lepcis Magna, on the other hand, the *spina* was elaborate and included a water channel like that at Rome. The Roman pattern of racecourse spread into the eastern part of the empire, where no doubt the better accommodation for spectators caused it to be preferred to the Greek hippodrome, though Greek writers continued to use the Greek word 'hippodrome' for any racecourse. The hippodrome at Istanbul is a Circus in the Roman tradition rather than a true Greek hippodrome like the one at Olympia. Recent excavations at Tyre have revealed a Circus with a semi-circular *meta* still *in situ*. At Alexandria in Egypt the hippodrome must have been constructed on the Roman model, surrounded with spectators' seats. The Third Book of Maccabees, a work not admitted even into the Apocrypha, relates how Ptolemy Philopator herded the Jews of Alexandria into the hippodrome and had them trampled to death by elephants intoxicated with incense. This would not have been possible if the racecourse had not been surrounded by very solid structures.[138]

Herod the Great, an admirer of all things Roman, had four Circuses built in his domains. The one at Caesarea Maritima is still to be seen, with the short obelisks of a turning-post lying on the ground, but it awaits excavation. The other three are known only through references to them in Josephus.

The Circus of Jerusalem lay to the south of the city; the site is unknown, but the buildings must have been solid and substantial, since the Jewish rebels thought it worth occupying as a military strong point at the beginning of their revolt in 4 BC. The Circus at Jericho must have been equally substantial; it was used as a concentration camp for prisoners of war in the same revolt. The fourth Circus was at Tarichaeae on the shores of the Lake of Galilee. Although this was a large city, its site is not certainly known; it was probably about four miles north of Tiberias, where a valley running down to the lake affords good conditions for chariot-racing.[139]

CHAPTER XI

THE ORGANIZATION OF
ROMAN RACING

THE HISTORY OF THE RACING in these Circuses falls naturally
into two periods, divided by the establishment of the Empire
just before the beginning of the Christian era. Of the organization in the Republican age we know little. It is reasonable
to suppose that it resembled the Greek set-up, with racing
controlled by wealthy owners who entered their teams at the
various meetings according to their chances of success and
the prestige or pecuniary advantage of victory at any particular festival. Even after racing had passed almost entirely
into the hands of professionals, an interest in horses continued
to flourish in the fashionable world. Among the scandals of
society at the end of the first century A D, Juvenal includes the
man who has squandered the family fortune on horses and
yet has the audacity to apply for a commission in the Army;
the poet adds a vivid description of the young spendthrift
driving at full pelt along the Flaminian Way as if he were
Achilles' charioteer, holding the reins himself and showing
off to his girl-friend in her guardsman's cloak. But in the
Roman world where racing was provided as entertainment
for spectators rather than to afford sport to owners, any
organization which depended on the whims of such men was
inadequate. A magistrate or politician promoting a festival
wanted to be sure of sufficient entries for his races to give the
crowd a good spectacle, and if personal animosity or political
prejudice caused private owners to boycott his Games, he
might be in a hopeless quandary. The need was met by the
establishment of great stables, prepared to furnish any required number of teams and drivers at any time. This was the

basis of Roman chariot-racing throughout its great period, the age of the Empire. The stables attracted passionate supporters in the crowds, just as modern football clubs do, and for this reason came to be known as factions; they were called by the names of the colours worn by their drivers. At first there were two, Reds and Whites. Early in the first century AD two others appear, Greens and Blues; the Greens are first mentioned in an inscription of AD 35. Dio Cassius tells us that the Emperor Domitian founded two new factions with the imperial colours of Gold and Purple, but this attempt to diversify the racing scene met with no success. A single inscription records that a charioteer who had won 178 races for the Reds was transferred to the Purples and won eight times for them; the Golds are never heard of again. Indeed, four factions proved too many for popular taste. The Romans were as fundamentally two-faction in racing as the British are two-party in politics. All four factions were still active at the beginning of the second century. Fifty years later the Blues had absorbed the Reds and the Greens had taken over the Whites; red and white tunics continued to be worn by the second drivers of the two major factions, but from now on, rivalry in the Circus was for the crowds a straight fight between Blues and Greens.[140]

From the beginning of the Christian era, statistics of performances in the Circus were as carefully kept as they are on the modern Turf or in cricket or baseball. At the end of their career, charioteers—or their families if the drivers were killed in accidents—erected monuments with the details of their achievements, and some of these have survived in various degrees of fragmentation. They record the number of starts, of wins and places, amounts of prize money for the more important races and totals for the driver's whole career. Even the tactics by which the races were won are included. One or two add lists of horses and the number of victories the driver won with each. Names, breeds, colours and sometimes the sires of the horses are given, but never the ages. As we should expect, these documents are full of technical terms, many of which cannot be certainly interpreted. To help in understanding them, literature affords one contemporary description of a race in the Circus Maximus. Unfortunately it is not an ordinary race for the professional drivers of the factions, but a special event for amateur charioteers. Nevertheless it throws much light on Roman racing. The account is in a poem addressed to a young friend by Sidonius Apollinaris, who was Bishop of Auvergne in the fifth century. The young friend, Consentius, has won a race of a kind which will be familiar to anyone who remembers the Oxford and Cambridge Sports of forty years ago. In those days the match was decided, not as now by points awarded for places, but by events, so that only first places counted, although two or three from each University competed in each race. In the Mile and Three Miles, this resulted in battles of tactics such as are rarely seen nowadays. The function of the second and third strings on each side was to attempt to dictate the pace of the race to suit their own champion and at the same time to unsettle their rivals' first string by every legitimate means, running at his shoulder or compelling him constantly to pass them on bends. In Consentius' race there are two teams of two chariots; each principal has a 'colleague' to help him. In modern racing, if it is to the advantage of a fancied horse to have a race run fast, a horse with no prospects of winning is sometimes entered from the same stable to ensure a good gallop in the early stages. A Roman chariot race, with thirteen tight turns round posts, obviously afforded far greater opportunities for a second or third string chariot to help the principal.

Sidonius first describes the occasion of the race and sets the scene:

On January the first it is the emperor's custom to promote Games called 'Private' with two sessions in the one day. A number of young men of the court practise a grim imitation of the *quadriga* race in the Olympics.

(*Carmina* XXIII, 360ff)

It is clear from the description that chariots and horses were provided by the authorities, and the competitors cast lots for them. When Consentius came forward among the whistling of the expectant crowd to draw his lot, the teams were already in the stalls. Only four traps of the starting-gate were needed, two on each side of the central passage which ran under the President's box. The drivers wore tunics of the traditional four colours of the Circus; no doubt Consentius and his rival had the Green and Blue, while their second strings carried the White and Red.

> When the draw was completed, you took the reins and stepped into your chariot; your colleague and the two drivers of the rival team did the same. Grooms were holding the horses by their bridles and smoothing down their plaited manes. They whispered encouragement to them, and with gentle pats on their necks they aroused their spirit for the coming race. The horses in the traps fretted and pressed against the bars. Their breath came through the still-closed gates, and even before the start the empty track was filled with their pantings. They pushed, they trembled, they tugged, they fought against the bit, they rampaged, they jumped, they terrified their rivals and were terrified by them. They could not stand still, but with flailing hoofs they lashed the iron-bound barrier. At long last the blare of the trumpet ended the suspense and sent the swift chariots dashing onto the track. Clouds of dust rose. The charioteers plied their whips, leaning forward so far over their teams as they urged on their yoke-horses that it was difficult to see whether the axle or the pole was taking their weight.

The poet imagines himself watching the race from a seat near the winning-post (X, Fig. 13, p. 189). He therefore has a good view of the start, but then the *spina* with its ornaments and devices partly conceals what is happening as the chariots run down the straight on the opposite side of the Circus:

When you had covered the open stretch of the track, the part where it narrows and is enclosed by the double wall of the long *spina* with its channel and lap-counter caught you from our gaze. But when the turn round the far post restored you to our view, your second string was in the lead; your two opponents had passed you, and you were lying fourth. The two drivers in the middle hoped that the leader would swing out to the right on one of the turns and allow them to slip inside him and secure the inner berth. You kept your horses reined back, reserving your effort for the seventh lap. Sweat flew from horses and drivers, and the roar of the crowd grew louder. Horses and chariot-eers alike were hot with exertion but at the same time chilled with apprehension.

For four laps there was no change in the position of the chariots. In the fifth, the leader realized that the pace had been too hot for his team and that his centre pair of horses was weakening; both chariots of the rival group passed him, and their drivers felt that they had the race in their hands. But now Consentius made his effort. He shook up his team and came up swiftly behind his opponent's second string just as he was going in to a turn. This so startled the driver that he lost con-trol of his horses and they ran out to the right, leaving Con-sentius in second place. His principal rival, ignorant of what had happened behind him and still confident that the race was his, now turned the last lap into a premature 'lap of honour', driving wide near the spectators' seats and waving to the crowd. Too late he became aware that Consentius had swept past inside him. He could see Consentius' chariot, but he hoped that his own partner was still leading in the cloud of dust on his left. Accordingly he came swooping across the track straight at Consentius in an attempt to achieve what in modern football is coming to be termed a tactical foul. Sidonius had been justified in calling this race a 'grim' imitation of the Olympic Games. However, the attempt failed. The driver merely crashed his own chariot, and to a roar from the crowd Consentius passed the post first. Prizes of crowns, silks and gold torques were awarded to both drivers of the winning combination, and consolation prizes to the two losers.

This passage of Sidonius is a great help in interpreting the inscriptions which are our fullest source of evidence for the organization of the Circus. It is clear from these that many of the events in the ordinary programmes for professional charioteers were team races, for teams of two, three or four chariots (*certamina binarum, ternarum, quaternarum*); the most highly esteemed, however, were the singles (*certamina singularum*), where it was 'every man for himself'. The most important of these inscriptions contains a very comprehensive set of statistics of the achievements of a charioteer named Diocles, whose career covered twenty-four years in the second century. The loss of a strip on the left side causes a few gaps in the account, but otherwise it is remarkably complete.[141]

Gaius Appuleius Diocles from Lusitania in Spain began his driving career in A D 122 with the Whites, and gained his first victory for that faction two years later. He transferred to the Greens in 128 and finally to the Reds in 131; he drove for that stable for fifteen years. With *quadrigae* he had 4,257 starts and was placed (*ad honorem venit*) 2,900 times—1,462 firsts, 861 seconds, 576 thirds and one fourth which won a prize of 1,000 sesterces; clearly only a very exceptional race had a fourth prize. He was unplaced 1,351 times. Of his 1,462 victories, 1,064 were in singles races, 347 in races for teams of two chariots like that described by Sidonius Apollinaris, and 51 in races for teams of three; the twelve traps in the Circus Maximus would accommodate a team of three from each of the four factions.

Most of Diocles' racing was done in *quadrigae*. With *bigae* he claims only 6 victories, with three-horse teams 4; the third horse in these races was presumably harnessed as a trace-horse on the off side, to help the left-hand turn round the post. In other unusual races he won twice from two starts in one day with six-horse teams, and he won with a team of seven horses on the first occasion on which such a race was ever held. He adds rather unnecessarily that he won this race without using his whip (*sine flagello*); a driver manipulating the reins of seven horses would hardly have a hand to spare for a whip. Harnessing six horses would demand two trace-horses on each side; with the team of seven the odd horse was probably on the off side.[142]

Next Diocles gives statistics about prize money. In major races for *quadrigae* he won 32 with a first prize of 30,000 sesterces, 28 at 40,000, 29 at 50,000 and 3 at 60,000. The ordinary (*pura*) first prize for *quadrigae* appears to have been 20,000 sesterces. With *bigae* he won 4 at 15,000, and this was the prize also for the three-horse races. For the six-horse races the first prize was 40,000 and for the seven-horse event 50,000. The grand total of Diocles' prize money was 35,863,120 sesterces. In an age of inflation and token currency it is impossible to give exact modern equivalents for these amounts; as a very rough and ready guide at the time of writing one might take ten sesterces as equal in purchasing power to one pound sterling.

The most intriguing but most puzzling section of the inscription is that which tabulates the statistics of tactics. They are as follows: *occupavit et vicit*, 815; *successit et vicit*, 67; *praemissus vicit*, 36; *eripuit et vicit*, 502; unclassified, 42. Of these technical terms, *occupavit et vicit* almost certainly means 'took the lead at the start and held it throughout'. *Successit et vicit* may be interpreted 'came from the rear to win'. Alone among the categories the total of '*eripuit*' victories is broken down thus: 'From Green 216, from Blue 205, from White 81'. The Reds, Diocles' chief faction, do not appear in this breakdown. This is intelligible if we take the phrase to mean 'Lay second throughout the race and snatched victory in the last stages'. The Greens, Blues and Whites are then the drivers deprived in this way of an expected win. To understand *praemissus vicit* (if that be the correct reading; the stone is imperfect at this point) we should perhaps fall back again on the parallel of the Oxford and Cambridge Sports of long ago. In the long-distance races it sometimes happened that the first string had an off day on the great occasion, and a second or third string who had been sent on ahead (*praemissus*) to make the pace went on and won. This must sometimes have occurred in the team races of the Circus, and Diocles may well have won victories in this way early in his career before he became first driver for his faction.

Next Diocles claims to have broken the records of several other great figures of the Circus, Teres and Thallus of the Reds, Commius, Venustus and Epaphroditus of the Blues, and Flavius Scorpus and Pompeius Musclosus of the Greens. He has to admit that other drivers surpassed him in the total number of victories, Scorpus for instance with 2,048 and Musclosus with 3,599, but he counterbalances these figures with the number of big prizes he has won. He points out that Scorpus, Musclosus and another Green charioteer whose name has been lost totalled between them 6,632 wins, but of these only 28 gained a prize of 50,000 sesterces. He himself with only 1,462 victories had won 29 at 50,000. These statistics, of course, do not prove Diocles' superiority as a driver; they merely show that by his time the number of big prizes had grown. Today with equal folly we are often invited to assess the ability of tennis or golf players by the amount of prize money they have won.

Diocles makes an interesting comparison of himself with Epaphroditus. The latter's total of victories was 1,467, five more than Diocles', but only 911 of them were in singles. Diocles' smaller total included 1,064 first places in singles. Epaphroditus *eripuit et vicit* 467 times, Diocles 502. Here is our evidence that victory in singles, where every man drove for himself alone, was more highly rated than a win in a team race, and that a win with the technique *eripuit* was particularly prized; this makes it all the more tantalizing that we do not certainly know what the technique was.

Finally Diocles tells us something of the horses he drove. This and other inscriptions suggest that in each team one horse was regarded as 'captain' and was usually harnessed as right yoke-horse. Charioteers, like jockeys, had their favourites. Nine of his horses Diocles drove in their hundredth victory, one in its two hundredth. In a year in which he won 127 firsts, three yoke-horses (*introiuga*), Abigeius, Lucidus and Pompeianus, participated in 103 of them; add to these two other horses, Cotynus and Galata, and the five accounted for 445 of the victories of Diocles' career, 397 of them in singles. One pair of these yoke-horses, Pompeianus and Cotynus, running together, won 99 times, the earliest record in any sport of a century so narrowly missed. Here again Diocles had to admit that his totals had been surpassed. Fortunatus of the Greens had won 386 firsts with his horse Tuscus; Diocles' best with a single horse was 152 with Pompeianus. But Tuscus had won only 9 prizes of 50,000 sesterces; Pompeianus won 10 at 50,000 and one at 60,000. The oddest record claimed by Diocles is that he was the best driver of African horses. Epaphroditus had won 134 firsts with his African Bubalus; Diocles' 152 with Pompeianus beat this. Were Africans perhaps more difficult to drive than other horses?

By a strange chance, Diocles turns up in another surviving inscription which records an offering made on his behalf by his son and daughter to the Temple of Fortuna at Praeneste. Such an offering might well have been made to the goddess on behalf of a charioteer in the middle of his career, in the hope of future favours. But it is also possible that Diocles had retired to end his days in this pleasant hill town, the modern Palestrina, and that this was a thank-offering from his family for his having escaped the perils of his calling.[143]

For our knowledge of the horses used in the races we owe most to two lists preserved in inscriptions. Each formed the last part of a monument celebrating the feats of a charioteer, but in both the first section with the driver's statistics has been lost. It is clear from these and other lists that the Romans did not share the Greek belief in the superiority of mares, and that whereas the Greeks thought that the best and most experienced horse of a team should be harnessed as right trace-horse, the Romans held that the decisive position was right yoke-horse. In the first inscription 74 names are legible, and only 3 of them are certainly mares. The list adds the breed or country of origin to each name; 46 of them are African, with a few each from Gaul, Mauretania, Spain, Sparta, Cyrenaica and Thessaly. The second inscription does not list the breed of each horse, but records that the unknown charioteer won 584 victories with Africans and 1,378 with Spanish horses. This puts him among the most successful known to us. The list names 122 horses, usually with the colour and often with the sire; only 7 of them are certainly mares. To each horse is added the number of victories the driver won with it, varying from 1 to 152, the number he achieved with a horse called Olympus. In this and similar documents more than 30 adjectives are used to describe the colour of a horse. The Romans obviously did not suffer from any such convention as that which compels us in horsey circles to refer to a pure white horse as a grey.[144]

The names are as various as with us. Sometimes a horse is called after a legendary character—Ajax, Arion, Daedalus, Argo, or Phaedrus. Sometimes the name describes the appearance or character of its bearer—Maculosus (Spotty), Candidus (Snowy), Petulans, Hilarus (Good-tempered), Peculiaris (Choosy), or Rapax (Greedy). Often it embodies the hopes of the owner who bestowed it—Advolans (Flier), Callidromus (Gorgeous Runner), Sagitta (Arrow), Victor, Palmatus, or Callinicus (Glorious in Victory). Sometimes it is fanciful, Gemmula, Pugio (Dagger), Passer (Sparrow), Hederatus (Ivy-crowned), Perdix (Partridge). The Romans had the same difficulty as we experience in finding new names, and they are often repeated. In the first of these lists there is a Spartan Romulus and an African Romulus, an African Lupus and a Spanish Lupus, a Thessalian Passer and an African Passer.

Another charioteer who has left a record of his achievements only a little less detailed than Diocles' is Publius Aelius

Gutta Calpurnianus. He drove for all four factions, in races for singles and for teams. His major successes may be tabulated thus:

	Whites	Reds	Blues	Greens	
Singles	83	42	334	116	
Teams of two	17	32	184	184	
Teams of three	2	3	65	64	
Teams of four	0	1	0	0	
	102	78	583	364	= 1,127

The victory for the Reds in a race for teams of four is the only example known to us. As there was not room in the starting-gate of the Circus for a team of this number from each of the four factions, the race was probably between two factions. Like Diocles, Calpurnianus puts on record the names of some of his favourite horses, and he claims that he drove one chestnut to victory in 429 races; appropriately it was called Victor. Some technical terms he shares with Diocles. Both give totals of the number of races they won 'straight from the procession' (a pompa). Every meeting in the Circus Maximus opened with a procession in which statues of the gods and goddesses were carried. It was obviously important. If the emperor was present he took part in it; on one occasion when Augustus was ill he was carried in it in a litter. Apparently the chariots engaged in the first race also drove in the procession and went straight from it into the traps; to win this opening race was clearly a distinction. This is a marked difference from our own practice, where the most important events in the day's programme are placed in the middle.[145]

Unlike Diocles, Calpurnianus claims no victories with *bigae* and only eight with three-horse chariots. He has one win *equorum anagonum*, which literally means 'horses that have never raced before', but may signify 'horses which have never won'. Another entry about a win *sacro quin-quennalis certaminis* [*sic*] suggests that Calpurnianus may have been hired on one occasion to drive in Greece in the Games at Olympia or Delphi.

The most marked difference between the careers of Calpurnianus and Diocles is that the former claims sixty-one victories *pedibus ad quadrigam*, 'on foot with the chariot'. This must refer to those events which required the charioteer to dismount from his chariot and cover the last part of the course on foot, as in the *Kalpē* of the early Olympics described by Pausanias. It may be that a fashion for such races coincided with Calpurnianus' career. Or perhaps Diocles avoiding competing in them; obviously a first-class driver who was not a good runner would not risk his reputation in this way if he could help it.

Another interesting feature of Calpurnianus' inscription is that four of his victories are described by the word *remissus*, 'sent back'. This term, which is found in other inscriptions but not in Diocles', should mean 'won after a re-run'. We know from Ovid that this sometimes happened, and that spectators demanded a recall by waving their cloaks, but we do not know what had to happen in a race to justify a re-run or at what stage a recall could take place. In a fragment of a lost speech, Cicero says, 'by that interruption we are recalled from the very finishing line'; such a metaphor, however, hardly constitutes firm evidence. The problem is complicated by the occurrence of the word *revocatus*, 'recalled', in the language of racing; it should mean the same as *remissus*, but this is by no means certain. The earliest charioteer's inscription which has come down to us records the achievements of Scirtus of the Whites in thirteen seasons of driving. They are set out in detail year by year, starting in AD 13. The totals are: firsts 7; *revocatus* 4; seconds 39; thirds 60. (This seems a poor tally compared with the thousands of a Scorpus or a Musclosus at the end of the century, yet Scirtus must have been a leading driver of his time to secure the tribute of this monument; clearly the number of races increased rapidly in this period.) From the way the statistics are set out, it is obvious that the four wins *revocatus* are not included in the seven firsts but are additional to them. In Scirtus' early years his wins are simple firsts; the victories *revocatus* come later and seem to confer a special distinction. In the world of the theatre, *revocatus* was used of an actor or singer who was recalled to the stage for an encore. If a charioteer was sometimes recalled to the track after a particularly brilliant performance to receive the applause of the crowd and perhaps do a 'lap of honour', it would be obvious why a victory *revocatus* should have been especially esteemed in Caligula's time. When the practice was discontinued, *revocatus* would become a natural synonym for *remissus*, as it appears to have been later.[146]

Scirtus' inscription includes another technical term, found nowhere else, whose interpretation can only be a matter of guesswork. In his total of successes, after his sixty third places, comes the entry '*Iustitiale* I'. Can it be that on one occasion Scirtus finished first but was disqualified after an objection? Such memories rankle for years.

Diocles and Calpurnianus both lived long enough to retire from the track; Calpurnianus in fact reveals that he arranged for his monument in his own lifetime (*vivus feci*). But most of the charioteers whose records have survived were less fortunate; their monuments were erected by their young widows. The life of a modern steeplechase jockey is hazardous enough, but if he is thrown he can at least hope to land on soft English turf or mud. Roman charioteers added to the obvious dangers of a track baked hard by the sun by their practice of looping the slack of the reins round their waists. When it became necessary to pull back the horses violently in an emergency or at the turns, it must have been useful to be able to throw the whole weight of the body into the action; reins can very easily slip through sweaty fingers. And drivers appear to have carried knives in their belts in the hope of being able to cut themselves free in a disaster. But in a racing world where part of the tactics of driving was deliberately to foul an opponent the mortality rate was obviously high. Certainly there was not always time for the driver to use his knife after a crash. One day when Nero was a boy, he was chatting with his friends about an accident in which a chariot-eer of the Greens had been dragged. The boys should have been working at the time, and their tutor asked them what they were talking about. The quick-witted Nero replied that they were discussing how the dead Hector had been dragged round Troy at the tail of Achilles' chariot.[147]

Part of the drivers' motive in winding the reins round their waists was probably sheer bravado, like that of a matador who stands on a handkerchief to play a bull. Showmanship was an element in a charioteer's make-up, as it is with any professional sportsman. A Greek treatise in praise of Demos-thenes tells of Anniceris, a charioteer from Cyrene, who dis-played his skill to Plato and his friends by driving round and round the Academy course in Athens, exactly superimposing his tracks after the manner of a modern figure-skater, so that only a single mark was left in the sand.[148]

Some of the monuments of young drivers add interesting details to our knowledge. There is the record of Fuscus of the Greens, who in AD 35 became the first man ever to win on his first day of racing. (Diocles, we have seen, had to drive for two years before his first victory.) Fuscus won fifty-three races in Rome, one of them *revocatus*. He is one of the few to record victories outside Rome, including one at Bovillae, thirty miles south of Rome, where three arches of the start-ing-gate of the Circus still stand. He died at the age of twenty-four. The tombstone of a driver who died even younger throws light on the early years of a charioteer's career. Crescens, a Moor, was twenty-two when he died after driving for the Blues for nine years. He must therefore have been a boy of thirteen when he first raced. His epitaph records that he won his first victory in his twenty-fourth race on 8 November AD 115, when the birthday of the Emperor Nerva was being celebrated. The names of the horses he drove that day are there, Circius, Acceptor, Delicatus and Cotynus; one's first success in a game always remains a vivid memory. Nine years later he drove in his last racc, on the anniversary of the birth of the Emperor Claudius, 1 August 124, the year in which Diocles scored his first win. Crescens' career was therefore that of an apprentice, and it is not surprising that in 686 starts he had no more than 47 firsts, with 130 seconds and 111 thirds. His 47 victories are broken down into 19 in singles, 23 in races for teams of two, and five for teams of three; one race was won *praemissus*, eight *occupavit*, and 38 *eripuit*. Naturally such a young charioteer would have fewer drives in singles, where victory was most highly prized, and more in team races, less esteemed by drivers with established reputations. Not all drivers started in childhood. One inscription records a charioteer, M. Nutius Aquilius, who died at the age of thirty-five after a career of twelve years.[149]

Most of these tombstones do not state directly that the young charioteers were killed in racing accidents, but this sometimes emerges in epigrams appended to the obituaries. One such stone, probably from the end of the second century, originally held the statues of two brothers, both charioteers; the statues have vanished, but the details of the careers remain:

> Marcus Aurelius Polyneices, born a slave, lived 29 years, 9 months and 5 days. He won 739 palms; for the Reds 655, for the Greens 55, for the Blues 12, for the Whites 17. 3 were for six-horse chariots, 8 for eight-horse, 9 for ten-horse.

> Marcus Aurelius Mollicius Tatianus, born a slave, lived 20 years, 8 months and 7 days. He won 125 palms; for the Reds 89, for the Greens 24, for the Blues 5, for the Whites 7.

A short Greek poem below reveals that they were the sons of a charioteer Polyneices, born and brought up in Rome, and both killed on the racecourse.[150]

Most of the great charioteers started life as slaves, born to slaves working in the racing stables. If they were successful drivers they could soon make enough money from gifts to buy their freedom, and thereafter accumulate large fortunes. The Greek names of many charioteers and the fact that the epigram of Polyneices' sons is in Greek remind us that many of these slaves were of Greek origin and probably spoke Greek as their first language. The Roman racing vocabulary included several latinized Greek words. It is clear also that there was a constant transfer of drivers from faction to faction, especially in the early part of their careers, but we do not know on what terms this was done. While they were still slaves they could be bought and sold, and no doubt managers of stables were often glad to get rid of young drivers who were getting above themselves because of a few successes. Once the charioteer had purchased his freedom and had become a popular favourite, he could sell his services in the open market, as the darlings of football crowds do today. A minor point of interest to emerge from the inscription is that during the career of the younger Polyneices there was obviously a vogue for races for chariots drawn by large numbers of horses.

One monument speaks for itself. It has a relief depicting a small boy falling from a *biga* in full career. There is a brief couplet, all the more pathetic for being in halting verse:

'Here am I, Florus, a child driver, falling; while I was trying to put on speed, I plunged into the shades of Lethe.' Januarius erected this to his beloved pupil.[151]

One of the greatest of these drivers who died young was Scorpus, recorded in Diocles' inscription as the winner of 2,048 races during the latter part of the first century. His career coincided with the lifetime of the epigrammatist Martial, who mentions him in a few poems, revealing that he had not attained twenty-seven years when he died. (The exigencies of poetic Latin compelled Martial to speak of him as 'snatched away in his ninth *triennium*'.) During the charioteer's lifetime Martial used him as an example when, in a fashion familiar to us today, he was deprecating the huge sums of money lavished on these sporting heroes while more deserving objects went begging. But after his death, the poet composed an epitaph for him:

> I am Scorpus, the glory of the roaring Circus, the object of Rome's cheers, and her short-lived darling. The Fates, counting not my years but the number of my victories, judged me to be an old man.
>
> (X, 53)

He also wrote a panegyric in more elaborate language:

> Let grieving Victory tear to pieces her Idumaean palms, and do thou, Adoration, beat thy naked breast with cruel hands. Let Honour put on mourning, and sad Glory cut her hair once crowned with victory, and throw it as an offering on the wanton flames of the pyre. Alas, foul trick of Fortune! Cheated of the flower of thy youth, Scorpus, thou art fallen, and all too soon dost harness the dark horses of Death. Why did the finishing post to which thou didst so often hasten with speedy course in thy chariot become the finish of thine own life?
>
> (X, 50)

The occurrence in the poem of technical terms of the Circus, *facinus* (foul), *fraudatus* (cheated) and *occidis* (crash) may be no more than a literary device, like the use of *Favor, coronatus* and *meta*. It does not necessarily mean that Scorpus was killed in an accident, but it is certainly not unlikely that he was.[152]

Not all crashes on the track were fatal, but the treatment applied to the wounds of the injured must have made some of these victims of accidents feel that death might have been preferable. The elder Pliny tells us something of the remedies:

> Sprains and injuries caused by a blow they treat with the dung of wild boars, collected in the spring and dried. The same remedy is applied to charioteers who have been dragged or injured by a wheel, or severely bruised in any other way; in an emergency it can be used fresh. Some

think that it is more efficacious if it is boiled in vinegar. They say too that powdered and taken with a drink it is a good cure for fractures and strained muscles, while for those injured in a crash it is better taken in vinegar. More cautious doctors burn it to ash and mix it with water; the Emperor Nero is said to have refreshed himself regularly with this cordial, trying even by this method to prove himself a real charioteer. If you cannot get wild boar's dung, the next best is that of the domestic pig.

(*NH* XXVIII, 237)

The fate of horses after their racing careers is less well established than that of their drivers. They started racing later than ours, generally at five years old, and went on longer. Stallions were not withdrawn permanently to stud after a few years on the track, as with us, but went on longer and were used for breeding during their racing careers. One instance is known of a horse running in a team with his own son. Interest in the details of breeding was widespread. Martial says that it was one of the accomplishments of the fashionable young man, the *bellus homo*, to know the pedigree of Hirpinus, a famous racehorse of his day; Juvenal, deprecating the importance attached to ancestry in men, points out that the offspring sired by this Hirpinus were soon sold off if they did not win races. The breeder's task must have been even more difficult in antiquity than it is today. To be a successful member of a team of four or more, a horse needed to combine the docility of a circus rosin-back with the spirit of a racer. Presumably the famous horses who were the favourites of the great charioteers possessed this remarkable combination of qualities; perhaps they could impart something of them to the horses who were harnessed alongside them. This would help to explain why the chief horse of a team was always one of the central pair (*introiuga*).[153]

Old racehorses were variously treated. The Greek poets did not overlook the tragic figure of the Derby winner ending his days as a cab-horse—with the Greeks he was turning a millstone:

> I, my friend, was once crowned at Olympia; twice I was proclaimed victor at the Castalian spring, I was shouted home at Nemea, and as a colt in the Isthmian Games I ran swift as the winged winds. Now in old age I am driven to turn the rotating millstone, a mocking imitation of the crowns I won.
>
> (*Anthologia Palatina*, IX, 20)

Two Roman poets give us a happier picture. When Cicero is arguing the possibility of a pleasant old age for a man who has led an active life in the world, he quotes a couplet from Ennius:

> Like a brave horse who has often won an Olympic crown in the last lap, and now, overtaken by age, passes a peaceful life.
>
> (Cicero, *De Senectute* V, 14)

And Ovid, pleading in exile for better treatment for himself in his declining years, contrasts the fate of the champions of the Circus with his own:

> So that he shall not come down in the world and bring disgrace on the many palms he won, the old racehorse lazily crops the grass in the meadows.
>
> (*Tristia* IV, viii.19)

These veterans of the Circus found an unexpected patron in the Emperor Nero. Dio Cassius tells us that he tricked them out in elegant rugs and gave money for their food.[154]

We have seen how the chariot teams of Cimon and Euagoras in Greece were accorded honourable burial. At Acragas in Sicily the graves of favourite horses were marked by marble pyramids. The Romans sometimes followed a similar practice, and a tombstone has survived with a metrical inscription commemorating an African mare named Speudusa (Hasty):

Sired on Gaetulian sands by a Gaetulian stallion, speedy as the wind, in thy life unmated, now, Speudusa, thou dwellest in Lethe.[155]

CHAPTER XII

CHARIOT-RACING IN THE SOCIAL LIFE OF ROME

THERE ARE STILL ENORMOUS GAPS in our knowledge of the organization of Roman racing. We do not know exactly where the prize money came from or how it was distributed —what proportion of the prize, for instance, went to the driver and how much to the stable. We know the titles of several officials in the factions, *dominus, conditor, hortator, medicus, doctor, sellarius,* but we do not know their exact functions or the relationship between them, still less the internal organization of each faction's finances. We do, however, know a good deal about the part which the racing in the Circus played in the social scene in Rome, particularly under the Empire, when it helped to meet a need. Under the Republic, the ordinary citizen of the working class had been able to take at any rate a nominal part in political life through the elections, and he had been liable to be called on for military service in the legions. Under the Empire these two avenues for his energies and interest were closed. The ranks of the legions were increasingly filled by a professional class born and bred in the military cantonments on the distant frontiers. The army was officered, the provinces governed and the higher posts in the civil service filled by representatives of the old governing class. In small country towns the man in the street may have been able to exercise some little influence on local government, but hardly in the great cities. This huge mass of people did not constitute a serious threat to imperial power, but it was to the interest of the authorities that they should be kept reasonably content and free from a disposition to riot. The recipe for securing this was, in Juvenal's memorable phrase, 'Bread and Games' (*panem et circenses*).[156]

The races in the Circus were one of the three great sources of public entertainment at the time. The others were the theatre—to judge from the slight evidence we have, as full of dirt and drivel as our own—and the bloodthirsty shows of gladiators and wild animals in the arena. On social and moral grounds, chariot-racing was probably the least open to criticism of the three. It was a sport in which all classes of society could share. Most emperors thought it wise to patronize the races, and with some of them the enthusiasm was genuine. Julius Caesar was regular in his attendance, but it was noticed that he was sometimes giving his attention to State documents and his correspondence rather than to the chariots. In contrast, Augustus went less often to the Circus, but while he was there he always concentrated on the racing. Tiberius was an embittered man when he succeeded Augustus, and was not often in Rome. Yet in happier days, as we have seen, he had been keen enough to enter a chariot at Olympia and to win. Caligula was as unbalanced in his passion for racing as in other things. In his youth he had improved his physique, especially his thighs, by riding. Later he encouraged chariot-racing for amateur drivers, instituting some events confined to senators; to mark the importance of these races, he had the track covered with bright red or green powder for them. He also interspersed fights with panthers between the races. He constructed a racecourse on the slopes of the Vatican hill, and to adorn its *spina* he brought from Egypt the obelisk which now stands in front of St Peter's. He was a fanatical supporter of the Greens and often visited their stables and dined with the charioteers; on one occasion he made a gift of two million sesterces to a driver of the Greens, Eutychus.[157]

Suetonius tells us that Vitellius, who reigned for a few months during the 'Year of the Four Emperors' which followed the death of Nero, suffered from a weak hip, the result of an accident when he was charioteering with Caligula. Vitellius affords an early example of the influence of sport on politics. He was able to make his bid for the purple because he was in command of an army in Germany. He owed this appointment to the support of Titus Vinius, a friend of his since both were ardent admirers of the Blues.[158]

The Emperor Claudius, as we should expect, was no great sportsman, but he promoted Games in the Vatican Circus with animal fights after every five races; he also improved the Circus Maximus by reconstructing the wooden front of the starting-gate and the tufa turning posts in marble. We are indebted to Suetonius' *Life* of him for one interesting piece of information. Claudius accorded divine honours to his grandmother Livia, and had her statue, together with that of Augustus, drawn by elephants in the processions which opened the meetings in the Circus Maximus.[159]

Of all the emperors Nero is the one most closely associated with chariot-racing. His earliest connection with the sport was unhappy; his father Domitius Nero promoted a race meeting during his praetorship but defrauded the winners of their prizes. As a boy the future emperor used to play a game with ivory chariots on a board, probably like the table-top race games of our own day, and he continued this practice at the beginning of his reign. He never missed a meeting in the Circus, even an unimportant one, if he was anywhere near the city. His addiction to the track cost his wife her life, for when Poppaea scolded the emperor because he came home late from the races one day he kicked her with fatal results. This treatment of his wife contrasts strangely with his kindness towards veteran racehorses.[160]

In the Circus he increased the number of races in the day's programme to fifty, divided into two sessions by an interval for refreshments. On one occasion, according to Cassiodorus, Nero dallied so long over his lunch that the people became restive. As soon as the emperor realized this, he threw his napkin out of the window of the dining room of the royal box as a sign to the crowd that he had finished. This was the origin of the custom by which the President of the Games used to drop a napkin (*mappa*) as a signal to the starter to open the traps (*Pl.* 77).[161]

Nero's patronage of racing had one unfortunate result. The charioteers and managers of the stables became ever more arrogant and rapacious, and refused to supply their services to the less important meetings. A praetor, Aulus Fabricius, who had undertaken to present Games in the Circus Maximus, found their demands so exorbitant that he refused to meet them. Reviving the old tough qualities which had made Rome great, he defied the stables and had teams of dogs trained to draw the chariots at his meeting. This caused the Red and White managements to climb down, but the Blues and Greens held out. Whenever an attempt is made to resist the greed of a trade union, there is always one employer prepared to sell the pass. This time it was Nero who weakly yielded to the demands of the Blues and Greens. Yet it is also recorded of him that he suppressed the hooliganism of the charioteers, who had a long tradition of terrorizing the streets of Rome. Fabricius' dog teams appear to have tickled the fancy of the spectators, for the emperor imitated him by promoting races between chariots drawn by camels.[162]

Nero, however, was not content to be merely a patron of racing; he was also an active participant. Apparently he converted Claudius' Vatican Circus into a private practice track on which he could prepare for his appearances as a charioteer in the Circus Maximus. His most conspicuous performances were given in Greece, where his sporting activities were combined with his feats as actor and musician. He had the 211th Olympic Games postponed from the year 65 to 67, and was thus able to take part in the Pythian and Isthmian festivals of that year as well. He insisted on musical and dramatic contests being added to the Olympic programme for the first and only time in the long history of the Games, and he won the crowns for harp playing and tragic acting. No lesser mortal could be allowed to proclaim the emperor's victories, so he acted as his own herald; he then entered, and of course won, the competition for heralds which had by this time become a regular feature of the festival. In the hippodrome he won the *quadriga* races for horses and colts. Although in a

62–5 Chariots and racing. *Above*, a *biga* is harnessed; *below, left*. a *biga* in full career on a gemstone; *centre*, a winning mule-cart on a coin of Rhegium in Southern Italy and, *right*, a winning *quadriga* on a Syracusan decadrachm. Both coins are *c*. 480 BC and refer to Olympic victories by tyrants.

66,67 Two Panathenaic amphorae, *c.* 500 BC. That below was a prize in the race for mule-carts. Note that the mule-cart driver sat while horse charioteers like the one driving a *quadriga*, *above*, invariably stood (cf. Plates 63-5,71).

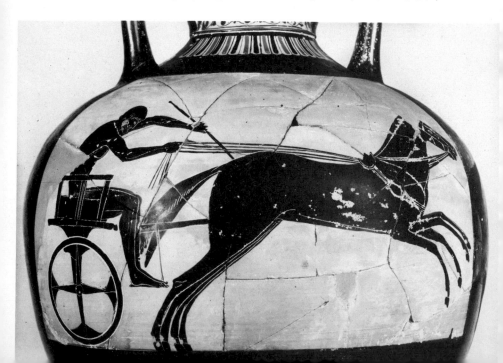

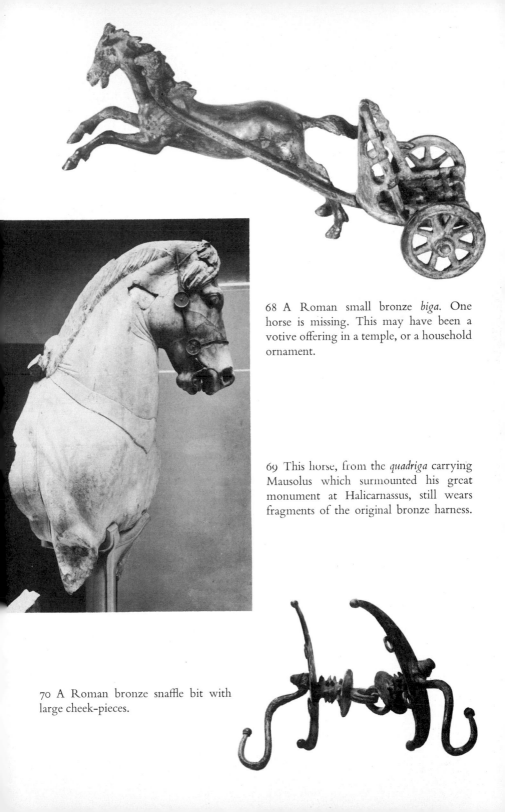

68 A Roman small bronze *biga*. One horse is missing. This may have been a votive offering in a temple, or a household ornament.

69 This horse, from the *quadriga* carrying Mausolus which surmounted his great monument at Halicarnassus, still wears fragments of the original bronze harness.

70 A Roman bronze snaffle bit with large cheek-pieces.

71-3 The Delphi Charioteer wears the typical long charioteer's robe (cf. Plates 63,66) whilst his Roman counterpart, on this small ivory figurine, wears a short tunic and carries the victor's palm. *Below*, the famous quartet of bronze horses outside San Marco in Venice once formed part of a chariot group.

74 Rome, the Circus Maximus from the air. The line of bushes down the centre marks the position of the *spina*.

75,76 *Above*, a reconstruction of the Circus Maximus and its surroundings in the Imperial period and, *below*, a race in the Circus Maximus portrayed on the side of a Roman sarcophagus.

77 The *mappa*, thrown down as the signal to start a race (pp. 215, 229), became in sculpture a conventional symbol to indicate a magistrate in Imperial times, and the practice was continued in the Byzantine Empire (cf. Plates 82,83).

78 Circus scene on a Roman mosaic from Tunisia. One chariot is going in the wrong direction, but this is probably only symbolic of the general confusion.

79 A detail from a marble relief of a circus scene, showing the dolphins used as lap-counters as a chariot flashes by.

80,81 Rome, the Circus of Maxentius. These two photographs were taken in May 1971, while the excavation of the Circus was still in progress. *Below*, the foundations of the *carceres* are seen between the two towers; in the centre is the wider opening for the processional entrance. *Above*, a view from the opposite end of the Circus. It shows the circular *meta*, the water channel in the *spina*, and the bulge in the spectators' seating on the left to give the wider front of entry to the chariots on the first lap (p. 187).

82,83 *Above*, a relief from the *spina* in the hippodrome at Istanbul, showing the emperor watching the races. *Below*, a scene in coloured marble inlay from a wall in the secular Basilica of Junius Bassus in Rome, built *c.* AD 330. The magistrate in the *biga* is about to throw down the *mappa*, not to start a race but more probably a game of polo (p. 102).

poem written earlier in his life he had rebuked Mithridates, King of Pontus, for his ostentation in driving a ten-horse chariot, he demanded that an event in that category should be included in the Games. In the early stages of the race, wanting the manage of his unruly jades, he was jolted out of his chariot. He did not remount but 'was replaced' in it (*rursus repositus*, one of Suetonius' prettiest touches); he did not complete the course even so, but was nevertheless awarded the crown. The authorities at Olympia took their revenge by refusing to admit the results of this Olympiad to the official canon.[163]

Nero's immediate successors were too busy restoring peace to the empire to have much time to devote to sport. Domitian revived the tradition of imperial patronage, but his innovations were not enduring. His two new factions, Purple and Gold, were short-lived. Oddly enough, neither of them enjoyed his support; like Nero, he was a fan of the Greens. He imitated several earlier emperors by giving 'Secular' Games. (These, as their name implies, were supposed to occur only once every century, but emperors, anxious not to be cheated of the opportunity of rivalling their predecessors, used to claim that the calculations had been wrongly done in the past.) For these he increased the number of chariot races in the day to one hundred, and to make such a massive programme possible reduced the number of laps in each race to five. Trajan added five thousand seats to the Circus Maximus, and Pliny congratulates him on reconstructing the imperial box there so that the spectators had a much better view of the emperor and his suite. The philosophical Emperor Marcus Aurelius was an exceptional figure; at the beginning of his *Meditations* he thanks his tutor for having taught him not to be a supporter of either Blues or Greens.[164]

At the other end of the social scale the mass of citizens showed no less enthusiasm for the factions. Some seats in the Circus were free (*gratuita loca*). According to Suetonius, Caligula was so disturbed one morning by the noise of the spectators who had come early to make sure of getting one of these seats that he gave orders for them to be cleared. This caused a riot in which a large number of people were killed, including twenty knights and twenty women. The mention of these free seats makes it clear that there must have been others for which the occupants paid, apart from the privileged places reserved for senators and knights. They were in fact seats in the covered stand, for Ovid tells of the awnings which shaded them and the perfumed spray with which they were cooled. The poet recommends a visit to the races as an excellent way for a young man to advance his suit with the lady of the moment, and he gives a delightful picture of the scene in the Circus, which we see through the eyes of the gay young spark chatting to his companion:

I'm no great student of horse-racing myself, but if you are keen on one of the drivers then he's my man too. I've come here so as to be able to sit by you and talk, and let you know how I feel about you. You look at the races. I'll look at you. Then we shall both be looking at what we like.

Whoever your favourite charioteer may be, what a lucky man he is! He is the one you care about. How I wish I were he! As soon as my team shot out of the traps, I would urge them on regardless. One moment I would give them their heads, the next I would ply the whip furiously, then graze the turning post with my near-side wheel. If I saw you among the crowd as I flashed past, I would pull back, and the reins would fall slack in my hands. How nearly Pelops failed in his race at Olympia because he gazed at his Hippodameia's face! Yet it was her support that brought him victory. I hope that I shall be inspired in the same way.

Why are you edging away from me? It's no use. We must keep inside our lines on the seats. That's the best of being in the Circus.

You, Sir, on the lady's right! Be careful. You are hurting her with your pushing. And you behind, keep your feet to yourself and don't poke your knee into her back.

Now your dress is trailing in the dust. Pick it up—or

rather let me; I can brush the dirt off it. It was too bad of that dress to hide such lovely legs. The longer I look, the lovelier they are. Atalanta's legs were like that when she ran against Milanion; yours are as beautiful as the pictures of Diana hunting. . . .

Would you like me to fan you with my race-card? Or perhaps it is my love that is so warm, not the day. . . . Look, a smut has fallen on your white frock; get away, filth, from this lovely figure.

But now the parade is coming. Now is the time to cheer and clap; the golden procession is here. First is Victory with her wings spread. Grant me, Victory, success in love. Here's Neptune. Let the sailors applaud him; terra firma is good enough for me. And I leave it to soldiers to cheer for Mars; I loathe violence, I'm all for love and leisure. . . . Next comes Venus; she's the one for my money, she and her Cupid with his bow. (Help my plans, Goddess. Put some sense into this new girl of mine, and tell her to encourage me). . . . Did you see? The statue bowed to me —a good omen. Now you simply must make good the promise Venus has just given me. I hope she won't mind, but you will be a greater goddess for me than ever she was.

But look, your legs are dangling, with nothing to rest them on. I'm sorry I forgot to bring a stool. If you like you can poke your toes through the holes in the railings in front. Let me put your cushion straight.

Now the track is clear for the big race. . . . The praetor has started them from the traps. I can see your man. With you as supporter, he's sure to win. Even his horses seem to know what you want.

But look! He has swung wide round the turn. What are you doing? The man just behind is coming up inside you. What are you doing, you fool? You are letting my lady down badly. For Heaven's sake, throw your weight into those left-hand reins. . . . I'm afraid, my dear, we've backed a lily-livered bungler.

Come on, chaps, demand a re-run. Toss up your cloaks

and show the praetor what you want.

Yes, it's a re-run. But all these waving cloaks are spoiling your hair-do. Snuggle up to me and let me protect you.

Now it's a fresh start, and the drivers' colours are flashing onto the course again. Do better this time; make the pace right from the start, and make my lady's prayers come true—and mine.

Well, my lady's prayers have been granted and her charioteer has won; mine remain to be gratified. He has his palm of victory. I have still to ask for mine. . . . She smiled, and her bright eyes flashed a promise. That is enough in the Circus; the rest awaits another place.

(*Amores* III, 2)

Ovid here reveals one or two points about Roman racegoing which would otherwise be unknown to us, and throws clearer light on others. There is the race-card or programme (*tabella*), and the tossing of cloaks by the crowd to demand a recall; unhappily the poet gives no clue to what justified the re-run in this race. His phrase 'make the pace right from the start' (*spatioque insurge patenti*, literally, 'press on in the open space') emphasizes the importance of the wide part of the track before the beginning of the *spina*.[165]

In strong contrast to Ovid's enthusiasm for racing is the view taken a century later by the younger Pliny in a letter to a friend. The cool eighteenth-century prose of William Melmoth's translation is admirably suited to the awe-inspiring priggishness of the original:

I have spent these several days past among my papers with the most pleasing tranquillity imaginable. You will ask how that can possibly be in the midst of Rome? Why, the Circensian Games were taking place; a kind of entertainment for which I have not the least taste. They have no novelty, no variety, nothing, in short, one would wish to see twice. I am the more astonished that so many thousands of grown men should be possessed again and again with a childish passion to look at galloping horses, and men standing upright in their chariots. If, indeed, they were attracted by the swiftness of the horses or the skill of the men, one could account for this enthusiasm. But in fact it is a bit of cloth they favour, a bit of cloth that captivates them. And if during the running the racers were to exchange colours, their partisans would change sides, and instantly forsake the very drivers and horses whom they were just before recognizing from afar, and clamorously saluting by name.

Such favour, such weighty influence, hath one cheap tunic—never mind it with the vulgar herd, who are more worthless than the tunics they wear—but with certain grave personages. When I observe such men thus insatiably fond of so silly, so low, so uninteresting, so common an entertainment, I congratulate myself that I am insensible to these pleasures; and am glad to devote the leisure of this season to literature, which others throw away upon the most idle employment. Farewell.

(*Epistles* IX, vi)

With trifling alterations the passage could be used of the crowds at a modern football match between two leading professional clubs. No doubt it is all quite true, but how regrettable!

Not all the members of Pliny's social class, as he indicates in his letter, took such a disapproving view of racing. His uncle tells us of a knight, Caecina, who was a director of one of the factions (*quadrigarum dominus*). He used to capture swallows on his country estate at Volterrae and take them to Rome. After a race he would smear their legs with paint of the colour of the winner and send them flying back to their nests, bearing the result to his friends at home.[166]

The furious partisanship of the racing crowds which Pliny denounces did not diminish as time passed. Two hundred years later, Ammianus Marcellinus depicts the Rome of the fourth century:

Now let me describe the mass of the people, unemployed

and with too much time on their hands. . . . For them the Circus Maximus is temple, home, community centre and the fulfilment of all their hopes. All over the city you can see them quarrelling fiercely about the races. . . . They declare that the country will be ruined if at the next meeting their own particular champion does not come first out of the starting-gate and keep his horses in line as he brings them round the post. Before dawn on a race day they all rush headlong for a place on the terraces at such a speed that they could almost beat the chariots themselves.

(XXVIII, iv.28)

The lengths to which this fanaticism could be carried are illustrated by a story told by the elder Pliny on the authority of official records (*acta*). At the funeral of Felix, a charioteer of the Reds, one of his fans threw himself on the pyre and was burnt to death. The supporters of the rival factions, furious that the Reds should achieve the glory of this act of devotion, spread the story that the man had been drugged by the incense (*copia odorum corruptus*) and had fainted, falling into the flames.[167]

CHAPTER XIII

BETTING ON CHARIOT-RACING

THE MOST IMPORTANT and most fundamental difference between Roman racing and our own lies in the amount of betting involved in each. The habit of gambling is almost universal, but its application is curiously varied. In its simplest form it is based on sheer chance, and the compulsive gambler wants the quickest machinery to enable him to repeat his bets; hence the toss of a coin, the throw of dice, the roulette wheel or the one-armed bandit. At the other end of the scale is the backing of skill or of a combination of skill and chance such as is found in most card games. Sometimes this can hardly be called gambling at all. A sweepstake, in which each competitor in a contest puts up an equal amount, the winner taking all, is scarcely to be distinguished from a competition where there are entry fees from which prizes are provided. But in most betting on sport, the gambler uses his skill to predict the result of a contest in which he takes no part himself.

The extent to which any particular sport or game is connected with gambling appears to be entirely a matter of accident and fashion. In Britain today, horse-racing and greyhound-racing are little more than part of a vast gambling industry. Yet show jumping, a near cousin to steeplechasing, has so far almost completely escaped the contagion. Time brings changes in fashion. At the beginning of the nineteenth century, cricket was rotten with betting; today in Britain—whatever may be true in Australia—there is very little betting on it. Athletics has on the whole freed itself in the same way.

There are many and various opinions about the ethics of gambling and about its effects on society and the individual. Even its fiercest defender, however, could not pretend that it does not constitute a danger to sport. In spite of popular belief, any intrusion of money into sport is bad for sport, and the worst offender is the hot money of the betting industry. Whenever large sums of money depend on the result of an event there is inevitably a temptation to bribery and corruption. In our racing the authorities take the most stringent precautions against it, yet bribery is sometimes detected and even more often suspected. In football, on which there is an enormous volume of gambling, the organization of the greater part of it in the form of pools minimizes the risk of corruption; even the largest syndicate could hardly bribe enough teams to ensure a winning coupon. Yet when there is betting on single matches, as a notorious example showed, corruption can intrude even into football. In other sports, where the result depends on the efforts of an individual and not on a team, bribery is obviously easier.

The Greeks gambled, the Romans gambled still more. In their betting both liked quick results, and their large-scale gambling appears to have been confined to dicing. At Rome it was regarded as a social evil, and as early as the Republican period the law tried to suppress it. An exception to the ban was allowed in the month of December, when the feast of the Saturnalia, the pagan forefather of our Christmas festivities, was thought to justify a relaxation. Such attempts to eliminate betting by laws have never succeeded anywhere. In Rome the highest in the land were known to flout them. Augustus was a confirmed gambler, rather surprisingly in view of his temperament. So too was the Emperor Claudius, who even wrote a book on the subject of play at the tables; unhappily it has not come down to us, nor have the poems on dicing mentioned by Ovid.[168]

Though most betting in antiquity was on dice, compulsive gamblers will bet on anything and are prepared to back their opinion on any subject under the sun. Greeks and Romans betted on sport as on many other things. We have seen the spectators at Homer's chariot race ready to wager on who was leading at one moment in the race. In this sphere the great difference between the ancient world and the modern is this. We have an enormous and well-organized gambling industry with bookmakers, totalizators, pools promoters and betting shops to encourage and facilitate gambling on sport. There is no evidence for anything of this kind in Greece or Rome. When their satirists deplore the ruination of men's lives by gambling, the losses are always suffered at the gaming tables, never on the racecourse. The absence of a gambling organization, helped perhaps by the big prizes and the lavish gifts bestowed on winning drivers, had one desirable result. Charioteers were accused by ancient authors of many vices, but hardly ever of accepting bribes. There is a solitary suggestion of 'pulling' in Martial; the epigrammatic brevity of the couplet leaves a wide field for conjecture:

> The horses of the Blues team are furiously lashed with the whip, but they show no turn of speed; you are doing a great job, Catianus.
>
> (VI, xlvi)

Was Martial perhaps having an oblique dig at the emperor, a fervent partisan of the Greens? Yet in another epigram, poking fun at charioteers of the Blues who had excused their failures by hinting that they were obliging Domitian, he points out that since the emperor's death the Greens have in fact won more races. On the whole, in spite of Catianus, it would seem that Roman charioteers were reasonably incorruptible. This is a very different state of affairs from that in Greek athletics at the time of the Roman Empire. There the competitors, especially the boxers, wrestlers and pankratiasts, were freely accused of taking bribes from an opponent to throw a match, or of collusion to produce a tame draw.[169]

Bets on chariot-racing at Rome appear to have been made informally. Petronius has a pretty picture of Trimalchio at dinner one evening making a bet with his cook on the result of the first race at the next meeting. Spectators in the Circus would make a bet with their neighbour on the next race. According to Juvenal, the two attractions which drew a young man to the races were a pretty girl at his side and the possibility of making 'rash bets' (*audax sponsio*). The phrase suggests a wager made on the spur of the moment rather than a calculated bet based on a cool study of the Racing Calendar. Ovid reveals that such bets were also made in the amphitheatre on the outcome of fights between gladiators. The Romans called a bet *pignus*, a 'pledge' of the gambler's confidence in his own opinion, or *sponsio*; the latter word is etymologically identical with 'sponsorship', but we use our word in a sporting context of a different kind of backing.[170]

Some light is thrown on the official Roman attitude to this problem by two items in the great *Digest* of Roman law compiled in the sixth century on the orders of Justinian. The first states: 'A decree of the Senate has forbidden games for money, except where a man engages in javelin-throwing or in a contest of running, jumping, wrestling or boxing held *virtutis causa*.' (This phrase, 'in pursuit of excellence', is not easy to render in terms comprehensible to a modern reader; perhaps it might be paraphrased 'as a bona fide sporting event'.) In the next section it is recorded on the authority of Marcianus that, 'By the law of Titius, Publicius and Cornelius it is also legal to make a *sponsio*; but by the other laws, if the contest is not a bona fide one [*pro virtute*], it is illegal to do so.'[171]

It would appear that Roman law would not have frowned on the half-crown between friends on their round of golf, but that it disapproved of any betting on other people's performances.

CHAPTER XIV

CHARIOT-RACING AND THE EARLY CHRISTIANS

CHRISTIANITY WAS BORN and grew up in the Roman empire. In the very earliest days of the Church belief in an imminent Second Coming was an inducement to its members to withdraw as much as possible from contemporary society. When it became clear that this was a mistaken belief the growing community of Christians was faced with the problem of coming to terms with the world around them and of trying to abolish its worst abuses and to reform other aspects of it. The Christian religion has always had to deal with the difficulty of some of the worthiest and most fervent of its adherents who believe that anything which affords pleasure must necessarily be sinful, and even today the most innocent forms of sport are liable to attack from this quarter. In the eastern part of the Roman empire, where Christianity originated, athletics were still the popular entertainment. Possibly because St Paul was a devotee they seem to have escaped condemnation by the Church; it afforded preachers of the new religion admirable illustrations for use in their sermons. The Christian life with its moral struggle was presented in terms of the athlete's, the strict ascetic discipline and training, the toughness of the contest, and the crown or palm of victory as the reward in the end. But the popular entertainments of the Western empire confronted Christians with a more serious dilemma. We are fortunate to possess one suggested solution of this problem in the *De Spectaculis* of Tertullian, written about AD 200.[172]

Tertullian was born in Carthage, grew up as a pagan and was trained as a lawyer. His conversion to Christianity came late in middle age. By this time the Church in Rome had become powerful and was increasing in numbers. Many of its members had been born of Christian parents and took their religion for granted; they were willing in many things to conform with the secular society in which they found themselves. This would not do for the ardent convert Tertullian. He denounced the Catholic Church for its readiness to compromise, and threw in his lot with the Montanists, who insisted that Christians should practise apartheid and form a close community withdrawn from contact with the outside world. The *De Spectaculis* is a contribution to this campaign. Its opening chapter makes it clear that there were plenty of Christians prepared to justify their enjoyment of public entertainments. Tertullian goes into the assault with the dialectical skill of a trained advocate and the resources of a master of language. He throws together the three major entertainments—the chariot races of the Circus, the plays of the theatre and the gladiatorial fights of the arena. The bloodthirsty horrors of the last were indefensible, and so could be used as a weapon in his attack on the other two.

As might be expected, his accusations against the Circus are based mainly on its pagan associations, and to prove these he plunges into the history of racing, including in his account some details of which we should otherwise be ignorant. Naturally he points to the procession which opened every festival, with the statues of the pagan deities carried in their cars. The 'eggs' of the lap-counter, he asserts, are in honour of Castor and Pollux, hatched from the egg of Leda. The dolphins of the other lap-counter sport in honour of Neptune. The obelisk is sacred to an Egyptian god. The horse is no doubt a useful animal, 'but when it was devoted to the purpose of racing, it ceased to be a gift of God and became an instrument of demons'. The very chariots are dedicated to heathen deities, the six-horse to Jupiter, the *quadriga* to the Sun, the *biga* to the Moon. Nevertheless Tertullian's disapproval does not prevent him from giving a very spirited description of the scene on a race day:

Then since passion [*furor*] is forbidden to us Christians, we are warned to hold aloof from every public entertainment, even from the Circus, because passion holds sway there. See how the people rush to the racecourse with frantic enthusiasm, a disorderly mob, blind and already in a fury of anxiety about their bets. The praetor seems to them to be wasting time; every eye is turned on him as he shakes in the urn the lots for the draw for stations. Thus they wait in desperate eagerness for the start. Then they go mad and roar as one man; you can tell they are mad because of their sheer silliness. The praetor drops the white cloth, and they all call out 'They're off', telling one another what everyone can see for himself. This shows how blind they are; they do not see what he has dropped. They think it is a white cloth; in fact it is a symbol of the devil thrown out of Heaven [*Pl.* 77].

When Nero threw his discarded table napkin out of the window, he can hardly have suspected that he was performing an act of deep theological significance.

So it goes on, bringing frenzy, anger and riots, and everything forbidden to the devotees of peace. Then come curses and abuse of the other side whom they have no reason to hate, and applause for their own champions who do not deserve their devotion. What are they going to achieve by all this, except escape from themselves?—but perhaps they want to escape from themselves. They are reduced to tears by another man's misfortune, they are in transports of joy through another man's success. What they long for and what they dread are equally outside themselves. Their enthusiasm for their own colour is without reason, their hatred of the other is not based on justice. . . . If any of these passions which rage in the Circus is anywhere else permissible for Christians, then it will be allowed them in the Circus; but if it is forbidden them elsewhere, then it will not be permitted them there.

(*De Spectaculis*, xvi)

A final glimpse of chariot-racing in the Roman West is afforded in the works of Cassiodorus soon after AD 500. A century earlier Rome had fallen to the barbarians, and a succession of Gothic emperors were trying to restore at least a semblance of authority. The ablest of them, Theodoric, succeeded in giving Italy some thirty years of law and order (493–526), using as his capital Ravenna, where his tomb incorporates one of the supreme architectural feats of antiquity. He was clearly a man of great practical ability, but he is said to have known little Latin—having spent ten years of his boyhood in Constantinople, he was probably more at home in Greek—and to have been unable to read or write. A Christian himself, he employed as his Latin secretary another Christian, Cassiodorus, a man of good family who had had a career in administration. Later in life Cassiodorus founded a monastery in South Italy, and for its library he edited all the documents for which he had been responsible during his political career. To make them more useful as historical sources, he obviously expanded some of them with explanatory material.

One of these documents concerns a charioteer, Thomas, who had come from the Eastern empire and whom Theodoric wished to recommend to Faustus, the Prefect of Rome, as a suitable recipient for a government grant. Cassiodorus wrote the letter of commendation; it is not difficult to distinguish those parts which embody Theodoric's direct instructions from the elucidatory passages which Cassiodorus added later:

> Since reliability and honesty are rare in public performers, it is all the more admirable when one of these men exhibits a good character; everyone likes to find something praiseworthy in an unexpected quarter. When the charioteer Thomas came recently from the East, We after due consideration bestowed on him a reasonable allowance, until We could prove his skill and character. Since he is acknowledged to have achieved the highest position in this sport,

and since of his own free will he has left his country and
chosen the seat of Our empire as his sphere of activity, We
have adjudged him worthy of a monthly grant, so that
We might leave no doubt of Our opinion of a man who
has recognized the primacy of Italy in the world.

His success on the track has made him famous, and he
has been carried to victory even more by the enthusiasm
of his admirers than by his chariots. He transferred his
services to the faction which had been going downhill
and which was the despair of its supporters; having himself been responsible for this by his efforts for their rivals
he now proceeded to gladden their hearts, sometimes
overcoming his opponents by his own skill, sometimes
defeating them by the speed of his horses. His frequent
success caused him to be accused of witchcraft; a reputation
for this appears to be a recommendation in racing circles.
For when victory cannot be attributed to the merits of a
driver, it must necessarily be put down to magic.

Thus far we can detect unmistakably the voice of Theodoric.
Now in later life Cassiodorus takes up the account:

This spectacle drives out sound morality and invites childish factiousness, it banishes honesty and it is an unfailing
source of riots. A past age included it among religious
observances; a factious later generation has turned it into
a plaything.

Cassiodorus then gives a history of chariot-racing, on
which we have already drawn for the lay-out of the Circus
and the story of Nero's napkin. To this he adds an interpretation of the symbolism of the races which shows that he had
studied Tertullian, but he goes far beyond his predecessor.
The twenty-four races of each session represent the hours of
the day, the seven laps the days of the week. The twelve
traps of the starting-gate are the signs of the Zodiac; the
turning posts are the tropics, and the three small obelisks on
each post represent the *decani*, the three important points in

each zodiacal month. The Egyptian obelisks on the *spina* are the Sun and Moon, as 'Chaldaean signs' on them betray. The *spina* itself is the symbol of the sufferings of the defeated. A *biga* represents the Moon, a *quadriga* the Sun, and they race round the Circus as the heavenly bodies race round the heavens, with the *metae* also representing the turning points of east and west. The water-channel down the *spina* symbolizes the sea, into which the dolphins of the lap-counter plunge. The 'eggs' of the other lap-counter appropriately stand for the fluttering birds hatched from them, symbols of the inconstant characters of racegoers. The ridden horses used by the Circus stewards who come out to announce that a race is about to be started symbolize Lucifer, the morning star which heralds the day.

Then Cassiodorus reiterates his disapproval:

> Most remarkable of all, in these beyond all other spectacles men's minds are carried away by excitement without any regard for dignity and sobriety. Green takes the lead, and half the crowd is plunged into gloom. Blue passes him, and a great mass of citizens suffer the torments of the damned. They cheer wildly with no useful result; they suffer nothing but are cut to the heart; they argue as if the state were in danger. No wonder that such a departure from sensible behaviour should be attributed to a superstitious origin.

Now the voice of Theodoric once again takes up the tale:

> We are compelled to support this institution by the necessity of humouring the people, who are mad on it. They love these entertainments and reject serious pursuits. Few men are led by cool reason, few care for any worthwhile occupation. The mob is drawn to whatever it has found by experience to dispel care. It thinks that anything which gives pleasure ought to be applied to increasing the happiness of the times. So We must be generous to racing, and must not always rule Our gifts by Our judgment. It

is prudent sometimes to relax from severity [*desipere*] so that in this way We can keep control of popular entertainment.[173]

(*Variae* III, 51)

In the opening words of this letter, Cassiodorus refers to charioteers as *histriones*; the word means 'stage actors'. He is thus among the first to recognize that these professional heroes of the stadium and Circus were not 'sportsmen' in any sense of that term, but public entertainers, a truth which the modern world is slow to acknowledge.

The name of the charioteer on whose behalf the letter was written is noteworthy. 'Thomas' is neither Greek nor Latin but Hebrew. He was presumably either a Jew or a Christian of some other nationality who had been named after the saint.

One detail in this passage is not recorded elsewhere—the appearance of the ridden horses to inform spectators that the race would soon start. The term used (*desultorius equus*) meant originally a horse used in those events in which the rider had to dismount and remount in the course of the race, a horse, in fact, like the rosin-backs of the modern circus. Such races are known to have been promoted by Julius Caesar in Rome, and we have seen examples of similar events in Greece also. The use of the word here suggests that the event had become obsolete and that the term was retained for utility horses kept at the Circus for miscellaneous purposes. Some of the mosaics and reliefs which depict the Circus show ridden horses galloping alongside the chariots during a race. The function of the rider was presumably to shout information to the charioteer about what was happening behind him. He may have been the *hortator* who is mentioned in an inscription among the employees of a racing stable. And these horsemen may well have been identical with Cassiodorus' riders whose appearance heralded the races.[174] By a curious coincidence there is a parallel to these horses in our own world. The nearest equivalent today to Roman chariot-racing is afforded by the Chuck Waggon races of the Canadian Rodeo. The waggons are drawn by four horses harnessed in the modern manner with two leaders and two wheelers, and each waggon is accompanied by outriders. Waggon and outriders form a team, and the first waggon to cross the finishing line is not necessarily the winner if its outriders have fallen too far behind. But there is no evidence that the ridden horses of the Roman Circuses performed any such function.

It is probably a mere accident that while Cassiodorus is obviously anxious to leave no weapon unused in his attempt to discredit chariot-racing, he does not follow Tertullian in mentioning betting as an undesirable element in the Circus. He does, however, call attention to one vice of charioteers not found in Tertullian when he says that Thomas was accused of owing his victories to black magic. There is a hint that this was why he found it convenient to leave the Eastern empire for the West.

Many players of games are mildly superstitious and are inclined to link their prospect of success with an article of clothing or a mascot, or with putting on the left boot before the right. All this is innocent and harmless enough; in so far as it has any conscious purpose, it is the positive one of trying to secure victory for the one who uses it. Roman drivers, on the other hand, invoked the powers of darkness to send disaster on their rivals. So prevalent was the practice in the racing world that charioteers were generally believed to have particular expertness in this field. Ammianus Marcellinus records that a charioteer named Hilarinus sent his young son to a friend to be taught 'certain illegal secret practices, so that without anyone knowing about it he might be helped by these mysterious aids'. The same historian also tells us of a debtor who, wishing to free himself of his creditors, had recourse to 'a charioteer who would risk any illegal practice'. As these passages show, the law attempted to suppress such activities. In the section of the *Codex* dealing with the matter it is specially laid down that charioteers bringing vexatious accusations on this score against their rivals will be subject to heavy penalties. Ammianus relates a case in which some men of senatorial rank (*clarissimi*) were accused of encouraging a charioteer, Auchenius, in this poisonous art (*veneficium*). By adding that the judge who acquitted them was a close friend of the Emperor Maximinus, the historian seems to be hinting that such practices extended to the highest in the state.[175]

Spells were believed to be most effective if they were committed to writing, preferably on the saturnine metal lead, and for this reason a few of them have survived. One was found at Hadrumetum in North Africa; it is in execrable Latin:

> I adjure you, demon whoever you are, and I demand of you from this hour, from this day, from this moment [*ex anc ora ex anc die ex oc momento*] that you torture and kill the horses of the Greens and Whites, and that you kill in a crash their drivers Clarus, Felix, Primulus and Romanus, and leave [*lerinquas*] not a breath in their bodies.

The combination of Greens and Whites here is evidence that these two factions were teamed together against the Blues and Reds.[176]

Another driver, who wrote his spell in Greek, was far more explicit about the powers he was addressing. The first fifty lines of his document are devoted to a list of divinities with their attributes. Among them are Neicharoplex, god of all places below the earth, Lailam, god of winds, Arourobaarzagran, god of necessity, Blableisphtheibal, first-born of Earth, Hermes, Semeseilam, who brings light and dark to the world, Souarminoouth, son of Solomon, and Thesthenothril, the god who bestows on mortals the movement of their joints. It is surprising to find Hermes in this company; appropriately he is invoked in virtue of his function of conducting the souls of the dead to the underworld. Then the writer goes on:

> Help me in the Circus on 8 November. Bind every limb, every sinew, the shoulders, the ankles and the elbows of

Olympus, Olympianus, Scortius and Juvencus, the charioteers of the Red. Torment their minds, their intelligence and their senses so that they may not know what they are doing, and knock out their eyes so that they may not see where they are going—neither they nor the horses they are going to drive.

To make sure that the curse shall not miss its mark, he goes on to list these horses; from this list we know that a horse Maurus and his sire Lampadius were both expected to run at the meeting on 8 November.[177]

An even more urgent spell, also in Greek, was found near Carthage. It is directed chiefly against a driver of the Blues, Victoricus, 'son of Earth, the mother of every living thing'— an unusual phrase for casting doubts on Victoricus' legitimacy. This curse was obviously accompanied by the sacrifice of a cock:

As this cock is bound, legs, wings and head, so bind the legs, hands, head and heart of Victoricus the charioteer of the Blues tomorrow, and the horses he is going to drive, Secundinus, Juvenis, Advocatus, Bubalus and Laureatus, Pompeianus, Baeanus, Victor and Eximius.

The conclusion of the spell shows that its writer knew something of the Hebrew scriptures:

I adjure you by the God of Heaven above, who sits on the Cherubim, who divided the land and set apart the sea, by Iao, Abriao, Arbathiao Adonai Sabao, that you bind Victoricus and Dominator, so that they may not come to victory tomorrow. Now. Now. Quick. Quick [ἤδη. ἤδη. ταχύ. ταχύ.].[178]

(A year or two ago we might well have supposed that such use of magic was a feature of ancient sport which had not survived to our own day. Recently, however, it has been revealed in our newspapers that witchcraft is as rife in African football as ever it was in Roman racing. 'Of the 200 clubs in Kenya, about 95 per cent hire witchdoctors to improve their chances.' 'Club wizards have various ways of spooking opposition teams. Herbal mixtures and tree sap are sometimes spread on the ball or left in the opponents' dressing rooms.' 'Clubs usually refuse to announce the names of their players in advance for fear that they might be bewitched.' 'Telling a club whether it is going to win its next match and, if necessary, casting a few spells on their opponents, pays Mr Abubakar well. . . . He explained that he invoked Allah and the Angels to help him win a match. . . . The Angels, he said, sometimes demanded a price for their services, and it would be necessary to sacrifice a goat or a chicken.' Here is a world in which a Roman charioteer would have felt completely at home.)[179]

These attempts to harness the powers of darkness might suggest that there was some justification for the Christian objections to racing. Certainly the objections had little or no effect. Christians, it is true, were largely responsible for ending the gladiatorial exhibitions of the arena, but the collapse of chariot-racing in the West was probably not due to them, as its history in the Christian Byzantine Empire of the East makes clear.

CHAPTER XV

CHARIOT-RACING IN THE BYZANTINE EMPIRE

WHEN CASSIODORUS WROTE HIS LETTER for Theodoric, Rome had long ceased to be the most important centre of chariot-racing. Two centuries earlier, soon after the division of the empire between the Latin West and the Greek Eastern halves, Constantine had refounded Byzantium as the capital of the East and had given it his own name, Constantinopolis. He had embraced Christianity in the later part of his life, and from its inception the Eastern Empire was fundamentally Christian. Among the splendid buildings which rose in the new city was a great Circus of Roman pattern. Byzantine historians, who wrote in Greek, generally called it by the Greek name, hippodrome, though the Latin word Circus, transliterated into Greek, is sometimes found. As we have seen, this was by no means the first Roman Circus in the Greek world, but it became by far the most famous. Today its site is a great open space, its surface some ten feet above the level of the ancient track. Three objects still stand where they were erected on the *spina* of the old course. Two of them are obelisks, in respectful imitation of the similar pair in the Circus Maximus in Rome. One of them is genuinely Egyptian; the other is an ersatz affair, built up of blocks and coated with stucco. The reliefs on the base of the former obelisk present us with a lively picture of the royal box on the course, with the guards and courtiers surrounding it, and the empress waiting with the crown in her hand to bestow on the winner (*Pl.* 82). The third object on the *spina* is of great historical interest. It is the lower part of the serpent column dedicated at Delphi in 478 BC to commemorate the victory over the Persians in the battle of Plataea; it was inscribed with the names of the cities which contributed contingents to the Greek army that day, and traces of the names can still be detected. Probably at the same time as he brought this trophy to adorn his hippodrome at Byzantium, Constantine also brought the monument with the four bronze horses which now stand on the façade of the cathedral of San Marco in Venice (*Pl.* 73).

The lay-out of the hippodrome with its starting-gate on the Roman model was not the only feature of Western racing introduced into Constantinople at this time. The factions came too, and the supporters of Blue and Green became even more fanatical in their partisanship than in Rome itself. Almost all the evidence suggests that these were the only two factions on the track at Constantinople, but one epigram in the *Greek Anthology* describes a famous Byzantine charioteer, Constantinus, as belonging to the Whites, and two others call Julianus a driver of the Reds. These three poems belong to a group describing the paintings on the ceiling of the imperial box in the hippodrome. The artist had depicted four chariots and probably for aesthetic reasons had shown the drivers in tunics of different colours. It may well be that the practice still continued on the course of putting the second charioteer of the Greens into a white tunic and the second string of the Blues into red. This would obviously have helped spectators to identify the chariots during a race, and in this way the memory of the old White and Red stables would have been kept alive. The ceiling has long since vanished, and we do not know whether it was the artist or the writer of the epigrams who ascribed to the drivers portrayed on it the names of the four best-known charioteers of the age. In the poems, Porphyrius is named as the driver of the Blue chariot, Faustinus of the Green. The honour of being the Green charioteer in the pictures was perhaps given to Faustinus on grounds of seniority; he was Constantinus' father, and so Constantinus was depicted as his second string. (We know from other sources that during his career Constantinus drove for both Blues and Greens). The name of the

last of the great quartet, Julianus, was ascribed to the charioteer pictured in red.[180]

So far as our evidence goes, there was no important difference between Byzantine and Roman racing. But for Constantinople there is none of the detailed statistical information
provided by the Roman inscriptions. In their place we have a
number of short laudatory epigrams in verse on Byzantine
charioteers. A few of these are the epitaphs inscribed on the
bases of their statues which were erected in the hippodrome
itself. The remainder are mostly the handling or re-hand-
ling of the same material by bookish versifiers, and all are of
doubtful value as evidence. Six charioteers are celebrated in
this way. Of one of them, Anastasius, the single epigram
devoted to him tells us nothing. Another, Julianus of Tyre,
retired in old age to the regret of all, and his statue was
erected by Emperor and Senate. Faustinus too was still
driving when an old man, and his son, also Faustinus but
better known as Constantinus, drove for fifty years. In the
long history of sport there appear from time to time professionals who command affection and respect for their
character as much as admiration for their skill. Constantinus
seems to have been one of these. The sixteen surviving
epigrams devoted to him insist on the gap which his death
has left. 'He was an ornament to the hippodrome, a legend
for posterity.' 'Since his death there has been no joy in racing,
no friendly argument about it in the streets.' 'Come back;
the other charioteers miss your advice and are like orphaned
children.' All very platitudinous, no doubt, but it is significant that these clichés are not applied to the other drivers.[181]

From five epigrams on Uranius we learn that he was
nicknamed Pelops, that one of his statues stood near those of
the Faustini, father and son, that he drove for twenty years
for the Blues and then retired but was tempted back to the
track by the emperor and thereafter drove for the Greens.
The trick of premature retirement and return has found
many imitators; farewell performances have always been
profitable to public entertainers. When the return could be

attributed to the emperor's intervention, the publicity value was enormous. Both devices appear in the career of the most famous of these charioteers, Porphyrius, who is the subject of thirty-four surviving poems. He was an African and started his driving with the Blues; he claimed that he was assigned to that faction by the emperor. His career on the track was interrupted by a period of military service, during which he fought with distinction in a sea battle. Apparently this was in a civil war, in which the emperor was supported by the Greens while the Blues favoured the rebels; thus far had faction spread beyond the partisanship of the racecourse. When the revolt had been put down Porphyrius returned to the hippodrome, but the political animosities of the war remained, and it was found expedient for obvious reasons to transfer him to the Greens; the emperor is said to have played a part in arranging this. At the same time, Porphyrius changed his name and was thereafter known as Calliopas. His success for his new faction made the Blues repent that they had let him go, and it would seem that at the end of his career he was once more a Blue driver.[182]

One feature of racing at Constantinople appears in these epigrams about Constantinus and Porphyrius for which there is no evidence at Rome—the challenge to a defeated opponent to exchange horses and re-run the race. A repetition of the victory was conclusive proof that success was due to the skill of the driver and not to the quality of his horses. One poem about Porphyrius says that he constantly exchanged horses with a 'friendly' driver (ὁμόφρων) and won again; this presumably means a driver of the same faction, possibly his second string in a team race. Such a success would not have been very remarkable. A stable's second driver no doubt 'knew his place' when he was in a race with his faction's leading star. But another epigram clearly states that he exchanged horses with his rivals and pleased Blues and Greens at the same time. He would still drive in his Blue tunic in the second race, but he would be driving a Green team, and so both stables could claim a share in his win. An epigram on Constantinus informs us that on one occasion he won 25 races in the morning and then in the afternoon with exchanged teams won 21 of the corresponding events. Apart from the evidence of skill with the reins, to drive fifty races in a day represents an extraordinary feat of physical endurance.

The building of the hippodrome at Constantinople and the introduction of chariot-racing on the Roman pattern appears to have started a revival of interest in the sport over most of the Greek world. We have noted how in the second and first centuries B C equestrian events at Olympia and other great centres declined in importance. The revival did not spread quickly, and it does not seem to have affected the Greek mainland at all. As might be expected, its chief centres were the great cities of the eastern Mediterranean, Alexandria and Antioch. But the mass of papyri from Oxyrhyncus in Egypt affords evidence that even so small a city had its hippodrome, around which there was a good deal of racing activity. Surviving documents deal with the management of racing stables, and there is a bill for the purchase of horse embrocation (μάλαγμα) for one of the stables. Most interesting of all is the programme of a day's racing in the hippodrome, diversified by other attractions. There are six chariot races. In the first interval comes the procession—which at Rome used to precede the first race—and a performance by singing tightrope dancers (καλοπαῖκται βοκάλιοι). In the second interval the dancers gave another show. After the third race there was a deer-hunt (δόρκος καὶ κύνες); after the fourth, actors or clowns (μῖμοι) had their turn. The interval before the last race was occupied by athletic events (ξυστός). This programme belongs to the sixth century A D.[183]

Another glimpse of chariot-racing in the Byzantine empire outside Constantinople is afforded by an incident in the Circus of Alexandria in the sixth century. A charioteer, whose mother's name was Mary, was thrown from his chariot during a race, but managed to remount, pass the driver who had fouled him and win. The crowd roared,

'The son of Mary has fallen and risen again and is victorious'. While they were still shouting, news was brought to the Circus that the Christian leader Theophilus had made himself master of the temple of Serapis in the city and overthrown the idol. The crowd instantly perceived the symbolic significance of the incident on the track.[184]

We have seen how the frenzied partisanship of Blues and Greens extended outside the hippodrome into the political life of the day. Even more remarkably it intruded into the contemporary theological controversies, which indeed were closely connected with politics, as in the sixteenth and seventeenth centuries of our own history. The great point at issue at that time was the exact nature of the divinity of Christ. The Monophysites believed that He had only one composite nature, and it was assumed that those who held this view would be supporters of the Green faction, while the Blues commanded the allegiance of all who adhered to the orthodox Trinitarian doctrine. This would be hardly credible to us, if we were not faced today with an exactly similar situation in football circles in Glasgow, where the two leading teams have come to symbolize rival theories of church government, the Celtic club carrying the hopes of those who accept Papal authority, while Rangers command the support of those who prefer the rule of presbyters. This confusion of loyalties makes it difficult, when rioting breaks out among spectators whether in ancient or modern times, to determine how far it is due to quarrels about the game or sport involved and how far it arises from quite different motives. Up to the present the modern world has not produced a parallel to the worst of these riots in Byzantine times. In January 512 rioting broke out in the hippodrome between Blues and Greens. It lasted for several days and ended in a massacre. The lowest contemporary estimate of casualties put the figure at 30,000 dead. Perhaps this carries a warning for our own day.[185]

ATHLETES AND
THEIR DREAMS

DREAMS AND THEIR INTERPRETATION have always exercised a powerful fascination on the human mind, from the time of Joseph and his Pharaoh to Freud. Homer and Herodotus bear witness to the importance attached to them from the earliest days of the Greek world. In the Hellenistic age the subject did not escape the attention of the encyclopaedists whose work is among the most characteristic features of the literature of the period, and we are fortunate to possess a considerable treatise on it, the *Onirocriticon* of Artemidorus of Daldis. Little is known of its author except that he lived in Asia Minor in the second century of the Christian era. His method is one used centuries earlier by the first Greek medical writers and adopted by Aristotle and his school, the collection and classification of masses of factual data as a necessary preliminary to forming explanatory hypotheses about them. Artemidorus' interpretations follow familiar lines. To some dreams the sequel in real life is a straight parallel; others 'go by opposites'. Sometimes he reveals his method by breaking away from his generalized classification and relating a specific dream of some individual on a particular occasion; these are among the most interesting parts of the work.

Apart from its importance in the history of the interpretation of dreams, the *Onirocriticon* is of great value for the accidental light which it throws on the everyday life of the Greek world under the Roman Empire. Then, as now, sport was part of this everyday life, and the student of Greek athletics will from time to time come across something in the pages of Artemidorus to add to the scanty literary evidence on the subject which has survived from antiquity. The relevant parts of the work fall readily into two divisions. Sometimes an athlete is the dreamer, and a dream about matters quite unconnected with athletics has for him a significance different from its meaning for other mortals. At other times athletics forms the subject matter of a dream, the dreamer not being necessarily a sportsman.

A typical example of the first class gives us the varied interpretations which Artemidorus places on a dream that one has lost the sight of both eyes. This may prognosticate the loss of children, brothers or parents: of children, because the eyes are beloved objects and the guides of the body, as children are to their parents in old age; of brothers, because the eyes are twin brothers; of parents, because our eyes are the cause of our seeing the light of day, as our parents are. But it is good for a prisoner to dream of blindness, or for anyone forcibly restrained or oppressed by poverty; for the former will no longer see the miseries which surround him, while the latter will have helpers to assist him, since a blind man is surrounded by plenty of helpers and is relieved of all distress. The dream is a warning not to travel and foretells that one who is abroad will not return home, for one cannot see either the foreign country or one's homeland without eyes. If anyone who is looking for a lost object has this dream he will not find it; if he is pursuing a runaway slave he will not recover him. But it is the best of dreams for poets, since when they are composing they need peace and quiet, and this is best secured if they are not distracted by shapes or colours. (The tradition that Homer was blind clearly operates here.) Then Artemidorus adds: 'For athletes who practise the heavy events (boxing, wrestling and the pankration) this dream foretells defeat, but to runners it promises victory. I know a sprinter who was about to compete in the Imperial Games celebrated in Italy for the first time by the Emperor Antoninus in honour of his father Hadrian. He dreamed that he had become blind, and then he won his race; the leader in a race, like a blind man, cannot see his rivals.'

In the same way, to dream that one is a baby is good for a poor man, since he will have someone to look after him, or for a slave, because it foretells that he will have a kind master who will forgive his mistakes; but it is unlucky for athletes, since babies can neither walk nor run nor injure anyone; this last is an obvious reference to boxers and pankratiasts. Should an athlete, a gladiator or anyone in training dream that he has milk in his breasts it foretells illness, for bodies which produce milk are female and therefore weak. For the same reason it is unlucky for an athlete to dream that he has been changed into a woman. A pankratiast dreamed shortly before a meeting that he had given birth to a baby and that it had been put out to nurse. He was hopelessly defeated in his fight, and his career was finished; he had dreamed that he performed the function not of a man but of a woman.[186]

To dream that one has a large head is good for a wealthy man who has never held office, for a poor man, a money-lender or a club secretary. The prognostication of good fortune depends on the fact that the Greek word for 'head' (κεφαλή) also meant 'sum total' of money. For a wealthy magistrate, a demagogue or a politician the same dream portends personal injury from mob violence and a head swollen by bruises; for an athlete it foretells success—his head will be made larger by the victor's crown.[187]

It is lucky for an athlete to dream that he has two or three heads; it shows the number of crowns he will win. To a poor man the dream foretells wealth, a wife and fine sons. To a wealthy man it signifies that his family will try to oust him; if the first head sticks out, they will fail; if the later heads out-top the first, it means danger and death for him. It is also a good omen for an athlete to dream that he has the head of a lion, a leopard or an elephant, since the dreamer, if he takes on what is beyond his normal powers, will succeed.[188]

To dream that one sees one's feet burning is bad for every-one alike. It signifies the loss and destruction of all one's property, especially children and slaves. The only people to whom this dream brings good are runners, when they see it just before competing; they will run like a cat on hot bricks.[189]

Another example which has a completely different significance for athletes from that which it has for all others is a dream that one has been turned into bronze. To everyone else it foretells death, but for an athlete it means victory, because victors were allowed to erect bronze statues of themselves.[190]

In the days of Greek independence, young men were subject to a year's pre-military training before they entered on their service in the army; during this year they were called ephebes. When Greece became part of the Roman empire, the institution of the *ephebeia* was continued as a useful climax to a young man's education. Many cities appointed special magistrates, called ephebarchs, to supervise these Youth Clubs, whose activities were largely sporting. To dream that one is an ephebe, according to Artemidorus, has many different meanings for different classes of people. For an old man or one past his prime it foretells death, for a lawbreaker it prognosticates conviction in the courts; but for an honest man it is good, 'for the ephebe is practically the epitome of an honest and healthy life'. If a young athlete has this dream before the entries for a meeting are scrutinized it is unlucky, since it means that his entry will be rejected on the ground of his age.[191]

It was the Greek custom to grant a winning athlete a civic reception, during which he rode into his city in a coach. It was therefore lucky for athletes in general to dream of riding in a chariot, but not for runners; to them the dream indicated that their own feet were inadequate, since they had to rely on horses.[192]

As thunder and lightning were believed to come straight from the gods it is not surprising that to dream of them had important and widely different significance. To an unmarried man it foretold marriage, to a married man separation. A slave distrusted by his master would be freed, a trusted and honoured slave would lose his master's favour. A poor man would become rich, a rich man poor. 'To dream of being struck by lightning brings fame to athletes, to lovers of literature and to those who wish to find themselves in the public eye.'[193]

Sometimes Artemidorus throws light on an allusion in Greek literature by referring to a long-forgotten custom. In the *Thesmophoriazusae* of Aristophanes, a character says, 'We take the cake for cunning'. Artemidorus tells us, 'It is lucky to dream of a cake, provided it is not a cheese-cake; cheese-cakes signify deceit and treachery. Sesame cakes and biscuits are lucky for everyone, *for cakes were formerly given as prizes in the Games.*'[194]

To dream of eating cooked meat is generally good, especially if it is roast pork. 'But to dream of eating raw flesh is by no means good; it foretells the loss of a valuable posses-sion. . . . Yet according to my own observation, the greatest and most outstanding good luck is to dream of eating human flesh, provided that it is not the flesh of a friend or relative. In that case, the dreamer will bury the one whose flesh he has dreamed he was eating. Most desperate of all is for a man to dream that he is eating the flesh of his own son; for that portends the immediate death of his son, unless he thinks he is eating those parts of the body by which the son earns his living—the feet of a runner, for instance, the hands of a craftsman or the shoulders of a wrestler; then this dream foretells prosperity for the son, and some advantage to the father from his son. For in a way, when men gain advantage from one another, they feed on one another'. This is good evidence of the extent to which professional athletics afforded a satisfactory livelihood in Artemidorus' time.[195]

A dream that one is crowned with a garland is interpreted according to the plant or flower of which the wreath is woven. Narcissus, violets, crocuses, roses, lilies, amaranth, thyme and melilot each have different significance. A crown of wild celery (*selinus*) brings death to the sick and those suffering from dropsy, because it is a plant of cold and damp places, and because this crown belongs to funeral games—it was the trophy at the Nemean meeting. It is good for athletes, but harmful to others. Palm and olive help athletes and the poor, bringing prosperity to the latter, fame to the former. The olive tree in dreams had an obvious connection with athletes, who always anointed themselves with olive oil before competing. The white poplar, like other trees which bore no useful fruit, was generally unlucky in dreams; it was advantageous only to athletes, because it was sacred to Heracles, who was a great patron of athletes and bore the epithet Victorious. For the same reason it was lucky for an athlete to dream of Heracles or of a statue of him. The other divine figure whose statue often stood in a gymnasium was Hermes, who also, if seen in dreams, brought good fortune to athletes and trainers; he did the same for lawyers, inspectors of weights and measures, and all engaged in trade.[196]

To dream of death is naturally significant. Rather surprisingly, Artemidorus links death with marriage, 'for each is a goal or end for a man' (τέλος; the Greek word has the same ambiguity as the English 'end'). The externals of each are the same—a procession of friends, wreaths, scents, myrrh, and the writing of documents, wills or marriage settlements. So to dream of death prognosticates marriage, while for a sick man to dream of marriage foretells his death. If a man dreams of death when he is at home, he will go abroad; if he has a similar dream abroad, he will return home, 'for a dead man is laid in earth, which is the common fatherland of us all'. A dream of death brings an athlete victory in the 'Sacred' Games, since the dead, like victors in races, 'have reached the end' (τέλειοι).[197]

Sometimes the significance of a dream is obvious. To see a lion fawning and approaching without attacking is good and brings advantage to a soldier from the emperor, to an athlete from his physical fitness, to a slave from his master, to a citizen from the magistrates. To dream that one is making human figurines in clay is good for athletic trainers and instructors, for in a sense they mould men, the former by 'giving them rhythm', the latter by improving them. 'A runner on the point of competing in a sacred festival dreamed that he found a watercourse full of mud and filth, and that he took a broom and cleaned and flushed it with a strong flow of water, making it free-running and clear. Next day, although his race was imminent, he took a stomach-pump to clear himself of all impurities; in the race he proved so nimble and light-footed that he won.'[198]

When Artemidorus comes to the section of his work dealing with dreams about athletics, he first interprets dreams about the pentathlon, the composite event consisting of the long jump, discus, javelin, running and wrestling. Of this he says: 'I have observed that to dream that one is taking part in the pentathlon invariably indicates firstly a trip abroad or movement from place to place, because of the race; next it signifies loss or unusual expenditure or unexpended disbursements, because of the discus, which is made of bronze and thrown from the hand. Often it portends suffering and the anxieties arising from it, because of the leaps in the long jump; for we say, when distress befalls a man suddenly, that "It comes leaping at him". Again, the pentathlon foretells riots and arguments because of the javelins with their whirring and speedy flight which resembles forceful language. Because of the wrestling, the pentathlon indicates for wealthy men a dispute about land, while to the poor it foretells sickness. A later passage will give the reason for this.'[199]

There are two points of interest in this passage for students of the techniques of Greek athletics. The plural in the phrase 'the leaps in the jump' (τὰ πηδήματα τὰ ἐν τῇ ἁλτηρίᾳ) strongly supports the view that the Greek jump was a double or triple long jump. The interpretation of the dream of javelin-throwing bears witness to the noisy buzz of the weapon in flight, caused by the strong rotation imparted to it by the thong; every cricketer has heard the same sound coming less loudly from a well spun cricket ball.

About running he writes: 'To dream that one is running a stade race (ἁπλοῦν δρόμον) is good for everyone except those who are ill, at any rate when they dream that they win.

For they come to the end of whatever they are attempting—
for this reason slaves are freed as a result of dreaming this—
whereas the sick come to the end of their lives and die. To
dream that one is running the quarter-mile (*diaulos*) foretells
the same result as the stade, but after a delay; the long-
distance race (*dolichos*) after many delays. An exception to
this is that for a woman to dream of the *dolichos* prognosticates that she will lead the life of a prostitute'. Technically the
most interesting feature of this passage is the use of the phrase
'single course' (ἁπλοῦς δρόμος) for the stade.[200]

Artemidorus' promise to deal further with wrestling is
redeemed thus: 'To dream that one is wrestling with a relative or friend means that one will quarrel with him and try
to outdo him. Where the quarrel already exists, whichever
party wins in the dream-wrestling will also prevail in real
life, unless the argument is about the possession of land. In
such disputes it is better to dream that one is thrown oneself,
unless the wrestler who throws his opponent finishes under-
neath; for the piece of land in dispute will fall to the one who
is nearest the ground. I know of one man who dreamed he
was wrestling, and, "making one from two fingers" as the
saying goes, threw his opponent. This man won a lawsuit by
laying his hands on documents written by his adversary.' The
phrase 'making one from two fingers (*or* toes)' (ἐκ δακτύλων
δύο περὶ μίαν ποιήσας) is otherwise unknown, and its force
cannot be determined; it is probably a slang term for some
wrestling trick.[201]

'To dream that one is wrestling with strangers portends
danger from illness, since the disease wants to do to the sick
man just what a wrestler tries to do to his opponent—to
"give him to the earth". So if he dreams he is thrown this
means death; if he dreams that he throws his opponent it
means recovery. For a man to dream that he is wrestling with
a boy is by no means good. If he dreams that he throws the
boy he will bury a member of his family; if he is thrown by
the boy, in addition to the waste of effort he brings on himself
ridicule and sickness—ridicule for obvious reasons, sickness

because he is overcome by a weaker body. But for a boy to dream that he defeats a man is good, for he will gain advantages beyond his hopes. However this is not so if the boy is an athlete, since in that case it indicates that his entries for boys' events will be rejected on account of his age. To dream that one is wrestling with a dead man foretells illness or a quarrel with the descendants or heirs of the dead man. In either case it is better to dream that one wins the bout.'[202]

Boxing is dealt with summarily: 'To dream that one is boxing is harmful to everyone, since in addition to the disgrace it portends injury; for the face is made ugly and there is a loss of blood, which is a symbol for money. This dream is good only for those who earn their living by blood—I mean doctors, sacrificers and butchers'. This is interesting evidence of the social position of boxers in Artemidorus' day. Wrestling was still a sport for schoolboys and for ordinary men in their leisure; boxing was confined to specialist athletes. Already the Greek word for 'boxer' ($\pi \acute{u} \kappa \tau \eta \varsigma$) and its derivatives were being used of gladiators.[203]

Even more important evidence for the place of athletes in the social scene comes in the interpretation of dreams of the pankration: 'The pankration in dreams has the same significance as boxing, but it portends deeper quarrels, because of the contention involved; in both it is better to dream that one wins. If a slave dreams that he competes in a 'sacred' festival and wins and is crowned, he will be publicly proclaimed a free man, since victory and crowning in a sacred festival are restricted to free men. It is important to remember that this is true only of a sacred meeting, for the rule does not apply elsewhere. To other men, to dream that one emerges from an athletic meeting with a crown signifies the end of something, whether good or bad.' In the second century A D there were two kinds of athletic meetings, 'sacred' games in which the prizes were crowns of olive, laurel, oak or some other plant, and 'thematic' games in which money prizes were given. From the competitors' point of view the difference between them was not great, since the winner of a crown was given a large monetary reward by his own city. But this passage of Artemidorus implies that there was a more fundamental distinction between them, that crown games were confined to free men, while thematic meetings were open to men of slave origin. The situation thus revealed is similar to that existing until recently in some fields of modern sport, in which there were two classes, amateur and professional, both making money from a game, but distinguished by considerations of social origin. Another passage of Artemidorus throws light on the social class from which the 'amateurs' of his day were drawn: 'If a woman dreams that she has given birth to an eagle, she will have a son; if he is a poor man, he will be a soldier; *if of the middle class [μέτριος], he will be a famous athlete*; if wealthy, a ruler or even a king.'[204]

Evidence of the relative numbers of sacred and thematic meetings is afforded by an inscription, also of the second century, recording the victories of a wrestler, Marcus Aurelius Hermagoras, who figured in a drawn final at the Olympic Games. He claimed 29 victories in sacred meetings, 127 in thematic. This gives roughly a proportion of four to one in favour of money-prize games, but we have to remember that an athlete of the status of an Olympic finalist would not condescend to appear at minor meetings; the preponderance of thematic games was therefore in all probability much higher.[205]

Artemidorus' interpretation of the race in armour is cursory, but it includes one interesting detail: 'To dream of the so-called armed race always portends delay to everyone, since this is the last event and open to all (τελευταῖον καὶ ἐπὶ πᾶσι). For the same reason the dream foretells death to the sick.'[206]

Already in the seventh century BC the Olympic Games included events for boys as well as men, and in the course of centuries there was an increasing tendency to separate boys and youths into classes by age. At many meetings in Artemidorus' time there were as many as five age-groups in each event. In the absence of birth certificates and demographic records, the scrutiny of entries for each group must have been difficult. So it is not surprising that the scrutiny figures both as the subject of dreams and as an element in their interpretation. Thus: 'To dream that one's entry is accepted for an age-group is good for everyone. Among athletes it is very significant for boys, since acceptance is a matter of age; for men it means nothing, as age-groups do not apply to them. To dream that one's entry has been rejected is bad for everyone and fatal to the sick. I know of one man who dreamed that his entry for the Olympic Games was rejected; he was condemned to the mines, because he was not allowed to take part in the sacred meeting.'[207]

Another anecdote in a later book gives further evidence of the anxieties of young athletes on this score. 'A boy wrestler who was worried about his eligibility for boys' events dreamed that at one meeting the umpire was Asklepios. In his dream the boy marched with the other boys in the preliminary parade [παροδεύων ἐν παρεξαγωγῇ], but then was excluded from the competition by the god. In fact he died before the Games. For the god excluded him, not from the Games, but from life, of which he is more properly considered the umpire.'[208]

Games outside the standard athletic programme sometimes appeared in dreams. Of most of these we know nothing except the name; the details have been completely lost. 'To dream that one is bowling a hoop means that the dreamer will encounter hardships from which he will eventually derive benefit. A hand-ball or large ball portends endless quarrels, and often love for a prostitute; both kinds of ball symbolize a prostitute, because they are always on the move and are passed from man to man. Jumping-weights and exercises with them foretell failure and hard work in the immediate future, followed later by leisure and success, since such exercises are simply preparation of the hands and arms. "Sacks" [θύλακοι], "wedges" [σφῆνες], leap-frog [ὑπεράλματα] and other such children's games prognosticate quarrels.' In a later book Artemidorus gives us an instance of

a dream about ball-play: 'A slave dreamed that he was playing a ball game with Zeus. Afterwards he had an argument
with his master and incurred his displeasure by using too free
language. Zeus signified the master, while the ball game was
a symbol of discussion and argument on equal terms, because
ball-players are trying to outdo one another, and every time
the ball comes to them, they hit it back.'[209]

After exercise athletes always took a bath, but the practice
was, of course, not confined to them, and in the Roman
empire the great public bath-houses became important social
centres. Artemidorus deals with dreams about them at some
length: 'Long ago, men thought that to dream of taking a
bath was unlucky, for they knew nothing of bath-houses,
since they used to wash in "tubs" [ἀσαμίνθοις] as we call
them. Later generations, even after bath-houses had come
into existence, thought that bathing was bad and that to
dream of a bath-house, even if one did not take a bath there
in the dream, was unlucky. They thought that the bath-house
indicated a riot, because of the uproar always coming from
it, and loss because of the loss of sweat there, also agony and
terror of soul, because in the bath-house a man changes colour
and exposes his body naked. Some of the present generation
follow the old opinion and come to the same conclusion, but
they are wrong and they disregard experience. Long ago it
was natural to think bath-houses evil, for men rarely took
baths and they did not have these great buildings; they took
a bath only to celebrate victory in war or after coming to the
end of some exhausting effort, and so the bath-house and the
bath itself reminded them of hard labour or of war. Nowadays some men will not eat unless they have had a bath, while
others take one even in the middle of a meal. Then too they
take a bath if they are going out to dinner. Today the bath is
simply the path to luxury. So to dream that one is having a
bath in a fine, well-lighted and airy bath-house is good and
foretells fortune and success to the healthy and recovery to
the sick, since it is healthy men who take a bath without
being compelled to do so. But it is unlucky to dream of

taking a bath in an unnatural way. For instance, if a man dreamed of going into the hot room in his clothes this would portend illness and great pain, since sick men are carried into the bath fully dressed, and those in great pain sweat in their clothes. It is bad for a poor man to dream of a bath with many attendants helping him. This prognosticates a long illness, since under no other circumstances is a poor man bathed with many to help him. In the same way it is bad for a rich man to dream of bathing alone. It is disturbing for anyone to dream that he cannot sweat or that the bath-house is open to the sky because it has lost its roof, or not to find water in the basins, since all these are unnatural. It means that the dreamer will not succeed in his hopes, especially if he earns his living among crowds or from crowds. I know a harpist who just before he competed in the sacred Hadrianic festival at Smyrna dreamed that he wanted to bath but found no water in the bath-house. In the competition he cheated and was detected, fined and expelled from the meeting. This was what the dream had foretold—that he would not attain what he wanted; the bath-house symbolized the theatre. To dream that one is bathing in hot water—I mean in natural hot springs—portends recovery for the sick but unemployment for the healthy, since men go to these hot springs either when they are convalescing or because they have nothing else to do. It is good to dream of bathing in springs and lakes, pools and rivers, provided that they have clear and transparent water, but not to dream of swimming in them, for swimming is bad for everyone and a symbol of danger and illness.

'Strigils, scrapers and towels are symbols of servants. So if anyone were to dream of losing one of them, he would lose a slave from among his personal attendants. In particular, scrapers signify loss, since they scrape off sweat and add nothing to the body. On occasion they have hinted at a prostitute, since a prostitute has the same effect on the body. An oil-flask or athlete's hold-all signifies sometimes a woman of the household or a trusted attendant, sometimes a useful slave.'[210]

In this passage it is tantalizing not to be told how the harpist cheated. Did he offer bribes to the judges, hire a claque to applaud his own performance and deride all others, or attempt to sabotage a rival's instrument? Artemidorus leaves us guessing.

By the beginning of the Christian era, athletics in the Greek world, like football in our own time, had become public entertainment rather than sport. This is brought out well in the interpretation of one class of dreams: 'To dream of making a public distribution is good for all entertainers, because those who make such distributions are popular with crowds. But to dream that at such a distribution one fails to obtain a portion is fatal, whether the share-out is public or private. It infallibly portends death, since no share can be given to the dead. I know of one man who went to Olympia to compete. He dreamed that the Stewards of the Games handed out loaves to the athletes, but that he was at the end of the queue and there was none left for him. Everyone else interpreted this as meaning that he would not get as far as competing [i.e. that his entry would be rejected]; I thought that it portended something worse than that, and I was right. For immediately after the entries were accepted, he died.'[211]

Our author uses another anecdote about a prominent athlete to illustrate a general statement: 'That light in dreams is preferable to darkness, except for those who wish to remain unobserved, you might deduce from this example. Not long before competing at Rome, the pankratiast Menippus of Magnesia dreamed that night came on in the middle of his contest. Not only was he hopelessly defeated in the Games at Rome, but as the result of a blow his hand was shattered.' Menippus' dream may well have been inspired by an incident recorded in an inscription found at Olympia. The ornate language of this inscription recounts that in the final of the Olympic pankration, Tiberius Claudius Rufus 'held on until the stars overtook him', with the result that, for the first time in history, a verdict of a draw was given at Olympia.[212]

A similar story in Artemidorus drives home the point that

while crowns round the head in dreams are lucky, those on any other part of the body are not merely not lucky but are downright bad. 'Zoilus took his two sons to Olympia to compete, one as a wrestler, the other as a pankratiast. He dreamed that they were wreathed with cultivated and wild olive round their ankles, and he was cock-a-hoop about this, since the prizes given at the Olympics were of sacred olive. But his sons died before the Games started. The crowns round their ankles were not far from the ground.'²¹³

One dream related by Artemidorus throws light on a recent discovery at Olympia. 'A runner who had won the boys' stade race at Olympia dreamed, just before he competed in another meeting, that he was washing his feet in his Olympic crown as if it were a bowl. He was badly beaten and left the stadium in disgrace, for he had treated his earlier crown with contempt.' Post-war excavations at Olympia uncovered two sets of 'sit-baths' with inset basins, the purpose of which has not always been understood. This anecdote removes all doubts.²¹⁴

In the section on the interpretation of dreams about death, we are given as an example: 'Menander of Smyrna on his way to compete at Olympia dreamed that he had been buried in the stadium there; he became an Olympic victor.' A further anecdote gives the reason for this: 'A man who had taken a boy wrestler to Olympia dreamed that the boy was murdered by the Stewards and buried in the stadium. The boy won an Olympic victory. This was the natural sequel to the dream. A dead man is given a eulogistic inscription on his tomb; so is an Olympic victor on his statue.' The same principle governs the interpretation of another curious dream: 'A man who had taken a boy pankratiast to Olympia dreamed that the boy was condemned to death and was about to be killed on the altar of Zeus. In his dream he succeeded by his prayers and entreaties in getting the boy reprieved. The boy's entry for the meeting was accepted, and he competed; but, although he had great hopes of victory, he failed. This was the natural outcome of the dream; he did not come

to the consummation of victory, just as in the dream he had
not come to death, the consummation of life. Nor did he
achieve public adulation; those who are sacrificed on behalf
of the state are accorded great public honours, as also are
Olympic victors.'[215]

Dreams, however, did not always go by opposites. 'A
man dreamed that he had been expelled from the gymnasium
by the *strategos* of his city. His father expelled him from his
house; for the father has the same function in his house as the
strategos has in the city.' Sometimes a dream of athletic
victory portended success in other fields. 'A man dreamed
that he won the men's wrestling at the Nemean Games and
was crowned. He happened to be engaged at the time in a
lawsuit about a piece of land in which there was a great marsh.
He won his case over the marshland, because victors at
Nemea are crowned with wild celery, which is a marsh
plant.' Equally a dream of misfortune was sometimes
followed by disaster: 'A man dreamed that he went into the
gymnasium of his city and saw a bust of himself which in
fact stood there. Then he dreamed that the whole surface of
the base of the bust crumbled. Someone asked him what had
happened to the statue, and in his dream he replied, "My
bust remains unharmed, but the base has been destroyed".
He became lame in both feet, the natural outcome of the
dream. The gymnasium was the symbol of the fitness of the
whole of his body, the bust signified the face and surrounding
parts, while the surface of the base was the remainder of his
body.'[216]

It was easy to misinterpret a dream. A pankratiast went to
Olympia with the intention of entering for the wrestling as
well as the pankration. He dreamed that both his hands had
been turned to gold. This might well have seemed an augury
of a double victory, but in the event he won neither crown,
'for he was doomed to find his hands as slow and useless as if
they had really been made of gold.'[217]

In the story of the harpist who cheated and was disqualified
we have had a hint of foul play in competition. Artemidorus

relates two other anecdotes which show how far corruption had penetrated the athletic meetings of his day. When dealing with dreams about death he warns us to take care that the dreamer has not imagined himself coming to life again, since that reverses the significance of the dream of death. To drive home the point he gives an example. 'Leonas the Syrian wrestler, just before a contest at Rome, dreamed that he died and was being carried out to be buried; a trainer met the cortège and was furious with the undertakers for burying the body in such irresponsible haste; he declared that the dead man could be brought back to life. Then he anointed the chest of the corpse with warm oil applied with a pad of wool and restored it to life. After this dream, Leonas wrestled superbly at the games and won several rounds, but when he was about to win the final he was prevented by the trainer, who put in an objection; for he had been bribed to stop Leonas from going through to ultimate success.'[218]

An even more outrageous piece of skulduggery is revealed in an unclassified dream recounted in Artemidorus' last book. 'A runner, shortly before competing in a sacred festival, dreamed that he went with a water-pot to a fountain to fetch water. As he approached the fountain the water was running, but when he reached it and was about to fill his pot the flow stopped. After a short time he tried again, but again just as he reached the water it stopped flowing. A third time the same thing happened. Finally the spring failed altogether; in a fury he hurled his pot to the ground and it was smashed to pieces. In his race, although there was some weight of opinion in his favour, the verdict was a dead heat and he had to re-run. For the second time he reached the finish at the same time as his rival. There was a third race, and despite the great weight of feeling on his side, he lost the crown. The fact was that the agonothete who was promoting the Games strongly favoured his opponent. We may say that the fountain was the symbol of the festival; the waterspout was the agonothete, the water stood for the crown, the pot was the athlete's training, and the failure to get water because the spring stopped running represented the failure to achieve the crown because of the pressure put on the judges by the agonothete; the wasted training corresponded to the breaking of the pot.'[219]

For the student of Greek athletics the great importance of this passage is that it affords incontrovertible evidence that after a dead heat a race was re-run, at any rate in Roman Imperial times. The incident throws light on an inscription recording the victories of Demetrius of Salamis in the pentathlon and stade about a century after Artemidorus' time. It tells us that among his other exploits 'he defeated Optatus in the fifth stade race after four dead heats with him [νεικήσας πέμπτῳ ἁπλῷ Ὀπτᾶτον ποιήσας αὐτῷ τετράκις σύνδρομον].' This statement has understandably evoked much comment from those who find it difficult to believe in four consecutive dead heats. Generally they have tried to resolve the difficulty by emending ἁπλῷ to ὅπλῳ or πάλῳ. Neither suggestion does anything to solve the problem of four dead heats, and emendation is quite unnecessary. ἁπλοῦς is used for the stade race by a scholiast on Pindar and by the paroemiographer Zenobius, and we have encountered it in that sense in Artemidorus. In the light of Artemidorus' anecdote the four dead heats of the inscription become much more plausible if we assume that, like the dreamer's opponent, either Demetrius or Optatus had bribed the judges. A corrupt judge might well hesitate to incur the fury of the spectators by awarding a race to a runner who had clearly, if narrowly, been beaten; but he might in such circumstances give his man another chance by announcing a dead-heat, and even repeat the stratagem more than once. In the excitement of a close finish much is forgiven. We may recall the story, no doubt apocryphal, of the verdict in the University Boat Race of 1877—'Dead heat to Oxford by seven feet'.[220]

NOTES

The abbreviations used for the names of authors, periodicals, etc. are those given in the Introduction to the latest edition of Liddell and Scott's *Greek Lexicon*, with the following additions:

AAW   E. N. Gardiner, *Athletics of the Ancient World* (Oxford, 1930).
GAA   H. A. Harris, *Greek Athletes and Athletics* (London, 1964).
IAG   L. Moretti, *Iscrizioni Agonistiche Greche* (Rome, 1953).

CHAPTER I

1 Homer: *Il.* XXIII, 262*ff*; *Od.* VIII, 97*ff.* Alexander: Arrian, *Anab.* II, v. 8; III, i. 4; III, vi. 1; III, xxv. 1; V, iii. 6; VI, xxviii. 3; VIII, xviii. 12 etc. Funeral Games: *ibid.*, VII, xiv. 10.
2 Shorts: Hom., *Il.* XXIII, 683; Thuc. I, 6; Paus. I, xliv, 1; Isid., *Orig.* XVIII, xvii. 2; Julius Africanus, *sub anno* 720 (*Ol.,* 15).
3 Dates of introduction of events at Olympia: Paus. V, viii. 5*ff.* For changes in the equestrian programme, see below, pp. 159–60.
4 Blows to head: Philostr., *Gym.,* 9. Shadow boxing: Paus. VI, x. 3; Plut., *Mor.,* 130e; D. Chrys. XXXII, 44.
5 Ear-guards: Plut., *Mor.,* 38b, 706c. σφαῖραι: Pl., *Leg.* VIII, 830a, 830e; Plut., *Mor.,* 825e. Punch-ball: Luc., *Lex.,* 5; Philostr., *Gym.,* 57; Ath. 668e.
6 Philo Jud., *Vit. Cont.,* 43. For

further discussion of boxing see *GAA,* 97*ff.* The evidence there given for boxing among the Minoans of Crete in the second millenium BC can now be supplemented from a fresco discovered recently by Professor Marinatos at the Minoan site in the island of Thera (Santorin). If it is correctly reconstructed this represents a pair of boxers in an attitude similar to that of boxers in Greek vase-paintings of a thousand years later. The fresco has some curious features. The athletes wear light blue caps, from which long tresses of black hair escape. Of the three hands which can still be seen, one is clearly and another probably wearing a black boxing-glove; the third appears to have no glove.
7 Lists of prize money: e.g. *CIG,* 2758. For further discussion

on the pankration, see *GAA*, 105*ff*.

8 For further discussion of the problems of the *husplex* see *GAA*, 67*ff*, Plates 26a and b.

9 Reconstruction of *husplex* at Athens: *IG*, II/III, 1035. Josephus, *BJ* III, 90. The best MS has ὑφ᾽ ὕσπληγος. Most editors emend unnecessarily to ἐφ᾽ ὕσπληγος.

10 Since this was written I have learned from Mr J. K. Doherty of Swarthmore, USA, that 'Ben Ogden, Temple University, Philadelphia, used an electric starting-gate in Madison Square Garden for some years. The sprinters leaned against canvas belts which were released electronically by the gun trigger.'

11 For the Würzburg vase, see *GAA*, Plates 4a and b.

12 Armed race: Aristoph., *Birds*, 291; Paus. II, xi. 8; VI, x. 4; Poll. III, 6.   Torch race: Aristoph., *Frogs*, 129*ff*, 1087*ff*; *Wasps*, 1204; *Frag.* 442; *Inscr. Delos* 1905, 1956, 1958; *Syll.*³, 667, 671, 958, 1068; *IG*, VII, 2871.   Alexander included torch races in the Games he promoted for his troops: Arrian, *Anab.* II, v. 8; II, xxiv. 6; III, xvi. 9.

13 Philostr., *Gym.*, 3.   All-rounder: DL IX, 37.   Second rate: Pl., *Amat.*, 135e; Suidas, s.v. Eratosthenes. Prizes: *CIG*, 2758.

14 'Victor in the first triad': see my articles, 'An Athletic ἅπαξ λεγόμενον', *JHS*, 1968, and 'The Method of Deciding Victory in the Pentathlon', *GR*,

1972.

15 Xen., *Eq.*, vii. 1; Ovid, *Met.* VIII, 365*ff*.   Man in arena: *AP* IX, 533. A rather obscure passage in Homer (*Il.* XV, 674*ff*) appears to describe Ajax as pole-jumping from one ship to another as they lay drawn up on shore, and to compare him with a trick rider performing the same feat on horses.

16 Jumps—52 ft (Chionis): Jul. Afric., *sub anno* 664 BC (*Ol.*, 29); 55 ft (Phaÿllus): Zenobius VI, 23. For further discussion of the Jump, see *GAA*, 80*ff*.

17 Cornel wood: Xen., *Cyr.* VII, 1. 2; *Str.* XII, vii. 3; Grattius, *Cyneg.*, 127*ff*; Bacchyl. VIII, 33; Theophr., *HP* IV, xi. 13.

18 Philo Jud., *Agr.*, 115.

19 Hom., *Il.* XXIII, 826*ff*. An inscription of the second century BC from Samos records among victors in other events the winner of a competition in stone-throwing (λιθόβολος) (*Syll.*³, 1061).

20 'Whirling round': e.g. Hom., *Il.* XXIII, 840.

21 Spartans: Plut., *Mor.*, 817b. Corruption: Paus. V, ii. 4; V, xxi. 3*ff*; VI, ii. 6; VI, iii. 11; VI, xviii. 6; *Syll.*³, 1076; Philostr., *Gym.*, 45; Plut., *Lycurg.*, xxii. 4; D. Chrys. XXXI, 119; Machon ap. Athen. XIII, 582b; Aul. Gel. V, 9; M. Aur. VI, 20; Themist., *Or.* I (*De Hum.*), 13a;   Crowd behaviour: D. Chrys. XXXII, 74; XL, 29.   Rhodes: Polyb. V, lxxxviii. 5; lxxxix. 4.

22 Paus. V, xvi. 2; Pl., *Leg.* VII, 804e; VIII, 833c.   Delphi inscr.: *Syll.*³, 802=*IAG*, 63.

Corinth: *Corinth* VIII, Pt. iii (Inscr. 1926/50), No. 153. Naples: *IG*, XIV. 755, Add. g; Suet., *Dom.*, iv. 4; Malalas, 287. 19*ff*. (Sophocles' Byzantine Lexicon translates βομβωνάρια as 'leggings', but, apart from the improbability of the rendering, the derivation of the word rules this out.) For further details of women's athletics in Greece, see *GAA*, Chapter IX.

23 Herod: Joseph., *BJ* I, 427; *Ant.* XVI, 149.   End of Olympic Games: Cedrenus, 326d. End of Antioch Games: Malalas, 417. 5.

24 Andreas: Procop. I, xiii. 30.

CHAPTER II

25 Hor., *Od.* III, xxix. 1.

26 Livy I, 35; VII, 2; XXVII, 21; XXXIX, 22. Other Greek Games—Sulla: App., *Bell. Civ.* I, 99.   Scaurus: Val. Max. II, iv. 7.   Pompey: Plut., *Pomp.*, 52.   Curio: Pliny, *NH* XXXVI, 120.   J. Caesar: Suet., *Jul.*, xxxix. Herod: Joseph., *BJ* I, 415; DH VII, lxxii. 2.

27 Failure of play: Terence, *Hec.*, Prologue.

28 Cicero to his brother: *QF* I, 1   Augustus: Suet., *Aug.*, xviii, xliii, xliv, xlv; Dio Cass. LVII, xi.

29 Augustus: Suet., *Aug.*, xlv.

30 Sybaris: Hor., *Od.* I, viii. Glycon: Hor., *Ep.* I, i. 30; *Inscr. Pergamum* 535=*IAG*, 58.

31 Atalanta: *Met.* X, 560*ff*. Achelous: *Met.* IX, 31*ff*.

32 Suet., *Gaius*, xviii, xx.

33 Verona: Pliny, *Ep.* VI, xxxiv.

34 Oil: Tac., *Ann.* XIV, xlvii. Statue: *ibid.* XV, xxii.   Wrestlers' powder: Suet., *Nero*, xlv; Pliny, *NH* XXXV, xlvii. 168. Patrobius: *SEG*, XIV, 613= *IAG*, 65; Dio Cass. LXIII, iii. I

cannot believe, as Moretti does (and Stein in *PW*), that there were two outstanding heavyweights called Patrobius active at the same time. Had there been, one of our authorities must surely have called attention to the fact, in order to show which Patrobius he had in mind.   Regulus: Plut., *Mor.*, 124c.   Commodus: SHA, *Comm.*, 17; Tertullian, *Ap.* xxxv, 9.

35 Suet., *Dom.*, iv. 4.

36 Pliny, *Ep.* X, xxxix, xl.

37 M. Aurelius: SHA, *M. Aur.*, iv. 9; Fronto II, xii. 1.

38 For a discussion of Statius' Funeral Games, see *GAA*, 55*ff*.

39 Atticus: Martial, Ep. VII, xxxii.   Juvenal: XIII, 96 (Ladas); II, 53; III, 76; VI, 246, 356, 421.

40 Nicostratus: Jul. Afric., *sub anno*; Paus. V, xxi. 11; Lucian, *Hist. Consc.*, 9.

41 Pharius: Sen., *Ep. Mor.* LXXXIII, 4*ff*.   High Jump: *Ep. Mor.* XV, 4.

42 Sen., *Ep. Mor.* XXXI, 4.

43 Ladas: L. Moretti, *Olympionikai* (Rome, 1957), 96.

44 Horace: *Od.* I, viii. 10.

CHAPTER III

45 Dio Chrys. IV, 48; Eustathius 1601, 30 on *Od.* VIII, 372.
46 Galen, *Nat. Fac.* I, vi. 17; Plato, *Phaedo*, 110b; Martial IV, xix; VII, xxxii; XIV, xlv–xlviii; Suet., *Aug.*, lxxxiii.   Isidorus: see below, p. 99.
47 Sophocles: Eustath., 1553. 63 on *Od.* VI, 101*ff*; Plato, *Ep.* XIII, 363d (συσφαιρισταῖς); *Theaet.*, 146a (ὄνος); *Euthyd.*, 277b; Plut., *Mor.*, 38e, 45e; Epict. II, v. 15.   Antigonus: Plut., *Mor.*, 182a.
48 Aristonicus: Ath. I, 19a; Inscr. *IG*², 385b; Plut., *Alex.*, xxxix. 3.
49 Theophrastus, *Char.* XXI, 15; *Delphi Inscr.*, 3862 (*BCH*, XXIII, 566*ff*).
50 Pliny, *Ep.* II, xvii. 11; V, vi. 27: Statius, *Silv.* I, v. 57; Centuripae: *CIL*, X, 7004.
51 Mucius: Cic., *De Or.* I, 127; Hor., *Sat.* I, v. 49.   Cato: Plut., *Cato*, L, i.   Vespasian: Suet., *Vesp.*, xx.   Galba: Quint. VI, iii. 62.
52 Pollux IX, 103*ff*.
53 The later Greeks identified

Homer's Phaeacia with Corcyra (Corfu).
54 Ath. I, 19.
55 Cloak: Martial IV, xix.
56 Spurinna: Pliny, *Ep.* III, i; Petronius, *Sat.*, 27.
57 Seneca, *Ep. Mor.*, LVI, 1. Inscription: *CIL*, IV, 1936.
58 Inscriptions: *CIL*, IV, 1905, 1926.
59 E. N. Gardiner, *AAW*, 234. W. B. Anderson: translation in the Loeb edition of Sidonius Apollinaris.
60 Cic., *De Senect.*, 58.
61 BM 'Pick-a-back' vase: Inv. 182.
62 Ps.-Plut., *Vit. Isoc.*, 839c. Etruscan painting: Tomba dei Giocoliari, Tarquinia, 2437.
63 For a discussion of these inscriptions, see M. N. Tod, 'Sparta Inscriptions', in *BSA Ann.* X, xiii, 212*ff*.
64 Plato, *Leg.* VII, 794d.
65 Secundus inscription: *CIL*, VI, 8997.
66 Metope XXVI from the Parthenon (BM) depicts a Lapith using this stab movement against a Centaur.

CHAPTER IV

67 Sphacteria: Thuc. IV, 26. Xerxes' fleet: *AP* IX, 296; Herod. VIII, 8; Paus. X, xix. 1.
68 Divers: Aristot., *Prob.* XXXI, 2–5, 11; Bacchylides, XVI.
69 Plut., *Ant.*, xxix; Shakespeare, *AC*, II. v.

70 Salamis: Herod. VIII, 89. Syracuse: Thuc. VII, 25. Races at Hermione: Paus. II, xxxv. 1.   Tisander: Philostr., *Gym.*, 43; Nonnus, *Dionys.* XI, 1*ff*, 407*ff*.
71 Enipeus: Hor., *Od.* III, vii. 25.   Hebrus: *Od.* III, xii. 7.

Sybaris: *Od.* I, iii. 8. Insomnia: *Sat.* II, i. 7. Aqua Virgo: Ovid, *Tr.* III, 12.
72 Ovid, *Her.*, xix. 43.
73 Julius Caesar: Suet., *Jul.*, lxiv; Plut., *Caes.*, xlix. Augustus: Suet., *Aug.*, lxiv. Cato: Plut., *Cat. Ma.*, xx. Alexander: Plut., *Alex.*, lviii. Caligula: Suet., *Gaius*, liv.
74 Clitumnus: Pliny, *Ep.* VIII, viii; Festus 260, 2. Maecenas: Dio Cass. LV, vii.
75 Nicarchus: *AP* XI, 243.
76 Pliny, *Ep.* II, xvii; V, vi.
77 At least one line appears to have been lost from the passage between 423 and 424. In 431, *pontum* cannot possibly be correct. It is a simple instance of dittography, caused by *ponto* earlier in the line. Manilius probably wrote some such word as *regnum, siccum,* or *terram.*
78 Inflated skins: Suet., *Jul.*, lvii; Hor., *Sat.* I, iv. 120. Odysseus: *Od.* V, 333ff.
79 Nausicaa: *Od.* VI, 96. Hydna: see above, p. 00. Cloelia: Livy II, xiii. Agrippina: Suet., *Nero*, xxxiv; Tac., *Ann.* XIV, v.

80 Women's baths: e.g. *AP* IX, 625. Domitian: Suet., *Dom.*, xxii.
81 Propertius I, xi; Pliny, *Ep.* VIII, viii; Catullus IV, iii.
82 Iphicrates: Xen., *Hell.* VI, xxviii. Xerxes' fleet: Herod. VII, xliv. Alexander: Arrian, *Anab.* VII, xxiii. 5. Nicocles: Isoc. IX, i.
83 Races at Hermione: Paus. II, xxxv. 1. Actia: Steph. Byz., *sub verbo.* Themistocles' monument: Plato Com. ap. Plut., *Them.*, xxxii. Sunium: Lys. XXI, v. Aristophanes has an oblique reference to these races at *Knights*, 551ff.
84 Philostr., *Her.*, x. 4; Dio Chrys. XXXVII, 15; Hom., *Od.* VIII, 246ff.
85 For a more academic account of the problems about these ships, see *Greek Oared Ships* by J. S. Morrison and R. T. Williams (Cambridge, 1968).
86 For a discussion of the Games in Virgil's *Aeneid*, see my paper in *Proceedings of the Virgil Society*, No. 8, p. 14.
87 Val. Flacc., *Arg.*, 475ff.

CHAPTER V

88 *Trochus*: The evidence for a distinction between τρόχος and τροχός is late and unconvincing. Hippocrates: Vict. II, lxiii; III, lxviii, lxxvi. From modern times we have the evidence of Gray that Eton boys bowled hoops in the eighteenth century: What idle progeny succeed / To

chase the rolling circle's speed / Or urge the flying ball? ('Ode on a Distant Prospect of Eton College').
89 Eur., *Medea*, 46; Dio Chrys. XII, 37; Sex. Emp. I, 106.
90 Theophrast., *Char.* XIV.
91 *Inscr. Priene*, 112.

92 Ovid, *AA* III, 383; *Tr.* III, xii. 19; Hor., *Od.* III, xxiv. 56. Add to these Strabo, who includes ball-play and hoop-bowling among the activities of young Romans in the Campus Martius (V, iii. 8).
93 Martial XIV, clxviii, clxix.
94 The author of the poem on ball games to whom Ovid refers here may well be the Dorcatius

quoted by Isidorus (see above p. 79). Dorcatius is otherwise unknown.
95 These mosaics are fully illustrated and discussed by G. Brett in *The Great Palace of the Byzantine Emperors* (Oxford, 1947).
96 P. Roulez, *Choix de vases peints du Musée d'Antiquités de Leide* (Ghent, 1854).

CHAPTER VI

97 Aelian XII, xxii.
98 L. Moretti: *IAG*, p. 4.
99 Hom., *Od.* XIII, 77.
100 Hiller von Gaertringen: on *IG*, XII³, 449.
101 Xerxes' bridge: Herod. IX, 121.   Dedications: *AP* VI, *passim*.   Xenophanes: ap. Athen. X, 413. Seneca (*Ep. Mor.*

XCV, 48) deprecates the practice of athletes dedicating their strigils to Jupiter.
102 *Inscr. Ol.*, 718.
103 'Leather Roof' etc.: Epict. III, xii. 9. τὸ στέγην δερματίνην καὶ ὅλμον καὶ ὕπερον περιφέρειν. Libanius: *Ep.*, 473. 3. ὅλμος, φασίν, ὑπὲρ κεφαλῆς.

CHAPTER VII

104 Telemachus: *Od.* III, 475. Nausicaa: *Od.* VI, 73.   Chariot race: *Il.* XXIII, 262*ff.*
105 Nestor in Elis: *Il.* XI, 698*ff.*
106 Dates of equestrian events

at Olympia: Paus. V, viii. 7*ff.*
107 Aristoph., *Birds*, 939*ff* and scholia.
108 Chariots at Delphi: Paus. X, vii. 5*ff.*   Races at Athens: *IG*, II/III, 2316.

CHAPTER VIII

109 Sparta Inscr. *IG*, V, i. 213 =*IAG*, 16.
110 Pind., *Pyth.* IV, 49; Soph., *El.*, 727.
111 Delos hippodrome: *IG*, II/III, 1638.
112 Lycaeus: Paus.   VIII, xxxviii. 5.
113 Dimensions   of   hippo-

drome at Olympia: MS in Istanbul. Text in *Jahrb. des arch. Inst.* XII (1897), p. 153.   Panathenaic hippodrome: *Etym Mag.*, s.v. ἐν Ἐχελιδῶν.   Delos: *Syll.*³, 697, 728; Pind., *Ol.* II, 50; VI, 75.
114 *Inscr. Pergamum*, 10=*IAG*, 37. For a full discussion of the

problems of the starting-gate at Olympia, see my articles, 'The Starting Gate for Chariots at Olympia', *GR*, 1968, and 'The Starting Gate for Chariots: a Postscript', *GR*, 1969.

115 Aristoph., *Clouds*, 25.

116 Herodorus: Ath. X, 414*ff*; Pollux IV, 89.

117 Taraxippus—At Olympia, Isthmia and Nemea: Paus. VI, xx. 15*ff*.   At Delphi: Paus. X, xxxvii. 4.

118 Hom., *Il.* XXIII, 368. Clogs: Eur., *Hipp.*, 1189. See my note on this line in *CR*, 1968, 259.

119 Sarcophagus: Visconti, *Museo Pio Clementino*, vol. V, Plate xliii.

CHAPTER IX

120 For details of these winners, see *Olympionikai* by L. Moretti (Rome, 1957).   Cimon's horses: Herod. VI, 103.

121 Diod. Sic. XIV, cix. 1; XV, vii. 2.

122 Mithridates: Chios Inscr. published by D. Evangelides in Ἀρχ. Δελτ., vol. XI; Plutarch, *Pompey*, xxxvii.   Olympia under a cloud: Joseph., *BJ* I, 427. In the next century, during the reign of Claudius, the people of Antioch paid the authorities at Olympia for the privilege of calling their Games 'Olympic' (Malalas, 248. 5).

123 Natalis: *Inscr. Ol.*, 236= *Syll.*[3], 840.   Prometheus: *IG*, II/III, 3769=*IAG*, 89.

124 Euagoras: Paus. VI, x. 8; Herod. VI, 103.

125 Dyspontium: Phleg., *Frag.* 6.   Argos: *P. Ox.*, 222. Lichas: Thuc. V, 50 and scholia; Xen., *Hell.* III, ii. 21; Paus. VI, ii. 2.

126 *Inscr. Corinth.*, 15.

127 Pliny, *NH* XVIII, lxvii. 263.

128 Alcmaeonidae: *IG*, I[2], 472

=*IAG*, 5;   Pind., *Pyth.* VI.

129 Cynisca: Paus. III, viii. 1; Xen., *Ages.*, ix. 6; Plut., *Ages.*, 20; *Inscr. Ol.*, 160=*IAG*, 16. Belistiche: *P. Ox.*, 2082; Paus. V, viii.   11;   Ath. XIII,   596e. Eleian women: *Inscr. Ol.*, 198– 204.   Kasia: *Inscr. Ol.*, 233.

130 Hedea: *Inscr. Delphi*, 1534 = *Syll.*[3], 802=*IAG*, 63;   Aristoph., *Clouds*, 28.   Panathenaea; *IG*, II/III, 2311, 2316.

131 Lycus: Paus. VI, xviii. 10. A story about runaway chariot horses at Rome, resembling Pausanias' account of Aura, is told by Pliny (*NH* VIII, lxv. 160). At the Secular Games of AD 47, Corax, a charioteer of the Whites, was thrown from his chariot in the starting traps. When the gates opened, his team behaved just as if they were being handled by a skilful driver, won the race, and stopped when they had crossed the line. Two other anecdotes about the strange behaviour of runaway teams at the Games are related in the next chapter of Pliny.

132 Torch races—Panath.: *IG*,

II/III, 2311, 2317.   Thessaly:
IG, IX, 2. 531=*Syll.*³, 1059.
ἀναβάται: Paus. V, ix. 2.
133 For a discussion of the
problem of the jockey and the
horse, see *Plastik der Griechen* by

E. Bucher (Munich, 1936/58),
and *Antike Reiterstandbilder* by
H. von Roques de Maumont
(Berlin, 1958).
134 Hyssematas: *Hesperia*,
1939, 165.

CHAPTER X

135 *Carceres*: Livy VIII, xx.
136 Pliny, *NH* XXXV, xlvii.
199.
137 'Eggs': Livy XLI, xxvii;
Dio Cass. XLIX, xliii.

138 3 *Macc.*, 4*ff.*
139 Jerusalem: Joseph., *BJ* II,
44; *Ant.* XVII, 255.   Jericho:
BJ I, 659; *Ant.* XVII, 174.
Tarichaeae: *BJ* II, 599.

CHAPTER XI

140 Juv. I, 58.   Greens: *CIL*,
VI, 33950; Dio Cass. LXVII, iv.
4.   Charioteer of Purple: *CIL*,
VI, 10062.
141 Diocles: *CIL*, VI, 10048.
142 An Etruscan relief of a
three-horse chariot in Florence
gives no real evidence of the
method of harnessing.
143 Praeneste inscr.: *CIL*, XIV,
2884.
144 Lists of horses: *CIL*, VI,
10053, 10056.
145 Calpurnianus: *CIL*, VI,
10047.   Augustus: Suet.,
Aug., xliii. 5.
146 *Remissus* and *revocatus*:
Ovid, *Am.* III, ii (see below, p.
219; *CIL*, VI, 33950, 10055.

Scirtus: *CIL*, VI, 10051.
147 Suet., *Nero*, xxii.
148 Anniceris: Ps.-Lucian,
Dem., 23.
149 Fuscus: *CIL*, VI, 33950.
Crescens: 10050.   Aquilius:
10065.
150 Polyneices: *CIL*, VI,
10049.
151 Florus: *CIL*, VI, 10078.
152 Scorpus: Martial IV, lxvii;
V, xxv; X, l, liii, lxxiv.
153 Horse competing with
own son: see below, p. 236;
Martial III, lxiii; Juv. VIII, 63.
154 Dio Cass. LXI, vi. 1.
155 Acragas: Pliny, *NH* VIII,
lxiv. 155.   Speudusa: *CIL*,
VI, 10082.

CHAPTER XII

156 Juv. X, 81.
157 Julius: Suet., *Aug.*, xlv.
Augustus: Suet., *Aug.*, xlv.
Caligula: Suet., *Gaius.*, iii, xviii,
xxvi. 4, lv.

158 Suet., *Vitell.*, iv, vii, xii,
xiv, xvii.
159 Suet., *Claud.*, xi, xx, xxi.
160 Domitius: Suet., *Nero*, v.
Board game; *ibid.*, xxii.   Pop-

paea: ibid., xxxv.
161 Fifty races: Suet., *Nero*, xxii; Tac., *Ann.* XV, lxxiv; Cassiodorus, *Var.* III, 51.
162 Fabricius: Dio Cass. LXI, vi. l.   Camels: Suet., *Nero*, xi.
163 Private track: Suet., *Nero*, xxii; Tac., *Ann.* XIV, xiv. Nero at Olympia: Suet., *Nero*, xxiv.
164 Gold and Purple: Suet., *Dom.*, vii.   Secular Games: ibid., iv.   Trajan: Pliny, *Pan. Traj.*, li. 3.   M. Aurelius: I, v.
165 Free seats: Suet., *Gaius*, xxvi.   Ovid: After writing this lively poem in the *Amores*, Ovid made use of the same

material in the *Ars Amatoria* (I, 135*ff*), putting it in the form of didactic advice to the young man. The treatment is much inferior, but it introduces one or two details not found in the *Amores*— the cushion and footstool, for instance. I have taken the liberty of including these in my version. There is a charming verse rendering of the earlier poem in *Ovid Recalled*, by L. P. Wilkinson (Cambridge, 1955).
166 Caecina: Pliny, *NH* X, xxxiv. 71.
167 Felix: Pliny, *NH* VII, liii. 186.

CHAPTER XIII

168 Augustus: Suet, *Aug.*, lxxi. Claudius: Suet., *Claud.*, xxxiii; Ovid, *Tr.* II, 471.
169 Domitius (called Nero in the epigram): Mart. XI, xxxiii. Procopius (II, xi. 31*ff*) has an amusing anecdote of Chosroes

at Apamea in the sixth century A D, shouting orders to the leading Blue charioteer to pull back in order to allow Green to win.
170 Petronius, *Sat.*, lxx; Juv. XI, 201; Ovid, *AA* I, 168.
171 *Digest* XI, v. 2.

CHAPTER XIV

172 For St Paul's attitude to athletics, see *GAA*, 129*ff*.
173 The use of *desipere* suggests that Cassiodorus is here recalling Horace's *dulce est desipere in loco*.
174 Hortator: *CIL*, VI, 10074/5/6.
175 Hilarius: Amm. XXVI, iii. 3.   Debtor: Amm. XXVIII, iv. 25; *Codex* IX, xviii. 9.

Auchenius: Amm. XXVIII, i. 27.
176 Spell from Hadrumetum: *ILS*, 8753.
177 Spell: Text in *Antike Fluchtafeln* by R. Wünsch (Bonn, 1907).
178 *ibid.*
179 Articles in *Daily Telegraph* and *The Times*, Feb. 22, 1971.

CHAPTER XV

180 *AP* XVI, 380–7.
181 Anastasius: *AP* XVI, 379.
Julianus: *AP* XV, 45; XVI, 386–
7. Faustinus: *AP* XVI, 363–
4, 382–3. Constantinus: *AP*
XV, 41–3; XVI, 365–75, 384–5.
182 Uranius: *AP* XV, 48–9;
XVI, 376–8. Porphyrius: *AP*
XV, 44, 46–7, 50; XVI, 335–62,
380–1.
183 *P. Ox.*, 138, 140, 145.
Programme: *P. Ox.*, 2707. According to Zosimus (II, 31) the

procession at the opening of the
Games (*pompa circensis*) was suppressed by Constantine. The
papyrus suggests that the ban
applied only to the capital.
184 *Apophthegmata Patrum, PG*
65, Col. 164. (In *Fontes Hist. Rel.*,
vol. 2, Bonn, 1922/25, 665.)
185 Nika riots: Procop. I, xxiv
(30,000 dead); Theophanes, 158
(35,000); Zonaras XIV, vi. 28
(40,000).

APPENDIX

186 Blindness: I, 26. Baby:
I, 13. Milk: I, 16. Wo-
man: I, 50. Pankratiast: V,
45.
187 I, 17.
188 Two heads: I, 35. Lion
etc.: I, 37.
189 I, 48.
190 I, 50.
191 I, 54. This is followed by a
passage which as it stands is un-
intelligible: παλαιστῇ δὲ ἀθλοῦντι
τὸ μὴ καταλαβεῖν τὸν ἀγῶνα
σημαίνει· εἰ δὲ καταλάβοι τὸ μὴ
ἀγωνίσασθαι · οὐ γὰρ ὑπερόριοι
οἱ ἔφηβοι ἀγωνίζονται ('To a
wrestler in training [it means]
that he should not enter for the
contest; if he does enter, that he
should not compete. For ephebes
do not compete beyond the
boundaries [of their own city]').
There appears to be no reason
why a wrestler should be different in this respect from any other

athlete, and no connection between the meaning of the dream
and ephebes not competing
ὑπερόριοι. Perhaps we should
read ἐν παλαίστρᾳ for παλαιστῇ.
The meaning would then be:
'For a man training in the gymnasium it means that he should
not enter for an open competition, or if he has entered, that he
should not compete; for ephebes
do not compete outside their
own gymnasium.' We should
then have to assume that the
competitors in the events for
youths in innumerable sports
meetings of the period were of a
different social class from that of
the ephebes.
192 I, 56.
193 II, 9.
194 Aristoph., *Thes.*, 94.
Artem. I, 72.
195 I, 70.
196 I, 77. II, 25, 37.

197 II, 49.
198 Lion: II, 12.   Figurines:
III, 17.   Choked   watercourse:
V, 79.
199 I, 57.
200 I, 58.
201 I, 60.
202 I, 60.
203 I, 61.   πύκτης for gladiator: e.g. II, 32.
204 I, 62; II, 20.
205 Inscription: *IG*, XIV, 739
=*IGR*, I, 444=*IAG*, 77.
206 I, 63.
207 I, 59.
208 V, 13. The occurrence here of the phrase παροδεύων ἐν παρεξαγωγῇ renders less probable the explanation of μόνον παροδεύσαντα in an inscription from Ephesus, which I suggested in 'Notes on Three Athletic Inscriptions', *JHS*, 1962.

209 I, 55; IV, 69.
210 I, 64.
211 II, 30.
212 IV, 42; *Inscr. Ol.*, 54, 55.
213 IV, 52.
214 V, 55. For a picture of these basins see *GAA*, Plate 31b.
215 IV, 82; V, 76; V, 75.
216 V, 36; V, 7; V, 3.
217 V, 48.
218 IV, 82.
219 V, 78.
220 Inscription: *SEG*, XII, 512
=*IAG*, 86. For a discussion of this inscription, see my 'Notes on Three Athletic Inscriptions', *JHS*, 1962. The view there put forward is strongly corroborated by this anecdote of Artemidorus, of which I was ignorant when I wrote the article.   Schol. Pind., *Pyth.* XI, 74; Zenobius, *Cent.* IV, 47; Artemidorus I, 58.

SOURCES OF ILLUSTRATIONS

MUSEUM LOCATIONS

A NOTE ON BOOKS

Of THE BOOKS RECOMMENDED in *Greek Athletes and Athletics*, the most useful to the general reader are E. Norman Gardiner's *Athletics of the Ancient World* (Oxford, 1930) and *History and Remains of Olympia* (Oxford, 1925), the latter now needing to be supplemented by E. Kunze's *Neue Ausgrabungen in Olympia* (Berlin, 1960). Two earlier works omitted from my list in 1964 are B. Schröder's *Der Sport im Altertum* (Berlin, 1927), particularly useful for its excellently chosen illustrations, and *Gymnasion* by J. Delorme (Paris, 1960); the latter is valuable for its examination of the buildings devoted to athletics.

Of the books on Greek athletics which have appeared since 1964, the most important is *Die athletischen Leibesübungen der Griechen* by Julius Jüthner. Jüthner was one of the three outstanding figures in the early study of the subject, ranking with J. H. Krause and E. Norman Gardiner. When he died in 1945 he left an immense collection of material, which the University of Vienna undertook to publish to commemorate the centenary of the birth of its distinguished son. The task of editing was entrusted to F. Brein. The work is to be completed in two volumes, of which Vol. I and Part i of Vol. II have so far appeared. It is for the specialist and the classical scholar rather than for the general reader, but its comprehensiveness renders it indispensable. Equally valuable is the reprint of Jüthner's 1909 edition of Philostratus' *Gymnastike*, making it once again readily available. Most of the rest of the output has been disappointing, especially *Olympia; Gods, Artists and Athletes* by Ludwig Drees (English edn., Pall Mall Press, 1968). The book is splendidly illustrated, but the section on the Games is out-dated and inaccurate. J. Ebert's *Zum Pentathlon der Antike*, which reached me too late for more than a brief mention in 1964, has proved on further examination and use to be a work of real merit.

On the other sports there is very little which it is possible to recommend. Several of them are dealt with in outline in Gardiner's *Athletics of the Ancient World*. Swimming has fared better than the others: E. Mehl's *Antike Schwimmkunst* (Munich, 1927) is a sound treatment. The few books which include ancient ball games show little inspiration in handling the evidence. Most surprising of all is the lack of books on chariot-racing. J. K. Anderson's *Ancient Greek Horsemanship* (1961), which deals admirably with those aspects of the subject it covers, does not touch chariots. The best modern account of chariot-racing is still to be found in the two articles, *Circus* and *Hippodrome*, in the Daremberg-Saglio *Dictionnaire des Antiquités*, now more than half a century old. They are much superior to the corresponding articles in Paully-Wissowa. The place of chariot-racing in the social life of the early Empire is well covered in J. P. V. D. Balsdon's *Life and Leisure in Ancient Rome* (1969), and there is a good account of the Nika riots in *Justinian and Theodora* (1971) by R. Browning. A full treatment of racing in the Byzantine Empire will soon be available in two books by A. D. Cameron. The first of these, *Porphyrius the Charioteer* (OUP), will probably be in the hands of readers before this book appears. A second, on the Circus Factions, is promised for the near future. A book dealing with all aspects of Greek sport, *Lo Sport nella Grecia antica* by R. Patrucco (Florence), has been announced for publication in 1971, but it has not yet reached me.

Many of the Greek and Latin authors cited in this book are published in the Loeb edition, with English translation opposite the original text. The Loeb library continues steadily to cover the more recondite authors, and this considerably facilitates the exploration of these writers for evidence of ancient sport. A Loeb edition of Manilius is promised. The Greek text of Artemidorus is available in the Teubner series, but there is no English translation.

GENERAL INDEX

INDEX OF GREEK AND LATIN AUTHORS